CQ

CQ

Learn the Secret of Lasting Love

Glenn D. Wilson and Jon Cousins

First published in Great Britain in 2003 by Fusion Press,
a division of Satin Publications Ltd.
101 Southwark Street
London SE1 0JF
UK
info@visionpaperbacks.co.uk
www.visionpaperbacks.co.uk
Publisher: Sheena Dewan

ISBN: 1–904132–28–6

2 4 6 8 10 9 7 5 3 1

Typeset by M Rules
Printed and bound in the UK by Mackays of Chatham Ltd,
Chatham, Kent

Contents

Preface

PARTIES, POLITICS AND PETS

Karen (26) and Andy (28) have been married for just nine months, having met at work around three years ago. They have one child, Jessica, who's just about to celebrate her first birthday and the three of them live in a new two-bedroom house on the outskirts of a big city. Karen and Andy were happy with their highly compatible CQ score of 122, after taking the confidential test as part of a trial, but thought that they might have some differences of opinion in one or two areas of their relationship. After taking the open test together, in order to determine where they don't necessarily see eye-to-eye, they were somewhat taken aback to discover that they had gaps in their views on three issues; parties, politics and keeping pets.

Karen is more of a party girl than Andy, but since having Jessica her socialising has been much reduced. When it comes to politics, Karen is right wing while Andy tends to follow his father, who emigrated to this country from Jamaica, was very active in the trade union world, and was staunchly left-wing. Their third area of conflict is over pets. Karen would love a dog but Andy isn't so sure.

Talking through the issues helps. Andy agrees to get a babysitter once a week so they can both get out to see friends at the pub. While it seems to bother Karen more than Andy that they have differing political outlooks, she understands that Andy has probably inherited his views from his father and she respects this. Andy's still not sure about the dog but they agree to rethink the situation once Jessica is a little older.

When people talk of true love, they often refer to those early stages of lust and intoxication when the world, and especially the partner, is seen through rose-tinted glasses – or perhaps even upside down as a result of all the emotional and physical cartwheels! We prefer to call this state 'infatuation', defining true love in terms of the value that remains after the first flush of passion has subsided and the rosy spectacles in all probability lie shattered on the ground. Temporary ecstasy is a fine thing, but long-term happiness depends on finding a soul-mate.

The Compatibility Quotient (CQ) Test described here, with a procedure for scoring yourself in relation to a current or potential partner, is an indicator of long-term compatibility. It will not tell you whether or not you are going to fall in love with another person in a compulsive, 'chemical' way, just whether or not it is a good idea if you do. We argue that traditional courtship, based on accidental meetings with people who happen to be handy, overplays immediate physical attraction at the expense of long-term prospects. Couples are often fatally snared before they have had a proper chance to consider their suitability as companions. With the advent of modern methods of meeting people, such as Internet dating, there is an opportunity to screen potential partners for compatibility before Cupid's dart strikes.

Chapter 1 reviews scientific evidence showing that we are better off matched with people who are similar to ourselves in certain key respects and explains why the popular, but misleading, belief that opposites attract is so appealing. Chapter 2 discusses the chemistry of human bonding, which, although not as rigid as that of swans, nevertheless helps to explain why we so often find ourselves hooked on the wrong partner, with all the consequent trouble this causes to the individuals concerned and society as a whole. Chapter 3 outlines the development of the CQ Test, as well as the scoring and validation methods that put it on a scientific footing.

Those who are interested only in assessing their compatibility with a particular partner may skip the first three background chapters if they wish and turn straight to Chapter 4. This contains all the information necessary for arriving at the CQ score and also offers other suggestions as to who you might take the test with. Chapter 5 tells you what your CQ scores mean.

The 'confidential' version of the test given in Chapter 4 is devised so that you can work out a CQ score without knowing your partner's answers. All you find out is your overall compatibility, without loss of privacy. However, some couples may wish to go on to compare their answers as a way of diagnosing particular areas of conflict; perhaps using this as a starting point for discussion to see whether some accommodation can be reached. This requires taking the CQ Test again together, as an 'open test', so that the particular points of disagreement can be highlighted. Chapter 6 guides you in your interpretation of these differences and how you might cope with them. We recommend that you don't begin with the open test, since it might invalidate the result if you feel that your partner is looking over your shoulder as you choose your responses. The loss of anonymity can be instructive, but possibly at the expense of validity.

Finally, Chapter 7 provides you with the means to discover how important any differences are, specifically relating to you and your partner. It might be, for instance, that although you don't see eye-to-eye over a particular issue, it matters to neither of you. On the other hand, a difference of opinion over some other item could indeed bother one − or both − of you. You'll be able to discover this using the 24 Tests of Importance.

Here's wishing you the very best of luck − while at the same time trusting you will need less of it in the future to ensure your happiness.

Glenn Wilson and Jon Cousins

CHAPTER 1

The similarity factor

WALKING THE DOG

Barry (63) and Vivienne (64) have been happily married for 39 years. Their son and daughter are both also married, with children of their own. After almost 40 years, Vivienne thinks she already knows just about everything there is to know about Barry but they decide to take part in the trials for the CQ Test more for fun than anything else.

A score of 131 shows them to be extremely compatible, with remarkably few areas of difference. When they do focus on those differences, just two stand out. They are a couple of points apart on the subject of exercise and also have differing views about their weights. Barry is a bit of a couch potato and perhaps not surprisingly also carries a spot of extra weight. Vivienne is the chief dog exerciser in the household, always keen to get out for walks, and perhaps this helps her keep slim as well. When they talk it through, they discover that Barry mistakenly thinks Vivienne wants to get out of the house with the dog so as to be alone, while Vivienne wishes that Barry would exercise a little more. Amused at having learnt something new about each other after so many years, they agree to walk the dog together in the evenings.

Throughout history there have been two main competing theories of partner attraction. One is the idea of 'complementation', summarised in the saying that 'opposites attract'. The other is the idea that we gravitate towards people who are like ourselves, as expressed in the proverb 'birds of a feather flock together'.

The complementation theory suggests that we seek others who can 'fill the gap' or compensate in some way for our own deficiencies. For example, if we ourselves are shy and introvert, then we might want to pair off with an extravert, so that they can do all the talking and be the life and soul of the party, thus covering for our inability to fulfil this role. Or more simply, the suggestion is that if one partner likes to do a lot of talking, the other had better be a good listener. Similarly, if one person likes to be the boss, then he or she should live with someone who falls easily into the role of servant; two people fighting for supremacy would be a recipe for disaster.

The similarity principle asserts quite the opposite. According to this view, what we really want is a 'meeting of true minds', in which two people enjoy each other's company because they have a great deal in common with respect to attitudes, interests and preferred activities. Certain fundamental differences can eat slowly at the heart of a relationship, and without common ground a couple are bound to drift apart progressively.

Research findings

So which of these theories is true? Do people, in practice, pair off with others who are opposites, or those who are more like themselves? And which kind of relationship lasts better or results in greater satisfaction? The argument is, of course, open to testing by scientific methods. There has been a great deal of research on these questions over the last few decades, and nearly all of it comes out in favour of the similarity principle, or 'homogamy' as the scientists call it (like marries like).

This research, reviewed by Glenn and Chris McLaughlin in their book *The Science of Love*, shows that established partners tend to be alike in age, race, religion, intelligence, education, social status, body measurements such as height and weight, physical attractiveness as rated by other people, personality, sex drive, attitudes, habits and leisure preferences. There is no area of behaviour yet discovered in which this 'assortative mating' is reversed.

More importantly, the research tells us that those partners who are most alike are more likely to stay together in the long-term and tend to report greater satisfaction with their relationship. Admittedly, many of the studies are 'cross-sectional', showing only that similar partners are happier at the time they took part in the study (rather than over a longer term). However, the few studies that have adopted the more ideal 'longitudinal' approach, following the same couples through time, confirm that couples who are more alike are both happier and stay together longer. Apparently, birds of a feather not only flock together, they also nest together.

Why this should be so is not entirely clear. Some argue that we marry people who are similar to ourselves because they are likely to be close and accessible (neighbours, workmates, etc). With this argument, we get on well with them because we understand and empathise with them better than people from different backgrounds. It also seems obvious that having a lot in common with our partner leads us to share more activities and hence find each other's company more rewarding.

Other psychologists think the matter is rather more

complicated; if heterosexual, either we fall (narcissistically) in love with an opposite-sex image of ourselves, or an image of our opposite-sex parent as they were when we were infants (the Oedipal imprinting hypothesis). There is some research support for such ideas; for example, a tendency for people to match the eye colour of their opposite-sex parent more often than the same-sex parent when choosing a partner. Whatever the precise reason, the positive effects of partner similarity on the prospects of a relationship are undeniable.

The complementation 'myth'

If the research findings are so clear, then why does the idea of complementation ('opposites attract') persist in the minds and arguments of so many people? Why does '*vive le difference*' ring such a bell in our head?

The probable reason is that there are senses in which the theory contains a grain of truth. One is that trade-offs sometimes occur in partnerships, the most conspicuous being that of male status combining with female youth and beauty. The spectacle of a rich and famous, however plain and elderly, man, marrying a 'pretty young thing' is easily recognisable. Less common, but equally recognisable, is the reverse case of a high status, middle-aged woman sporting a 'toy boy'. Among their several marriages, Elizabeth Taylor and Joan Collins have both experimented with younger, handsome men of lesser social power than themselves. Each party to these arrangements may obtain something they want, but the relationships have poor prognoses and seldom last very long.

Another sense in which complementation (of a kind) does apply concerns the strongly gendered characteristics, those on which many men and women typically differ.

Within the context of traditional heterosexual part-nerships, one partner may contribute a male quality and the other its female flip-side. This is a pattern that goes beyond just genital anatomy; it applies to many other physical and psychological traits.

Research has shown that where there is typically a male–female difference within the population at large; partnerships that display this average difference within themselves tend to be more stable. Take height for example: men are on average taller than women by around 5 to 6 inches, and so a couple with this degree of difference works best. Note that tall women still pair off with tall men and short women with short men, so the similarity principle is relative (it still operates when coefficients of correlation are calculated), but it is a 'cardinal rule' of dating that he be taller than her. The exceptions, like Tom Cruise (5 foot 7 inches) and Nicole Kidman (5 foot 11 inches), are inclined to be unstable.

The same applies to personality traits on which men and women typically differ. Research shows that men are, on average, more cold and competitive (occasionally even psy-chopathic), while women are relatively emotional and empathic (volatile and sensitive to the feelings of others). Some have described this difference as 'instrumental' versus 'expressive'. Men are typically active and like to 'get things done', whereas women are more inclined to be commu-nicative. Research shows that partnerships where these personality differences are in the conventional direction are usually more stable and happy.

Sex roles also lend themselves to separation of tasks and skills. For example, women do most of the cooking and cleaning, while men do more carpentry, car maintenance and heavy lifting. Wives often learn a great deal about family health and education, while their husbands acquire expertise with computers and technology. If all tasks and learning are equally divided and conducted in parallel, then there may be little point in forming a partnership in the first place. Bringing different knowledge, skills and enthusiasms to the relationship provides a kind of glue.

There are, then, certain senses in which complementation does apply, or may have applied in the past, but they are more difficult to quantify and less significant than similarities when predicting success and happiness in partnerships.

Key areas of similarity

Given that similarity is important, in what areas of personality and lifestyle is it most salient? Perhaps the most obvious case is that of attitudes towards sexual permissiveness, pornography and infidelity.

For some people, sex is a precious and private 'gift' that must remain totally exclusive within the relationship. For others, it is just 'fun', a kind of recreation that can be enjoyed in many forms and with many people, without necessarily impinging on the love for one's partner. Clearly, two individuals coming from different ends of this spectrum of viewpoints are bound to clash. Hillary Clinton could apparently tolerate Bill's peccadilloes; others might not.

The same applies to attitudes in other sensitive areas such as religion and politics. People who are deeply religious are bound to be uncomfortable with avowed atheists and those who are politically conservative rub badly with extreme liberals.

Intelligence and cultural preferences are other areas that

are important for long-term compatibility. Unless people can connect intellectually, their conversations will be empty and unsatisfactory. It has been said that this may have contributed to the breakdown of the marriage between Prince Charles and Diana Spencer. His interests span science, agriculture, ecology, classical architecture, art and music, whereas she was more preoccupied with compassionate issues, fashion, partying and interpersonal intrigues. Charles and Diana may have had other problems, but these differences would not have helped.

IQ connects with educational level, social class and artistic preferences, but is not synonymous with any of them. It thus needs to be assessed from many different angles. Musical taste is important in its own right, but it may also be used as an indirect indicator of IQ, since people who prefer classical and jazz tend to be more intelligent than those who favour pop and heavy metal. Similarly, people who prefer documentaries on TV tend to be higher in IQ than those who choose quizzes and soaps.

Then there are simple matters of lifestyle. Clearly, a person who cannot abide the smell of cigarette smoke will not get on with a chain smoker, nor an alcoholic with a teetotaller. One who is allergic to pets has difficulty cohabiting with a cat-lover, and a person who wants children is unsuited to someone who has several already and/or no desire to start a new family. A woman who hankers for exotic food and restaurants is badly matched with a man who likes home cooking every night. And so on. Research and clinical experience over the years has identified key areas, such as those described above, where differences are particularly likely to be troublesome in a long-term relationship.

No doubt some people will say 'that may be so, but don't we enjoy discovering how our partner views things differently from ourselves and their ability to introduce us to interests and activities that we have not previously tried?' Can we not value our differences as life-enhancing? Rather than destroy our relationship, these differences may be an antidote to boredom. Truly, some differences are positive and make life together more colourful, but we also need a certain amount of common ground, and this is much more difficult to find. However many points of contact we establish, there will always be plenty of differences to celebrate, and it is better that they do not fall in vital areas where they are likely to be irreconcilable.

The thrust of all the evidence to date is that we are better suited to partnerships with people who are like ourselves. This may sound narcissistic, as though we are seeking a reflection of ourselves in the mirror (albeit usually an opposite-sex version). But the truth is that rapport depends upon the ability to see things from the point of view of the other person. Empathy is easier when that person thinks along similar lines to ourselves. On a more practical note, if a couple cannot agree on what TV programme to watch, what movie or play to go to, or what outdoor activities to engage in, they are bound to go their separate ways for much of the time, and so drift apart. This is why it is so important to share similar intelligence, attitudes, sense of humour, tastes and leisure preferences. Research has repeatedly confirmed that 'those who play together stay together.'

CHAPTER 2

Why do we fall in love with the wrong people?

YOURS UNFAITHFULLY

Simon (46) and Paula (44) were married for 19 years but have been divorced for the past three. Their two daughters (15 and 17) live with Paula in the family home while Simon lives with Kate, whom he met through work. While Paula was understandably bitter when Simon left her and the girls for Kate, the anger has subsided enough for her to realise that it may have been for the best, and she respects Simon's determination to do all he can to maintain contact with his daughters.

A little surprisingly they both agreed to take part in trials for the CQ Test; partly to see where they went wrong, but also to see how they can make things easier for each other over the next few years until the girls leave home.

Their CQ score after taking the open test was 86, below average, which suggests that they might have thought more seriously before getting married all those years ago. Among many differences, they learn that Paula felt she was an inexperienced lover. It never bothered her, but Simon had always felt uncomfortable about the situation.

Not surprisingly Paula saw sexual fidelity as being essential, while Simon thought you had to expect affairs. Their discussion brings to light her concern that the girls could well grow up with a diminished view of the importance of remaining faithful within a relationship, and Simon agrees to talk things through with them, letting the girls know he now regrets his infidelity.

Although couples that stick together usually have a great deal in common, many mistakes are made along the way. A cursory glance at the ever-escalating divorce statistics reminds us that many couples discover somewhere down the line that they have made a ghastly error and would be better off with someone else, or even living alone. Does our willingness to tie the knot with unsuitable partners simply represent carelessness or the triumph of hope over experience, or are there forces at work that push people positively toward disaster? Is there a devil that seeks to tempt people and ensnare them in unsuitable marriages?

The short answer is 'yes', and that devil is a chemist. We share with other animals certain brain circuits, hormones, pheromones, enzymes and neurotransmitters (nerve-signalling chemicals) that have evolved to attract us to others (usually fertile members of the opposite sex). Another array of brain chemicals seems calculated to persuade us to bond with them for a certain period of time, the evolutionary purpose being to ensure that our offspring have the support of two parents during their most vulnerable early years.

Sex hormones

The initial attraction phase of a relationship, often referred to as lust in its early 'hungry' stages, has a lot to do with hormones. Men, especially young men, are notoriously predatory in their sex drive and capable of being aroused by female nudity and visual stimuli of the unsubtle, 'pornographic' kind, and various infantile reminiscences of important female figures in their childhood. This is not due to social learning or peer pressure but is a direct result of male hormones. The main offender is a hormone called testosterone, which even before birth primes the brain to seek sexual stimuli. This latent desire is powerfully reactivated in later life, particularly around puberty and early adulthood.

Women also experience some degree of lust, perhaps because they also have a small supply of testosterone. Whereas with men testosterone is secreted by the testes, in women it is produced mainly by the adrenal cortex, though the ovaries also contribute. Women are by no means immune to the sight of a hunk with a promising 'lunch-box'; the main difference with women is that they are most attracted to men who display signs of dominance; not just physical strength but, more importantly with human females, social status and accomplishment. Dominance is important to women because it signals earning power and hence capacity to provide resources to support them through pregnancy and the early stages of motherhood. Oestrogen is probably more important in determining this preference for provider males, also guiding females towards partners who are available, generous and caring (sensitive).

Interestingly, women seem to have cyclical preferences for different types of men. Women who are ovulating (and therefore likely to become pregnant) are more attracted to 'sensitive' men with softer features, compared with women who are taking oral contraceptives, who favour more 'macho' features. The psychologists at St Andrews and Stirling universities, where these discoveries were made, point out that 'where a woman chooses her partner while she is on the pill, and then comes off it to have a child, she may find she is married to the wrong man' (*Sunday Times*, London, 12 January 2003). Clearly, there are certain dangers in allowing ourselves to be hostages to our hormones.

Pheromones

Similar to hormones, but affecting other people rather than ourselves, are chemicals called pheromones. These are emitted from certain nooks and crannies of the body, notably the armpits and crotch region, and are carried in the air until arriving at the nasal receptors of potential partners. These pheromones affect us both at a conscious 'smell' sensation level and at an unconscious level, of which we are not aware.

The complexity of these effects is considerable. There is evidence, for example, that we are attracted to partners whose pheromones indicate that their immune system is different from our own. This would have the evolutionary function of broadening the immune spectrum of any offspring the couple may go on to produce. Our children thus gain 'hybrid vigour' and are resistant to a greater variety of diseases. However, this effect is mainly observed in women who are ovulating, and hence more likely to get pregnant. When menstruating, already pregnant, or taking oral contraceptives, women are more likely to be attracted to partners who emit 'familial' pheromones. Presumably, the survival value of this tendency is that genetic similarity signals altruistic, supportive behaviours. Men, in the meantime, gravitate towards partners who are young, novel and in mid-cycle.

None of these natural forces are geared towards attracting us to partners who would be good for us in the long-term. On the contrary, they may trick us into associations with people who will ultimately make us unhappy.

Neurotransmitter substances

As people begin to experience sexual attraction and fall in love, they become tongue-tied, feel their pulse racing and their face flushing, and they experience a great variety of other symptoms, such as sweaty palms and a heightened perception of colour, sound and fragrance. These effects are down to other 'activating' brain chemicals, such as dopamine, nor-epinephrine, and phenylethylamine (PEA). The latter is similar to some of the stimulants contained in chocolate, which may help to explain why people who are feeling deserted and unloved often develop a craving for chocolate.

The desperate sensation that lovers often experience – the need to be with the other person virtually all the time, and to miss them whenever they are absent – seems to be connected with low levels of another neurotransmitter chemical, called serotonin or 5HT. Donatella Marazziti and colleagues at the University of Pisa have established that this is a condition that the most infatuated lovers share with patients suffering from obsessional-compulsive disorder. Their comparison has prompted some psychologists to argue that romantic love is best understood as a mild form of neurosis, or even insanity. It would follow that drugs that act in such a way to raise serotonin levels in the brain (Prozac being the most famous of them) should be a way of 'curing' both conditions. Indeed, Prozac-type drugs have shown promise as a treatment for obsessional-compulsive disorder but, not surprisingly, few people approach doctors seeking a cure for having fallen in love.

Bonding hormones

As romantic love usually leads to intense sexual activity and orgasm, a new, longer-lasting bonding force comes into operation. This depends on increased secretion of other chemicals, notably endorphins (the brain's internally generated opiates), and two hormones called oxytocin and vasopresin. These chemicals have the effect of 'gluing' the couple together (psychologically speaking) in a manner parallel to the bond that quickly develops between a mother and her new-born infant. Indeed, the mother-infant attachment shares much of the same brain chemistry.

This bonding tendency does not depend upon religious or moral values; it is part of the genetic heritage of our species. Evidence for this comes from experiments in which non-human species that are monogamous are rendered promiscuous (or vice versa) by genetic engineering in which critical genes concerned with secretion of hormones such as oxytocin are transferred from one to the other. In other words, faithfulness – whether in swans, voles or human couples – seems to arise from genetically determined hormone secretions and the effect that these have on our brain, instincts and behaviour. Humans are not the most monogamous among animals, but a certain degree of bonding does, nevertheless, take place.

The human bonding process may only take us in hand for a few years – long enough for our children to become less dependent. The idea of a 'seven-year itch' gained support from a MORI poll of nearly 1,000 married couples, conducted for *Reader's Digest* in 2001. Asked 'Have you ever wished you could just wake up one morning and not be married any more?', around one in five wives and one in seven husbands said 'yes'. Couples in the first five years of marriage and those who had reached their golden wedding anniversary were most stable, with only one in ten wishing they were single again. But of those who had been married for between five and nine years, one third would gladly opt out. Thus hormonal bonding may be good for a few years, after which some companionate qualities will be needed to carry us through.

Who wants to be a robot?

Many people find information such as this rather cold and disturbing. It somehow seems to remove the mystery and romance from human relationships, stripping us of dignity and reducing us to robots without free will. Yet there is no real reason why understanding the biological forces underlying our passions should render them less real. We can still enjoy the experience of falling in love, just as much as the student of chemistry who knows that water is comprised of H_2O molecules still enjoys a good swim on a hot summer day. More than that, knowing the mechanism of human bonding might enable us to treat it with respect and help us to avoid some of its more adverse consequences.

For most people, the experience of being 'head-over-heels in love' is one of the most memorable and ecstatic feelings they will ever enjoy, so the 'devil' in our brain is not necessarily a sworn enemy. We are not arguing that falling in love is an experience to be resisted at all costs. This is probably impossible and certainly not desirable. What we are arguing is that so long as we do retain some semblance of control, we might organise our circumstances in such a way that when the lightning strikes we are not standing barefoot in water. If we contrive to meet and mix with people to whom we are suited as long-term friends and companions then the magic, when it does happen, is less likely to hook us into a union with a bleak or non-existent future. If 'addiction' is inevitable, we are surely better to experiment with 'drugs' that have fewer harmful side-effects.

Falling in love 'at random'

Gilbert and Sullivan's operetta *The Sorcerer* provides a salutary moral tale. This concerns a well-meaning young couple whom, deeply in love themselves, desire to see everyone else in the village equally happily paired. Thus they lace the teapot at the vicar's garden party with a potion that causes each individual to fall helplessly in love with the first person they encounter upon wakening from their elixir-induced sleep. Inevitably the result is chaos, each character falling for a patently inappropriate mate. Clearly 'chemical' love, though it may appear to be some kind of poetic ideal, is usually an unmitigated disaster. In the absence of any rational basis to a relationship, infatuation may be the better name for it.

Interestingly, there is some research indicating that human partnerships are established fairly randomly, as in *The Sorcerer*. An American psychologist called David Lykken reasoned that if there was any kind of logic to mate choice, then identical twins should marry partners who are more alike than the partners of non-identical twins. This did not turn out to be the case, however. In a sample of 738 middle-aged couples, Lykken could find no evidence of genetics influencing the traits of their partners, leading him to conclude that mate-choice is essentially random. According to Lykken, it simply depends on 'where you are when Cupid's arrow strikes'.

But is this the way it really ought to be? What we prefer to call 'true love' is not a flash in the pan, however momentarily exhilarating, but something of lasting value. That is what the CQ was developed in order to facilitate.

CHAPTER 3

Development of the CQ Test

PORN PROBLEMS

Jill (32) and Mark (35) spent a year or so dating, until eventually Jill sold her place and moved in with Mark, taking her cat with her. They have been officially living together for 18 months. The early head-over-heels passion of their relationship has cooled a little but they're still happy together and are pleased with their initial CQ score of 116, showing them to be very compatible.

It must be said, however, that they were fairly surprised by a couple of the differences that were brought to light when they took the open test. Principally, they differ in the areas of chivalry and their attitudes towards pornography. Jill believes that chivalry is an essential part of life, while Mark regards it as something that is 'OK sometimes'. On the subject of pornography, meanwhile, Jill prefers to avoid it while Mark finds it a great turn-on. Both of these mismatches suggest that they could face problems in later life, and Mark readily agrees to try to behave in a more chivalrous manner.

However, Jill was upset and hurt about Mark's revelations about pornography since she felt it meant he didn't find her sexy and attractive. When they talked things through, however, they both acknowledged that they have sexual fantasies, and Jill saw that Mark's liking for pornography was no more threatening to their relationship than her enjoyment of romantic novels. After 'confessing' (nearly) all to each other, they decided to introduce some experimentation into their lovemaking.

Early history of compatibility testing

In the early 1980s Glenn Wilson was approached by Ivan Berg Software Ltd to devise a partner compatibility test for the first generation of home computers, which included Sinclair, BBC, Acorn and Commodore. The package Wilson constructed, called *Matchmaker*, consisted of 25 items that would each yield 'discrepancies' of between 0 and 4 points (totalling a possible 100). Subtracting the total discrepancy score from 100 yielded a 'percentage compatibility'. Scored in this way, *Matchmaker* became a popular parlour game, a sort of 'electronic spin-the-bottle' that people used for amusement at dinner parties. Just how many relationships were established, consolidated or possibly disturbed, by this test is hard to know.

The test also appeared on a national TV show called *Where There's Life*, hosted by Dr Miriam Stoppard, with members of the audience completing the test on arrival and being introduced to 'compatible' strangers to see how well they would get on. To the author's knowledge, at least one lasting relationship resulted from this TV programme. More recently, in a TV programme concerned with prediction of the future, the same measure showed itself superior to astrology in predicting which of several courting couples would still be together six months later in the new millennium.

The modern CQ Test

Matchmaker was the forerunner of the CQ Test. When in 2000, Jon Cousins approached Glenn Wilson with the idea of starting a partner introduction web site founded on scientific principles, the test was quickly pulled from Wilson's files as the starting point for discussion. Between them, Glenn and Jon updated and revised the items and decided that the percentage scoring system was not satisfactory because people did not know how to interpret it. In particular, couples found their scores disappointing low, even when they were more than averagely compatible. The typical range of scores, around 60-80%, based on the experience of school-exam marks, seemed rather mediocre.

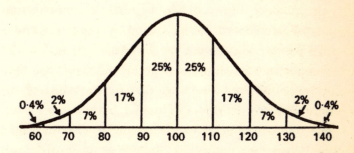

Jon Cousins then came up with the idea of modelling our scoring procedure on the IQ distribution, with which people already have some familiarity. This assumes a 'normal' (rainbow-shaped) distribution with a mean at 100 (by definition). The dispersion (spread of scores) is defined by a standard deviation of 15 points above and below that mean. (This number was chosen rather arbitrarily because it corresponded to the natural spread of 'raw' scores emerging with the pioneer IQ test, the Stanford-Binet.) A characteristic of this distribution (see diagram above) is that half the scores fall in the range of 90 to 110, while scores of 70 and 130 may be considered particularly low and high respectively. In the case of the CQ Test, scores close to 100 indicate average compatibility, while 70 and 130 signify very low and high compatibility.

Standardising the CQ

In order to arrive at proper norms for assigning CQ scores of this type, it was necessary to administer the test to a large sample of men and women. For this we used a random sample of 2,159 adults over the age of 18, representing individuals who had completed the CQ Test on entry to the Cybersuitors.com web-site by the end of October 2002. There were 1,234 men and 925 women. Discrepancies (a total of 1.14 million) between all male–female combinations within this sample were calculated and an empirical formula derived that would convert these discrepancy scores into the normal distribution described above. This formula was then used to calculate the table shown on page 196 which allows conversion of raw discrepancies into CQ scores with a 'floor' of 28 (a point the same distance below the mean as the ceiling of 172 is above the mean), where the two members of the pair answer all questions identically. One of the reasons for doing this was that it would eliminate the risk of having to deal with negative CQs (however infrequent these might be).

Validity studies

The next step was to validate the CQ as a predictor of partnership satisfaction. This was done by having 125 married couples complete the CQ Test in trials, working independently of each other (on the confidential test), along with a standard marital happiness questionnaire, the 'Locke-Wallace Marital Adjustment Test'. The latter asks individuals a variety of questions along the lines of: 'If you had your life to live over again, would you marry the same person?', 'Do you ever wish that you had not married?', 'How would you rate the degree of happiness, everything considered, of your present marriage?'

Overall, our married sample of professional counsellors and alternative therapists were fairly content with their marriages, as indicated by higher than average Locke-Wallace scores and CQs averaging 116. This was 16 points higher than the mean for randomly paired couples from the same group, indicating quite a strong tendency toward compatibility in the established couples. This in itself could be considered validation of the CQ score.

Nevertheless, there was some variance in quality of the different marriages as assessed by the Locke-Wallace Test, some being seen by the individuals as less satisfactory than others, and this variation was found to correlate with the CQ measure (.33 for men and .28 for women). In other words, both men and women who expressed less satisfaction with their marriage tended to be in partnerships with lower CQs, while those with higher CQs were more content. This could not have been due to couples growing more alike with time, because CQ scores were unrelated to the duration of the relationship.

An analysis of which CQ questions might be most critical for men and women revealed some interesting differences as to which discrepancies were most likely to diminish satisfaction. The top seven items for each gender were as follows:

Men	Women
1 Sexual fidelity	1 Sexual fidelity
2 Physical attractiveness	2 Preferred type of relationship
3 Preferred type of relationship	3 Liking for parties
4 Liking for parties	4 Tolerance of smoking
5 Taste for exotic food	= 5 Political views
6 Sexual experience	= 5 Libido
7 Libido	7 Attitude towards pornography

Sexual fidelity, preferred type of relationship (casual vs committed), liking for parties and libido emerged as particularly important areas of concern for both men and women. However, other areas seemed to be of greater import to one gender than the other. Men seemed to be more disturbed by disparities in physical attractiveness, food preferences and sexual experience; while smoking, politics and pornography were more important areas of concern for women. There were no items at all on which differences between the two members of the partnership were beneficial to the happiness of the relationship, again confirming the predictive value of similarity and the failure of complementation theory.

Comparisons of happiness

The above analysis was based on the strength and significance of correlation coefficients, which involves some understanding of statistics. But there is another way of looking at the differences between men and women that is perhaps easier to appreciate. If our married couples are divided into two broad groups designated 'happy' and 'unhappy' on the basis of the overall Locke–Wallace rating, then we can examine what percentage of couples within each of these groups yield a significant (2 points or more) difference on each of the CQ items. This enables us to make the following statements:

1 Couples sharing the same view on sexual fidelity are five times as likely to be happy as couples with different views on this issue.
2 Couples who enjoy the same type of TV programmes are almost three-and-a-half times as likely to be happy as those who disagree on TV viewing.

3   Couples with similar views on children are more than 3 times as likely to be happy as those with differing views.

4   Couples with similar tastes in food are almost three times as likely to be happy as those with different tastes.

5   Couples with similar sex drives are almost three times as likely to have happy marriages as those with differing libidos.

6   Women married to men who share the same view on pornography as themselves are eight times more likely to express happiness with their marriage. Men's satisfaction does not seem to be affected by whether or not their wife has similar attitudes toward pornography.

7   Women whose husbands have the same political view are 60% more likely to be happy than women who differ politically from their husband. Again, men do not seem to be affected by their wife's political preferences.

8   Men whose wives have substantially different levels of sexual experience from themselves are almost 40% more likely to have an unhappy marriage, whereas women are not affected by any differences between themselves and their husband as regards sexual experience.

These statements give a better idea of the strength of the relationships that were found in our research. Numerical details may be seen in the table overleaf. Note that because this is a different form of analysis, the items that emerge as most salient are not always those that showed the strongest correlations. What the two methods of analysis concur on is that partners who are similar across a range of different domains are more likely to express satisfaction with their marriage.

To whom important	Issue (CQ item)	Percentage showing major differences*		Factor by which happy and unhappy couples differ
		Unhappy couples	Happy couples	
Both men and women	Sexual fidelity	25.0%	4.8%	x5.2
	Food	20.8%	7.2%	x2.9
	Libido	50.0%	18.3%	x2.7
	Type of relationship	54.2%	31.3%	x1.7
Women only	Pornography	15.4%	1.9%	x8.1
	Politic	15.4%	9.6%	x1.6
Men only	Sexual experience	45.5%	32.7%	x1.4

* A gap of two or more points on the item in question

Reliability checks

A way of checking on the reliability of the CQ Test is to have the same person answer the questions a second time after an interval of about a month. By this time they have mostly forgotten the details of how they answered the first time around, so there are a few slight differences in their responses. CQs produced by this test–retest method, where the compatibility of the person is scored against the same person (rather than a partner), typically generate exceedingly high scores of around 150, which is almost equal to 100% compatibility, so this gives an idea of the absolute ceiling for scores that could be found in practice.

Another interesting approach is to have identical twins who have grown up separately complete the test. When this was done by one twin pair at the request of a TV company, the CQ score between the twins turned out to be 154. In other words, although they grew up apart from each other, these two twins might as well have been the same person completing the test twice after a short interval, again supporting the reliability of the test.

What the CQ doesn't tell us

The research outlined above gives us reasonable confidence that the CQ Test is a good summary measure of the similarity between pairs of individuals across a variety of domains that are important in predicting stable part-nerships. Of course, it does not cover all areas that may be important to couples seeking guidance on compatibility.

For one thing, there are certain traits that are threatening to the stability of relationships whichever partner con-tributes them, and it is even worse if both partners have them. High levels of emotional volatility, uncontrollable anger, self-centredness, irresponsibility, unreliability and psychopathic indifference to the feelings of others make people a bad risk generally and a convergence of them within a partnership is even more destructive. It is best to avoid people with such traits altogether.

Some key demographic markers such as age, gender, sexual orientation, race and geographical location were deliberately omitted because it was felt that people would be better left to choose their own parameters (or 'defaults' in computer-speak). Men very often want women younger than themselves, whereas many women are just as happy with an older man. Because there are such variations in this matter, it is better that people are left to determine their own limits.

The same applies to nationality and ethnic group: people differ greatly with respect to the partnerships they would contemplate, or how far they would be prepared to travel to meet a partner who is theoretically very suitable, and their ideas are often quite inflexible. Therefore, the choice of race and location are also best left in the hands of the individual. Sexual preference is another salient matter to most people; only a small minority of people are truly bisexual. In constructing the CQ Test, we did our best to devise items that would apply to gay men and lesbian women as well as heterosexual couples and, although we have not specifically researched the matter, we believe that the same principles of similarity would apply to homosexual couples.

As noted in Chapter 2, the other important area that is not assessed by the CQ Test is that broadly described as 'chemistry'. Even with an extremely high CQ, some couples will not feel comfortable with each other upon meeting and would never be inclined to fall in love in any circumstances. Nor do we deny the importance of these instincts, which are rather harder to define and predict. The first clue will be the reaction to a photograph, and other feelings will emerge after an actual meeting. Our argument is not that such human emotions should be set aside, but that the more practical issues might be taken account of in advance, so that when we do fall in love it is likely to result in a union with lasting value.

CHAPTER 4

Take the CQ Test

FAMILY PLANNING

Emma (24) met David (26) four months ago at a friend's wedding. They've been spending a lot of time together; David is madly in love and Emma's very happy too, although perhaps not as committed as her boyfriend seems to be.

They agreed to take the CQ Test as a way of finding out more about one another, quite certain that their score would go off the scale. It therefore surprised them both when they scored just 103, a very 'average' result. Keen to find out more about the things they disagree about, Emma arranges for them both to retake the test so they can determine where their 'gaps' are. There are quite a few but, perhaps most significantly, they learn that while Emma is set upon having a family, David is not that keen on children. It's something they've not talked about before.

Because David says he loves her, Emma had assumed that he'd want them to have children together, but now she's not so sure. Seeing things in a different light helps Emma. A couple of months later, their passion has noticeably cooled and they drift apart, although they remain good friends. Emma resolves to take the CQ Test sooner when her next relationship starts.

The chances are you picked up this book because you're curious to discover how compatible you are with someone you already know. If so, you'll be eager to take the test, but first of all a few words of explanation may prove helpful.

As we've already seen, the CQ Test was originally designed for use in a 'dating game' computer program, then turned into the partner-matching system that forms the foundation of online dating agency Cybersuitors.com. In both these instances, those taking the test do so anonymously. There's no chance of someone else seeing how you answer individual questions. This anonymity is important, particularly in those areas of the test that ask questions about sensitive subjects; and of course different people can be sensitive about different things. (It may be that you are actively keen to discover where your strengths and weaknesses are as a couple, and if this is the case you'll find a way in which you can do this in Chapter 6.)

For the printed version of the CQ Test, we still wanted to preserve each partner's confidentiality. But in calculating a CQ score, it is necessary for one (or both) of the partners to compare the way each person taking the test has answered each question. If we simply assigned letters or numbers to each answer, a curious partner could check back quite easily to discover how his or her partner had answered the questions.

'Substitution cryptography' came to the rescue. We've assigned combinations of numbers and letters, scrambling the order to make anyone's test results pretty secure, save to a tenacious code-breaker who might well need access to an Enigma machine. Take it from us, your answers to the CQ Test's questions, particularly those more sensitive ones buried away in the centre of the test, should be safe from prying eyes.

How to get the most from the test

When we set out to write this book its main purpose was to help those who were already dating or still looking for Mr or Ms Right; the CQ Test was developed as a means of providing dating couples with a more in-depth view of each other.

However it became progressively clear that there are other circumstances that would benefit from the CQ Test. You may think of still more ways in which the test could be put to work, in which case the authors would be pleased to hear from you.

If you're already dating

You might want to take the CQ Test with someone with whom you are currently romantically involved. In this case it's likely that you already know that there is a 'spark' between you. It would be surprising if you find that you achieve only a low CQ score when you take the test. If you are happy to be together, you almost certainly have many things in common.

But what happens if your score is low? While it's probably not cause to ride off into the sunset on your own, it will almost certainly be useful for you to go back through your individual answers to see which items represent your relationship's strengths and which its weaknesses (see Chapter 6).

It may be worth looking at any areas of difference even if you've got a high CQ score. It would be a rare thing indeed for a couple to have absolutely no points of conflict and, if you're thinking about a long-term relationship, it would be emotionally healthy to go into it with your eyes open.

If you're looking for love

You may have met someone with whom the 'chemistry' is right and you want to find out if you're suited as a couple. The trouble with 'chemistry' is that we rapidly lose all sense of realism and practicality. Before you know it, you can be swept off your feet and head-over-heels about someone who could easily turn out to be the wrong person (see Chapter 2). The CQ Test can be a great way for two people to find out more about each other.

Remember that our research found that happily married couples also tend to have high CQ scores. It can prove fascinating to take the test with someone you don't know very well, particularly if you are both willing to compare and discuss your answers once you have taken the confidential test. You may find yourselves discussing matters that you would otherwise have been extremely unlikely to talk about at such an early stage of getting to know someone. You'd have to be a very self-possessed person to ask someone you hardly knew for their views on sex, for instance. Take the test and the chances are that you'll be in for an interesting conversation.

If you're already married

If you've managed to persuade your other half to take the CQ Test, your relationship is probably not a total disaster area. An argumentative couple would be unlikely to co-operate enough to take the test in the first place. So what should you do if, as a married couple taking the CQ Test, you get a low score? It doesn't necessarily mean that the relationship is on the rocks. Our aim is not to put the kiss of death on bad relationships but instead to celebrate good ones, and also to enable those who are less happy to learn more about where things are going wrong, with a view to putting them right.

If you have been married for some time it would be surprising indeed if you discovered something about your partner that came as a true revelation. It is possible, however, that it might bring to the surface a fundamental difference (or perhaps several) that you have been doing your best to ignore.

Pretending that a problem doesn't exist won't make it go away, so it is better to recognise that you have opposite views about some things. Either rejoice that you're not so identical that life would be boring, or see if you need to find some middle ground over the conflict (see Chapter 6).

Finally, if you think you may have serious differences that are difficult to resolve, we can't stress enough the value of seeking professional counselling, which could save your relationship.

Relationship counsellors

When we conducted our research among married couples, we made a donation to the marriage guidance organisation Relate for each questionnaire returned, by way of thanks. We also shared our findings with Relate, because we believe the CQ Test to be a powerful tool that professional counsellors can use to encourage couples to open up (to the counsellor or to each other).

There are two ways to use the book in counselling. If partners are being counselled together, the confidential test can be used to obtain an overall score in such a way that no one present will know on which items the couple have scored high or low. A session following the test might be built around asking the couples to suggest where their strengths and weaknesses are.

Alternatively, a counsellor may decide to apply the open test (see Chapter 7). In such a case, the counsellor will discover where the couple's strengths and weaknesses are and can use these as discussion points, revealing them or not according to the occasion.

Among friends

Since the CQ Test first saw the light of day as a kind of 'spin the bottle' game to amuse dinner-party guests, there is no reason why this book cannot achieve similar objectives, provided the adults are consenting.

In a group situation you may wish to calculate the compatibility of everyone in the group with everyone else. If a group of good friends take the test you could expect the scores to be high. Wherever you get a social group of people, you'll have relationships; and exploring who's got most in common with whom can be both an education and an entertainment.

Each person in the group should take the confidential test. Simply follow the directions on page 34 to calculate the CQ scores of each 'couple' that interests you. As well as investigating opposite-sex heterosexual partners, it can also be revealing to look at same-sex couplings, whether gay or straight. The CQ Test doesn't suggest that, just because you score highly with someone, you have to leap into bed with them. It just means you have a great deal in common. What should you do when you've calculated the results? Perhaps that one's best left to you.

If you're on a training course or in Further Education

The CQ Test is based on a consideration of how much two people have in common. It looks at people's self-perception, values and views about critical issues in life. It could therefore be valuably applied as an ice-breaking activity at the beginning of a training course or further education class. It will enable the group member to find which others they have most in common with and highlight those who are different; an opportunity, perhaps, to celebrate diversity.

When a larger group of people takes the test, it may prove helpful to provide photocopies of Table 1 and Table 2 on pages 195 and 196, as well as the instructions. Write up each person's string of results next to their name on a large sheet of paper, so that all group members can calculate their compatibilities with everyone else.

Other ways of using the CQ Test

A test such as this, exploring how much people have in common, is an effective way of forecasting how well those people are likely to get on if they are to spend a substantial amount of time in each other's company.

The test might be used to assign rooms in shared accommodation (eg at college) or offices when work teams are being organised. Organisers of singles holidays could use the test to plan suitable introductions. Friends considering a holiday together could do the test to see how they'd be likely to get on. Think about your own life and you will almost certainly be able to think of other ways in which you can use the CQ Test.

When you're ready to take the test, follow the directions on the next page. The process shouldn't take long; fifteen minutes or so for two people. As with any test of this nature, it will pay you to not think too hard about your answers. Once you have read the question and scanned its five possible answers, try to choose the response that immediately seems most appropriate. Although further consideration might cause you to change your mind, the best answer tends to be the one you selected first.

If you want an honest evaluation of your CQ (and plainly that is the ambition of this book) it will pay you both to be as honest you can with your answers. Some questions concern themselves with highly personal matters, but then any close human relationship involves such issues and a compatibility test that ducked them would be one that failed to meet its purpose.

How to take the CQ Test

1 The test works out the compatibility of two people, so that's the first requirement: a pair of willing participants. You'll also need this book, and a pencil and paper. The instructions may look a little complicated, but the process is really quite straightforward once you've got the hang of it.

2 Prepare for the test by drawing yourself a table with four rows and eight columns:

3 Label the rows and columns as follows, placing the names of the two people taking the test in the positions indicated by Person 1 and Person 2:

	(i)	(ii)	(iii)	(iv)	(v)	(vi)	total
Person 1							
Person 2							
Score							

4 Each person in turn should take the test as follows:

5 Begin on page 39 with Question 1. Select one of its five answers that most closely matches your view of yourself, then move on to the next question as directed. There's no need to remember or make a note of which answer you chose. If you come across a question that doesn't have any answer you feel is completely right, just select the one that is nearest.

6 Continue this process, answering four questions in total until you arrive at Result (i), which will consist of two

letters. Enter these under heading (i) in the row of the table with your name on it. Here's what you'd do if your score was N L, for example:

	(i)	(ii)	(iii)	(iv)	(v)	(vi)	total
Person 1	N L						
Person 2							
Score							

7   Now go back to page 39 and answer Question 2, then follow the same process, moving through another set of four questions until you've reached Result (ii), which will be another pair of letters. Enter them in the column under the heading (ii).

8   Repeat for Questions 3, 4, 5 and 6 on page 39. The table should now look something like this:

	(i)	(ii)	(iii)	(iv)	(v)	(vi)	total
Person 1	N L	R F	P C	D M	N O	L G	
Person 2							
Score							

9   Hand the book to the other person taking the test and ask him or her to follow the same procedure until you each have six pairs of letters:

	(i)	(ii)	(iii)	(iv)	(v)	(vi)	total
Person 1	N L	R F	P C	D M	N O	L G	✕
Person 2	A D	E P	B P	S O	B G	T B	✕
Score							

10 Now use Table 1 on page 195 to compare the two sets of results. Start by taking the first letter of each person's results in column (i), then look up the corresponding number in Table 1. For example, say that Person 1 has a result of N L and Person 2 a result of A D. Their first letters are N and A (it doesn't actually matter in which order you look up the letters in Table 1), which gives you a figure of 2. Enter this figure at the left hand side of the box at the foot of column (i) labelled Score.

11 Now do the same with the second letters (L and D in the example, which produce a figure of 4). Write this figure at the right–hand side of the box at the foot of column (i).

	(i)	(ii)	(iii)	(iv)	(v)	(vi)	total
Person 1	N L	R F	P C	D M	N O	L G	✕
Person 2	A D	E P	B P	S O	B G	T B	✕
Score	2 4						

37

12 Repeat the process in columns (ii), (iii), (iv), (v) and (vi).

13 Add together the 12 digits in the bottom row of the table and place the total in the bottom right-hand corner of the table.

14 Finally look up this total in Table 2 on page 196 to determine your CQ score.

Take the CQ Test

1   **How would you describe your height?**

I'd say I am quite tall.	Go to Question 7
I'm above average.	Go to Question 13
My height is about average really.	Go to Question 19
I'm below average height.	Go to Question 25
I'd describe myself as quite short.	Go to Question 31

2   **What sort of sex drive do you have?**

My sex drive is pretty non-existent.	Go to Question 8
I'd say my sex drive is reasonably low.	Go to Question 14
I'd describe my sex drive as about average really.	Go to Question 20
I think my sex drive is above average.	Go to Question 26
To be honest I'm absolutely insatiable.	Go to Question 32

3   **How would you rate your appearance?**

I think I'm very attractive.	Go to Question 9
I'd call myself rather attractive.	Go to Question 15
Compared to other people, I'd say I'm average.	Go to Question 21
I'd describe myself as rather plain.	Go to Question 27
I'm very plain really.	Go to Question 33

4   **How essential to you is sexual fidelity in a relationship?**

To me it's essential.	Go to Question 10
I'd say it is important.	Go to Question 16
I suppose the odd lapse is OK.	Go to Question 22
I think you have to expect affairs.	Go to Question 28
I'd want to have an open and swinging relationship.	Go to Question 34

5   **Which of the following best describes your view of parties?**

I actually prefer being alone.	Go to Question 11
Small groups are OK.	Go to Question 17
I think a few parties are OK.	Go to Question 23
I'm quite fond of parties.	Go to Question 29
I love wild parties.	Go to Question 35

6   **In your view, is money important?**

No, you can't buy happiness.	Go to Question 12
I just need enough money to live.	Go to Question 18
I want to be comfy.	Go to Question 24
I'd like to be rich.	Go to Question 30
Yes, I want to be very rich.	Go to Question 36

7 | **Being honest, which of these best describes you?** |
--- | --- | ---
| I'm really quite overweight. | Go to Question 37
| I'd say I am a little overweight. | Go to Question 43
| Compared to other people's my weight is about average. | Go to Question 49
| I'd describe myself as slim. | Go to Question 55
| I'm pretty skinny really. | Go to Question 61

8 | **What do you think about children?** |
--- | --- | ---
| I dislike them to be honest. | Go to Question 38
| I think other people's children are OK. | Go to Question 44
| I've no strong feelings one way or the other. | Go to Question 50
| I may want my own children one day. | Go to Question 56
| I definitely want my own (or already have them). | Go to Question 62

9 | **Which of the following best describes your view of drinking?** |
--- | --- | ---
| It's completely unacceptable. | Go to Question 39
| It's OK for other people but not for me. | Go to Question 45
| I drink occasionally. | Go to Question 51
| I drink quite often. | Go to Question 57
| To be honest I think I drink a bit too much. | Go to Question 63

10 | **What do you think of pornography?** |
--- | --- | ---
| I think it's disgusting. | Go to Question 40
| To be honest I prefer to avoid it. | Go to Question 46
| It's OK sometimes. | Go to Question 52
| It's harmless fun really. | Go to Question 58
| I actually think it's a great turn-on. | Go to Question 64

11 | **What is your view of smoking?** |
--- | --- | ---
| I think it's totally intolerable. | Go to Question 41
| I feel it's fairly undesirable. | Go to Question 47
| It's OK for other people to smoke. | Go to Question 53
| I'm a light smoker. | Go to Question 59
| I'd describe myself as a heavy smoker. | Go to Question 65

12 | **Which of the following best describes the type of relationship you'd prefer?** |
--- | --- | ---
| A casual friendship is fine. | Go to Question 42
| I'd prefer a lasting friendship. | Go to Question 48
| I would favour a short-term affair. | Go to Question 54
| My preference would be for an intimate long-term relationship. | Go to Question 60
| I would choose marriage. | Go to Question 66

13 **Being honest, which of these best describes you?**

I'm really quite overweight.	Go to Question 67
I'd say I am a little overweight.	Go to Question 73
Compared to other people's my weight is about average.	Go to Question 79
I'd describe myself as slim.	Go to Question 85
I'm pretty skinny really.	Go to Question 91

14 **What do you think about children?**

I dislike them to be honest.	Go to Question 68
I think other people's children are OK.	Go to Question 74
I've no strong feelings one way or the other.	Go to Question 80
I may want my own children one day.	Go to Question 86
I definitely want my own (or already have them).	Go to Question 92

15 **Which of the following best describes your view of drinking?**

It's completely unacceptable.	Go to Question 69
It's OK for other people but not for me.	Go to Question 75
I drink occasionally.	Go to Question 81
I drink quite often.	Go to Question 87
To be honest I think I drink a bit too much.	Go to Question 93

16 **What do you think of pornography?**

I think it's disgusting.	Go to Question 70
To be honest I prefer to avoid it.	Go to Question 76
It's OK sometimes.	Go to Question 82
It's harmless fun really.	Go to Question 88
I actually think it's a great turn-on.	Go to Question 94

17 **What is your view of smoking?**

I think it's totally intolerable.	Go to Question 71
I feel it's fairly undesirable.	Go to Question 77
It's OK for other people to smoke.	Go to Question 83
I'm a light smoker.	Go to Question 89
I'd describe myself as a heavy smoker.	Go to Question 95

18 **Which of the following best describes the type of relationship you'd prefer?**

A casual friendship is fine.	Go to Question 72
I'd prefer a lasting friendship.	Go to Question 78
I would favour a short-term affair.	Go to Question 84
My preference would be for an intimate long-term relationship.	Go to Question 90
I would choose marriage.	Go to Question 96

19   **Being honest, which of these best describes you?**

I'm really quite overweight.	Go to Question 97
I'd say I am a little overweight.	Go to Question 103
Compared to other people's my weight is about average.	Go to Question 109
I'd describe myself as slim.	Go to Question 115
I'm pretty skinny really.	Go to Question 121

20   **What do you think about children?**

I dislike them to be honest.	Go to Question 98
I think other people's children are OK.	Go to Question 104
I've no strong feelings one way or the other.	Go to Question 110
I may want my own children one day.	Go to Question 116
I definitely want my own (or already have them).	Go to Question 122

21   **Which of the following best describes your view of drinking?**

It's completely unacceptable.	Go to Question 99
It's OK for other people but not for me.	Go to Question 105
I drink occasionally.	Go to Question 111
I drink quite often.	Go to Question 117
To be honest I think I drink a bit too much.	Go to Question 123

22   **What do you think of pornography?**

I think it's disgusting.	Go to Question 100
To be honest I prefer to avoid it.	Go to Question 106
It's OK sometimes.	Go to Question 112
It's harmless fun really.	Go to Question 118
I actually think it's a great turn-on.	Go to Question 124

23   **What is your view of smoking?**

I think it's totally intolerable.	Go to Question 101
I feel it's fairly undesirable.	Go to Question 107
It's OK for other people to smoke.	Go to Question 113
I'm a light smoker.	Go to Question 119
I'd describe myself as a heavy smoker.	Go to Question 125

24   **Which of the following best describes the type of relationship you'd prefer?**

A casual friendship is fine.	Go to Question 102
I'd prefer a lasting friendship.	Go to Question 108
I would favour a short-term affair.	Go to Question 114
My preference would be for an intimate long-term relationship.	Go to Question 120
I would choose marriage.	Go to Question 126

25   **Being honest, which of these best describes you?**

I'm really quite overweight.	Go to Question 127
I'd say I am a little overweight.	Go to Question 133
Compared to other people's my weight is about average.	Go to Question 139
I'd describe myself as slim.	Go to Question 145
I'm pretty skinny really.	Go to Question 151

26   **What do you think about children?**

I dislike them to be honest.	Go to Question 128
I think other people's children are OK.	Go to Question 134
I've no strong feelings one way or the other.	Go to Question 140
I may want my own children one day.	Go to Question 146
I definitely want my own (or already have them).	Go to Question 152

27   **Which of the following best describes your view of drinking?**

It's completely unacceptable.	Go to Question 129
It's OK for other people but not for me.	Go to Question 135
I drink occasionally.	Go to Question 141
I drink quite often.	Go to Question 147
To be honest I think I drink a bit too much.	Go to Question 153

28   **What do you think of pornography?**

I think it's disgusting.	Go to Question 130
To be honest I prefer to avoid it.	Go to Question 136
It's OK sometimes.	Go to Question 142
It's harmless fun really.	Go to Question 148
I actually think it's a great turn-on.	Go to Question 154

29   **What is your view of smoking?**

I think it's totally intolerable.	Go to Question 131
I feel it's fairly undesirable.	Go to Question 137
It's OK for other people to smoke.	Go to Question 143
I'm a light smoker.	Go to Question 149
I'd describe myself as a heavy smoker.	Go to Question 155

30   **Which of the following best describes the type of relationship you'd prefer?**

A casual friendship is fine.	Go to Question 132
I'd prefer a lasting friendship.	Go to Question 138
I would favour a short-term affair.	Go to Question 144
My preference would be for an intimate long-term relationship.	Go to Question 150
I would choose marriage.	Go to Question 156

31 Being honest, which of these best describes you?

I'm really quite overweight.	Go to Question 157
I'd say I am a little overweight.	Go to Question 163
Compared to other people's my weight is about average.	Go to Question 169
I'd describe myself as slim.	Go to Question 175
I'm pretty skinny really.	Go to Question 181

32 What do you think about children?

I dislike them to be honest.	Go to Question 158
I think other people's children are OK.	Go to Question 164
I've no strong feelings one way or the other.	Go to Question 170
I may want my own children one day.	Go to Question 176
I definitely want my own (or already have them).	Go to Question 182

33 Which of the following best describes your view of drinking?

It's completely unacceptable.	Go to Question 159
It's OK for other people but not for me.	Go to Question 165
I drink occasionally.	Go to Question 171
I drink quite often.	Go to Question 177
To be honest I think I drink a bit too much.	Go to Question 183

34 What do you think of pornography?

I think it's disgusting.	Go to Question 160
To be honest I prefer to avoid it.	Go to Question 166
It's OK sometimes.	Go to Question 172
It's harmless fun really.	Go to Question 178
I actually think it's a great turn-on.	Go to Question 184

35 What is your view of smoking?

I think it's totally intolerable.	Go to Question 161
I feel it's fairly undesirable.	Go to Question 167
It's OK for other people to smoke.	Go to Question 173
I'm a light smoker.	Go to Question 179
I'd describe myself as a heavy smoker.	Go to Question 185

36 Which of the following best describes the type of relationship you'd prefer?

A casual friendship is fine.	Go to Question 162
I'd prefer a lasting friendship.	Go to Question 168
I would favour a short-term affair.	Go to Question 174
My preference would be for an intimate long-term relationship.	Go to Question 180
I would choose marriage.	Go to Question 186

37 How would you say your IQ compares to other people's?

I'd describe myself as bright.	Go to Question 187
I'm somewhat more intelligent than average.	Go to Question 193
My level of intelligence is about average.	Go to Question 199
I'd say I am a bit below average.	Go to Question 205
I think of myself as being a little dull, really.	Go to Question 211

38 What job do you do (or plan to)?

I'm a professional; eg doctor, teacher.	Go to Question 188
My role is managerial; eg business manager, police inspector.	Go to Question 194
My job is clerical, in admin or in customer service; eg secretary, chef.	Go to Question 200
I'm a skilled tradesperson; eg motor mechanic, decorator.	Go to Question 206
I work in a manual job; eg labourer, cleaner.	Go to Question 212

39 How would you describe your political views?

I'd describe myself as being far left.	Go to Question 189
You could label me left of centre.	Go to Question 195
I'm pretty neutral really, or not interested in politics.	Go to Question 201
I would say I am right of centre.	Go to Question 207
The best description of me would be far right.	Go to Question 213

40 How do you feel about keeping pets?

I hate them (or am allergic to them).	Go to Question 190
I don't really like them.	Go to Question 196
Some I like, others I don't.	Go to Question 202
I enjoy them if it's practical and acceptable where I live.	Go to Question 208
I can't imagine life without having a pet.	Go to Question 214

41 How religious would you say you are?

I'm active and committed to my religion.	Go to Question 191
I go to church or a place of worship sometimes.	Go to Question 197
I worship in private.	Go to Question 203
I'm not really religious and never worship.	Go to Question 209
I'd say I was actively anti-religious.	Go to Question 215

42 How experienced are you sexually?

I am still a virgin.	Go to Question 192
To be honest I'm rather inexperienced.	Go to Question 198
I've had no complaints so far.	Go to Question 204
I would class myself as an experienced lover.	Go to Question 210
I'd say I'm really hot stuff.	Go to Question 216

43 How would you say your IQ compares to other people's?

I'd describe myself as bright.	Go to Question 217
I'm somewhat more intelligent than average.	Go to Question 223
My level of intelligence is about average.	Go to Question 229
I'd say I am a bit below average.	Go to Question 235
I think of myself as being a little dull, really.	Go to Question 241

44 What job do you do (or plan to)?

I'm a professional; eg doctor, teacher.	Go to Question 218
My role is managerial; eg business manager, police inspector.	Go to Question 224
My job is clerical, in admin or in customer service; eg secretary, chef.	Go to Question 230
I'm a skilled tradesperson; eg motor mechanic, decorator.	Go to Question 236
I work in a manual job; eg labourer, cleaner.	Go to Question 242

45 How would you describe your political views?

I'd describe myself as being far left.	Go to Question 219
You could label me left of centre.	Go to Question 225
I'm pretty neutral really, or not interested in politics.	Go to Question 231
I would say I am right of centre.	Go to Question 237
The best description of me would be far right.	Go to Question 243

46 How do you feel about keeping pets?

I hate them (or am allergic to them).	Go to Question 220
I don't really like them.	Go to Question 226
Some I like, others I don't.	Go to Question 232
I enjoy them if it's practical and acceptable where I live.	Go to Question 238
I can't imagine life without having a pet.	Go to Question 244

47 How religious would you say you are?

I'm active and committed to my religion.	Go to Question 221
I go to church or a place of worship sometimes.	Go to Question 227
I worship in private.	Go to Question 233
I'm not really religious and never worship.	Go to Question 239
I'd say I was actively anti-religious.	Go to Question 245

48 How experienced are you sexually?

I am still a virgin.	Go to Question 222
To be honest I'm rather inexperienced.	Go to Question 228
I've had no complaints so far.	Go to Question 234
I would class myself as an experienced lover.	Go to Question 240
I'd say I'm really hot stuff.	Go to Question 246

49 **How would you say your IQ compares to other people's?**

I'd describe myself as bright.	Go to Question 247
I'm somewhat more intelligent than average.	Go to Question 253
My level of intelligence is about average.	Go to Question 259
I'd say I am a bit below average.	Go to Question 265
I think of myself as being a little dull, really.	Go to Question 271

50 **What job do you do (or plan to)?**

I'm a professional; eg doctor, teacher.	Go to Question 248
My role is managerial; eg business manager, police inspector.	Go to Question 254
My job is clerical, in admin or in customer service; eg secretary, chef.	Go to Question 260
I'm a skilled tradesperson; eg motor mechanic, decorator.	Go to Question 266
I work in a manual job; eg labourer, cleaner.	Go to Question 272

51 **How would you describe your political views?**

I'd describe myself as being far left.	Go to Question 249
You could label me left of centre.	Go to Question 255
I'm pretty neutral really, or not interested in politics.	Go to Question 261
I would say I am right of centre.	Go to Question 267
The best description of me would be far right.	Go to Question 273

52 **How do you feel about keeping pets?**

I hate them (or am allergic to them).	Go to Question 250
I don't really like them.	Go to Question 256
Some I like, others I don't.	Go to Question 262
I enjoy them if it's practical and acceptable where I live.	Go to Question 268
I can't imagine life without having a pet.	Go to Question 274

53 **How religious would you say you are?**

I'm active and committed to my religion.	Go to Question 251
I go to church or a place of worship sometimes.	Go to Question 257
I worship in private.	Go to Question 263
I'm not really religious and never worship.	Go to Question 269
I'd say I was actively anti-religious.	Go to Question 275

54 **How experienced are you sexually?**

I am still a virgin.	Go to Question 252
To be honest I'm rather inexperienced.	Go to Question 258
I've had no complaints so far.	Go to Question 264
I would class myself as an experienced lover.	Go to Question 270
I'd say I'm really hot stuff.	Go to Question 276

55 **How would you say your IQ compares to other people's?**

I'd describe myself as bright.	Go to Question 277
I'm somewhat more intelligent than average.	Go to Question 283
My level of intelligence is about average.	Go to Question 289
I'd say I am a bit below average.	Go to Question 295
I think of myself as being a little dull, really.	Go to Question 301

56 **What job do you do (or plan to)?**

I'm a professional; eg doctor, teacher.	Go to Question 278
My role is managerial; eg business manager, police inspector.	Go to Question 284
My job is clerical, in admin or in customer service; eg secretary, chef.	Go to Question 290
I'm a skilled tradesperson; eg motor mechanic, decorator.	Go to Question 296
I work in a manual job; eg labourer, cleaner.	Go to Question 302

57 **How would you describe your political views?**

I'd describe myself as being far left.	Go to Question 279
You could label me left of centre.	Go to Question 285
I'm pretty neutral really, or not interested in politics.	Go to Question 291
I would say I am right of centre.	Go to Question 297
The best description of me would be far right.	Go to Question 303

58 **How do you feel about keeping pets?**

I hate them (or am allergic to them).	Go to Question 280
I don't really like them.	Go to Question 286
Some I like, others I don't.	Go to Question 292
I enjoy them if it's practical and acceptable where I live.	Go to Question 298
I can't imagine life without having a pet.	Go to Question 304

59 **How religious would you say you are?**

I'm active and committed to my religion.	Go to Question 281
I go to church or a place of worship sometimes.	Go to Question 287
I worship in private.	Go to Question 293
I'm not really religious and never worship.	Go to Question 299
I'd say I was actively anti-religious.	Go to Question 305

60 **How experienced are you sexually?**

I am still a virgin.	Go to Question 282
To be honest I'm rather inexperienced.	Go to Question 288
I've had no complaints so far.	Go to Question 294
I would class myself as an experienced lover.	Go to Question 300
I'd say I'm really hot stuff.	Go to Question 306

61 **How would you say your IQ compares to other people's?**

I'd describe myself as bright.	Go to Question 307
I'm somewhat more intelligent than average.	Go to Question 313
My level of intelligence is about average.	Go to Question 319
I'd say I am a bit below average.	Go to Question 325
I think of myself as being a little dull, really.	Go to Question 331

62 **What job do you do (or plan to)?**

I'm a professional; eg doctor, teacher.	Go to Question 308
My role is managerial; eg business manager, police inspector.	Go to Question 314
My job is clerical, in admin or in customer service; eg secretary, chef.	Go to Question 320
I'm a skilled tradesperson; eg motor mechanic, decorator.	Go to Question 326
I work in a manual job; eg labourer, cleaner.	Go to Question 332

63 **How would you describe your political views?**

I'd describe myself as being far left.	Go to Question 309
You could label me left of centre.	Go to Question 315
I'm pretty neutral really, or not interested in politics.	Go to Question 321
I would say I am right of centre.	Go to Question 327
The best description of me would be far right.	Go to Question 333

64 **How do you feel about keeping pets?**

I hate them (or am allergic to them).	Go to Question 310
I don't really like them.	Go to Question 316
Some I like, others I don't.	Go to Question 322
I enjoy them if it's practical and acceptable where I live.	Go to Question 328
I can't imagine life without having a pet.	Go to Question 334

65 **How religious would you say you are?**

I'm active and committed to my religion.	Go to Question 311
I go to church or a place of worship sometimes.	Go to Question 317
I worship in private.	Go to Question 323
I'm not really religious and never worship.	Go to Question 329
I'd say I was actively anti-religious.	Go to Question 335

66 **How experienced are you sexually?**

I am still a virgin.	Go to Question 312
To be honest I'm rather inexperienced.	Go to Question 318
I've had no complaints so far.	Go to Question 324
I would class myself as an experienced lover.	Go to Question 330
I'd say I'm really hot stuff.	Go to Question 336

67 **How would you say your IQ compares to other people's?**

I'd describe myself as bright.	Go to Question 337
I'm somewhat more intelligent than average.	Go to Question 343 ✓
My level of intelligence is about average.	Go to Question 349
I'd say I am a bit below average.	Go to Question 355
I think of myself as being a little dull, really.	Go to Question 361

68 **What job do you do (or plan to)?**

I'm a professional; eg doctor, teacher.	Go to Question 338
My role is managerial; eg business manager, police inspector.	Go to Question 344
My job is clerical, in admin or in customer service; eg secretary, chef.	Go to Question 350
I'm a skilled tradesperson; eg motor mechanic, decorator.	Go to Question 356
I work in a manual job; eg labourer, cleaner.	Go to Question 362

69 **How would you describe your political views?**

I'd describe myself as being far left.	Go to Question 339
You could label me left of centre.	Go to Question 345
I'm pretty neutral really, or not interested in politics.	Go to Question 351
I would say I am right of centre.	Go to Question 357
The best description of me would be far right.	Go to Question 363

70 **How do you feel about keeping pets?**

I hate them (or am allergic to them).	Go to Question 340
I don't really like them.	Go to Question 346
Some I like, others I don't.	Go to Question 352
I enjoy them if it's practical and acceptable where I live.	Go to Question 358
I can't imagine life without having a pet.	Go to Question 364

71 **How religious would you say you are?**

I'm active and committed to my religion.	Go to Question 341
I go to church or a place of worship sometimes.	Go to Question 347
I worship in private.	Go to Question 353
I'm not really religious and never worship.	Go to Question 359
I'd say I was actively anti-religious.	Go to Question 365

72 **How experienced are you sexually?**

I am still a virgin.	Go to Question 342
To be honest I'm rather inexperienced.	Go to Question 348
I've had no complaints so far.	Go to Question 354
I would class myself as an experienced lover.	Go to Question 360
I'd say I'm really hot stuff.	Go to Question 366

73 **How would you say your IQ compares to other people's?**

I'd describe myself as bright.	Go to Question 367
I'm somewhat more intelligent than average.	Go to Question 373
My level of intelligence is about average.	Go to Question 379
I'd say I am a bit below average.	Go to Question 385
I think of myself as being a little dull, really.	Go to Question 391

74 **What job do you do (or plan to)?**

I'm a professional; eg doctor, teacher.	Go to Question 368
My role is managerial; eg business manager, police inspector.	Go to Question 374
My job is clerical, in admin or in customer service; eg secretary, chef.	Go to Question 380
I'm a skilled tradesperson; eg motor mechanic, decorator.	Go to Question 386
I work in a manual job; eg labourer, cleaner.	Go to Question 392

75 **How would you describe your political views?**

I'd describe myself as being far left.	Go to Question 369
You could label me left of centre.	Go to Question 375
I'm pretty neutral really, or not interested in politics.	Go to Question 381
I would say I am right of centre.	Go to Question 387
The best description of me would be far right.	Go to Question 393

76 **How do you feel about keeping pets?**

I hate them (or am allergic to them).	Go to Question 370
I don't really like them.	Go to Question 376
Some I like, others I don't.	Go to Question 382
I enjoy them if it's practical and acceptable where I live.	Go to Question 388
I can't imagine life without having a pet.	Go to Question 394

77 **How religious would you say you are?**

I'm active and committed to my religion.	Go to Question 371
I go to church or a place of worship sometimes.	Go to Question 377
I worship in private.	Go to Question 383
I'm not really religious and never worship.	Go to Question 389
I'd say I was actively anti-religious.	Go to Question 395

78 **How experienced are you sexually?**

I am still a virgin.	Go to Question 372
To be honest I'm rather inexperienced.	Go to Question 378
I've had no complaints so far.	Go to Question 384
I would class myself as an experienced lover.	Go to Question 390
I'd say I'm really hot stuff.	Go to Question 396

79 **How would you say your IQ compares to other people's?**

I'd describe myself as bright.	Go to Question 397
I'm somewhat more intelligent than average.	Go to Question 403
My level of intelligence is about average.	Go to Question 409
I'd say I am a bit below average.	Go to Question 415
I think of myself as being a little dull, really.	Go to Question 421

80 **What job do you do (or plan to)?**

I'm a professional; eg doctor, teacher.	Go to Question 398
My role is managerial; eg business manager, police inspector.	Go to Question 404
My job is clerical, in admin or in customer service; eg secretary, chef.	Go to Question 410
I'm a skilled tradesperson; eg motor mechanic, decorator.	Go to Question 416
I work in a manual job; eg labourer, cleaner.	Go to Question 422

81 **How would you describe your political views?**

I'd describe myself as being far left.	Go to Question 399
You could label me left of centre.	Go to Question 405
I'm pretty neutral really, or not interested in politics.	Go to Question 411
I would say I am right of centre.	Go to Question 417
The best description of me would be far right.	Go to Question 423

82 **How do you feel about keeping pets?**

I hate them (or am allergic to them).	Go to Question 400
I don't really like them.	Go to Question 406
Some I like, others I don't.	Go to Question 412
I enjoy them if it's practical and acceptable where I live.	Go to Question 418
I can't imagine life without having a pet.	Go to Question 424

83 **How religious would you say you are?**

I'm active and committed to my religion.	Go to Question 401
I go to church or a place of worship sometimes.	Go to Question 407
I worship in private.	Go to Question 413
I'm not really religious and never worship.	Go to Question 419
I'd say I was actively anti-religious.	Go to Question 425

84 **How experienced are you sexually?**

I am still a virgin.	Go to Question 402
To be honest I'm rather inexperienced.	Go to Question 408
I've had no complaints so far.	Go to Question 414
I would class myself as an experienced lover.	Go to Question 420
I'd say I'm really hot stuff.	Go to Question 426

85 **How would you say your IQ compares to other people's?**

I'd describe myself as bright.	Go to Question 427
I'm somewhat more intelligent than average.	Go to Question 433
My level of intelligence is about average.	Go to Question 439
I'd say I am a bit below average.	Go to Question 445
I think of myself as being a little dull, really.	Go to Question 451

86 **What job do you do (or plan to)?**

I'm a professional; eg doctor, teacher.	Go to Question 428
My role is managerial; eg business manager, police inspector.	Go to Question 434
My job is clerical, in admin or in customer service; eg secretary, chef.	Go to Question 440
I'm a skilled tradesperson; eg motor mechanic, decorator.	Go to Question 446
I work in a manual job; eg labourer, cleaner.	Go to Question 452

87 **How would you describe your political views?**

I'd describe myself as being far left.	Go to Question 429
You could label me left of centre.	Go to Question 435
I'm pretty neutral really, or not interested in politics.	Go to Question 441
I would say I am right of centre.	Go to Question 447
The best description of me would be far right.	Go to Question 453

88 **How do you feel about keeping pets?**

I hate them (or am allergic to them).	Go to Question 430
I don't really like them.	Go to Question 436
Some I like, others I don't.	Go to Question 442
I enjoy them if it's practical and acceptable where I live.	Go to Question 448
I can't imagine life without having a pet.	Go to Question 454

89 **How religious would you say you are?**

I'm active and committed to my religion.	Go to Question 431
I go to church or a place of worship sometimes.	Go to Question 437
I worship in private.	Go to Question 443
I'm not really religious and never worship.	Go to Question 449
I'd say I was actively anti-religious.	Go to Question 455

90 **How experienced are you sexually?**

I am still a virgin.	Go to Question 432
To be honest I'm rather inexperienced.	Go to Question 438
I've had no complaints so far.	Go to Question 444
I would class myself as an experienced lover.	Go to Question 450
I'd say I'm really hot stuff.	Go to Question 456

91 **How would you say your IQ compares to other people's?**

I'd describe myself as bright.	Go to Question 457
I'm somewhat more intelligent than average.	Go to Question 463
My level of intelligence is about average.	Go to Question 469
I'd say I am a bit below average.	Go to Question 475
I think of myself as being a little dull, really.	Go to Question 481

92 **What job do you do (or plan to)?**

I'm a professional; eg doctor, teacher.	Go to Question 458
My role is managerial; eg business manager, police inspector.	Go to Question 464
My job is clerical, in admin or in customer service; eg secretary, chef.	Go to Question 470
I'm a skilled tradesperson; eg motor mechanic, decorator.	Go to Question 476
I work in a manual job; eg labourer, cleaner.	Go to Question 482

93 **How would you describe your political views?**

I'd describe myself as being far left.	Go to Question 459
You could label me left of centre.	Go to Question 465
I'm pretty neutral really, or not interested in politics.	Go to Question 471
I would say I am right of centre.	Go to Question 477
The best description of me would be far right.	Go to Question 483

94 **How do you feel about keeping pets?**

I hate them (or am allergic to them).	Go to Question 460
I don't really like them.	Go to Question 466
Some I like, others I don't.	Go to Question 472
I enjoy them if it's practical and acceptable where I live.	Go to Question 478
I can't imagine life without having a pet.	Go to Question 484

95 **How religious would you say you are?**

I'm active and committed to my religion.	Go to Question 461
I go to church or a place of worship sometimes.	Go to Question 467
I worship in private.	Go to Question 473
I'm not really religious and never worship.	Go to Question 479
I'd say I was actively anti-religious.	Go to Question 485

96 **How experienced are you sexually?**

I am still a virgin.	Go to Question 462
To be honest I'm rather inexperienced.	Go to Question 468
I've had no complaints so far.	Go to Question 474
I would class myself as an experienced lover.	Go to Question 480
I'd say I'm really hot stuff.	Go to Question 486

97 | **How would you say your IQ compares to other people's?**

I'd describe myself as bright.	Go to Question 487
I'm somewhat more intelligent than average.	Go to Question 493
My level of intelligence is about average.	Go to Question 499
I'd say I am a bit below average.	Go to Question 505
I think of myself as being a little dull, really.	Go to Question 511

98 | **What job do you do (or plan to)?**

I'm a professional; eg a doctor or teacher.	Go to Question 488
My role is managerial; eg business manager, police inspector.	Go to Question 494
My job is clerical, in admin or in customer service; eg secretary, chef.	Go to Question 500
I'm a skilled tradesperson; eg motor mechanic, decorator.	Go to Question 506
I work in a manual job; eg labourer, cleaner.	Go to Question 512

99 | **How would you describe your political views?**

I'd describe myself as being far left.	Go to Question 489
You could label me left of centre.	Go to Question 495
I'm pretty neutral really, or not interested in politics.	Go to Question 501
I would say I am right of centre.	Go to Question 507
The best description of me would be far right.	Go to Question 513

100 | **How do you feel about keeping pets?**

I hate them (or am allergic to them).	Go to Question 490
I don't really like them.	Go to Question 496
Some I like, others I don't.	Go to Question 502
I enjoy them if it's practical and acceptable where I live.	Go to Question 508
I can't imagine life without having a pet.	Go to Question 514

101 | **How religious would you say you are?**

I'm active and committed to my religion.	Go to Question 491
I go to church or a place of worship sometimes.	Go to Question 497
I worship in private.	Go to Question 503
I'm not really religious and never worship.	Go to Question 509
I'd say I was actively anti-religious.	Go to Question 515

102 | **How experienced are you sexually?**

I am still a virgin.	Go to Question 492
To be honest I'm rather inexperienced.	Go to Question 498
I've had no complaints so far.	Go to Question 504
I would class myself as an experienced lover.	Go to Question 510
I'd say I'm really hot stuff.	Go to Question 516

103 **How would you say your IQ compares to other people's?**

I'd describe myself as bright.	Go to Question 517
I'm somewhat more intelligent than average.	Go to Question 523
My level of intelligence is about average.	Go to Question 529
I'd say I am a bit below average.	Go to Question 535
I think of myself as being a little dull, really.	Go to Question 541

104 **What job do you do (or plan to)?**

I'm a professional; eg doctor, teacher.	Go to Question 518
My role is managerial; eg business manager, police inspector.	Go to Question 524
My job is clerical, in admin or in customer service; eg secretary, chef.	Go to Question 530
I'm a skilled tradesperson; eg motor mechanic, decorator.	Go to Question 536
I work in a manual job; eg labourer, cleaner.	Go to Question 542

105 **How would you describe your political views?**

I'd describe myself as being far left.	Go to Question 519
You could label me left of centre.	Go to Question 525
I'm pretty neutral really, or not interested in politics.	Go to Question 531
I would say I am right of centre.	Go to Question 537
The best description of me would be far right.	Go to Question 543

106 **How do you feel about keeping pets?**

I hate them (or am allergic to them).	Go to Question 520
I don't really like them.	Go to Question 526
Some I like, others I don't.	Go to Question 532
I enjoy them if it's practical and acceptable where I live.	Go to Question 538
I can't imagine life without having a pet.	Go to Question 544

107 **How religious would you say you are?**

I'm active and committed to my religion.	Go to Question 521
I go to church or a place of worship sometimes.	Go to Question 527
I worship in private.	Go to Question 533
I'm not really religious and never worship.	Go to Question 539
I'd say I was actively anti-religious.	Go to Question 545

108 **How experienced are you sexually?**

I am still a virgin.	Go to Question 522
To be honest I'm rather inexperienced.	Go to Question 528
I've had no complaints so far.	Go to Question 534
I would class myself as an experienced lover.	Go to Question 540
I'd say I'm really hot stuff.	Go to Question 546

109 **How would you say your IQ compares to other people's?**

I'd describe myself as bright.	Go to Question 547
I'm somewhat more intelligent than average.	Go to Question 553
My level of intelligence is about average.	Go to Question 559
I'd say I am a bit below average.	Go to Question 565
I think of myself as being a little dull, really.	Go to Question 571

110 **What job do you do (or plan to)?**

I'm a professional; eg doctor, teacher.	Go to Question 548
My role is managerial; eg business manager, police inspector.	Go to Question 554
My job is clerical, in admin or in customer service; eg secretary, chef.	Go to Question 560
I'm a skilled tradesperson; eg motor mechanic, decorator.	Go to Question 566
I work in a manual job; eg labourer, cleaner.	Go to Question 572

111 **How would you describe your political views?**

I'd describe myself as being far left.	Go to Question 549
You could label me left of centre.	Go to Question 555
I'm pretty neutral really, or not interested in politics.	Go to Question 561
I would say I am right of centre.	Go to Question 567
The best description of me would be far right.	Go to Question 573

112 **How do you feel about keeping pets?**

I hate them (or am allergic to them).	Go to Question 550
I don't really like them.	Go to Question 556
Some I like, others I don't.	Go to Question 562
I enjoy them if it's practical and acceptable where I live.	Go to Question 568
I can't imagine life without having a pet.	Go to Question 574

113 **How religious would you say you are?**

I'm active and committed to my religion.	Go to Question 551
I go to church or a place of worship sometimes.	Go to Question 557
I worship in private.	Go to Question 563
I'm not really religious and never worship.	Go to Question 569
I'd say I was actively anti-religious.	Go to Question 575

114 **How experienced are you sexually?**

I am still a virgin.	Go to Question 552
To be honest I'm rather inexperienced.	Go to Question 558
I've had no complaints so far.	Go to Question 564
I would class myself as an experienced lover.	Go to Question 570
I'd say I'm really hot stuff.	Go to Question 576

115 **How would you say your IQ compares to other people's?**

I'd describe myself as bright.	Go to Question 577
I'm somewhat more intelligent than average.	Go to Question 583
My level of intelligence is about average.	Go to Question 589
I'd say I am a bit below average.	Go to Question 595
I think of myself as being a little dull, really.	Go to Question 601

116 **What job do you do (or plan to)?**

I'm a professional; eg doctor, teacher.	Go to Question 578
My role is managerial; eg business manager, police inspector.	Go to Question 584
My job is clerical, in admin or in customer service; eg secretary, chef.	Go to Question 590
I'm a skilled tradesperson; eg motor mechanic, decorator.	Go to Question 596
I work in a manual job; eg labourer, cleaner.	Go to Question 602

117 **How would you describe your political views?**

I'd describe myself as being far left.	Go to Question 579
You could label me left of centre.	Go to Question 585
I'm pretty neutral really, or not interested in politics.	Go to Question 591
I would say I am right of centre.	Go to Question 597
The best description of me would be far right.	Go to Question 603

118 **How do you feel about keeping pets?**

I hate them (or am allergic to them).	Go to Question 580
I don't really like them.	Go to Question 586
Some I like, others I don't.	Go to Question 592
I enjoy them if it's practical and acceptable where I live.	Go to Question 598
I can't imagine life without having a pet.	Go to Question 604

119 **How religious would you say you are?**

I'm active and committed to my religion.	Go to Question 581
I go to church or a place of worship sometimes.	Go to Question 587
I worship in private.	Go to Question 593
I'm not really religious and never worship.	Go to Question 599
I'd say I was actively anti-religious.	Go to Question 605

120 **How experienced are you sexually?**

I am still a virgin.	Go to Question 582
To be honest I'm rather inexperienced.	Go to Question 588
I've had no complaints so far.	Go to Question 594
I would class myself as an experienced lover.	Go to Question 600
I'd say I'm really hot stuff.	Go to Question 606

121 **How would you say your IQ compares to other people's?**

I'd describe myself as bright.	Go to Question 607
I'm somewhat more intelligent than average.	Go to Question 613
My level of intelligence is about average.	Go to Question 619
I'd say I am a bit below average.	Go to Question 625
I think of myself as being a little dull, really.	Go to Question 631

122 **What job do you do (or plan to)?**

I'm a professional; eg doctor, teacher.	Go to Question 608
My role is managerial; eg business manager, police inspector.	Go to Question 614
My job is clerical, in admin or in customer service; eg secretary, chef.	Go to Question 620
I'm a skilled tradesperson; eg motor mechanic, decorator.	Go to Question 626
I work in a manual job; eg labourer, cleaner.	Go to Question 632

123 **How would you describe your political views?**

I'd describe myself as being far left.	Go to Question 609
You could label me left of centre.	Go to Question 615
I'm pretty neutral really, or not interested in politics.	Go to Question 621
I would say I am right of centre.	Go to Question 627
The best description of me would be far right.	Go to Question 633

124 **How do you feel about keeping pets?**

I hate them (or am allergic to them).	Go to Question 610
I don't really like them.	Go to Question 616
Some I like, others I don't.	Go to Question 622
I enjoy them if it's practical and acceptable where I live.	Go to Question 628
I can't imagine life without having a pet.	Go to Question 634

125 **How religious would you say you are?**

I'm active and committed to my religion.	Go to Question 611
I go to church or a place of worship sometimes.	Go to Question 617
I worship in private.	Go to Question 623
I'm not really religious and never worship.	Go to Question 629
I'd say I was actively anti-religious.	Go to Question 635

126 **How experienced are you sexually?**

I am still a virgin.	Go to Question 612
To be honest I'm rather inexperienced.	Go to Question 618
I've had no complaints so far.	Go to Question 624
I would class myself as an experienced lover.	Go to Question 630
I'd say I'm really hot stuff.	Go to Question 636

127 How would you say your IQ compares to other people's?

I'd describe myself as bright.	Go to Question 637
I'm somewhat more intelligent than average.	Go to Question 643
My level of intelligence is about average.	Go to Question 649
I'd say I am a bit below average.	Go to Question 655
I think of myself as being a little dull, really.	Go to Question 661

128 What job do you do (or plan to)?

I'm a professional; eg doctor, teacher.	Go to Question 638
My role is managerial; eg business manager, police inspector.	Go to Question 644
My job is clerical, in admin or in customer service; eg secretary, chef.	Go to Question 650
I'm a skilled tradesperson; eg motor mechanic, decorator.	Go to Question 656
I work in a non-skilled manual job; eg labourer, cleaner.	Go to Question 662

129 How would you describe your political views?

I'd describe myself as being far left.	Go to Question 639
You could label me left of centre.	Go to Question 645
I'm pretty neutral really, or not interested in politics.	Go to Question 651
I would say I am right of centre.	Go to Question 657
The best description of me would be far right.	Go to Question 663

130 How do you feel about keeping pets?

I hate them (or am allergic to them).	Go to Question 640
I don't really like them.	Go to Question 646
Some I like, others I don't.	Go to Question 652
I enjoy them if it's practical and acceptable where I live.	Go to Question 658
I can't imagine life without having a pet.	Go to Question 664

131 How religious would you say you are?

I'm active and committed to my religion.	Go to Question 641
I go to church or a place of worship sometimes.	Go to Question 647
I worship in private.	Go to Question 653
I'm not really religious and never worship.	Go to Question 659
I'd say I was actively anti-religious.	Go to Question 665

132 How experienced are you sexually?

I am still a virgin.	Go to Question 642
To be honest I'm rather inexperienced.	Go to Question 648
I've had no complaints so far.	Go to Question 654
I would class myself as an experienced lover.	Go to Question 660
I'd say I'm really hot stuff.	Go to Question 666

133 How would you say your IQ compares to other people's?

I'd describe myself as bright.	Go to Question 667
I'm somewhat more intelligent than average.	Go to Question 673
My level of intelligence is about average.	Go to Question 679
I'd say I am a bit below average.	Go to Question 685
I think of myself as being a little dull, really.	Go to Question 691

134 What job do you do (or plan to)?

I'm a professional; eg doctor, teacher.	Go to Question 668
My role is managerial; eg business manager, police inspector.	Go to Question 674
My job is clerical, in admin or in customer service; eg secretary, chef.	Go to Question 680
I'm a skilled tradesperson; eg motor mechanic, decorator.	Go to Question 686
I work in a manual job; eg labourer, cleaner.	Go to Question 692

135 How would you describe your political views?

I'd describe myself as being far left.	Go to Question 669
You could label me left of centre.	Go to Question 675
I'm pretty neutral really, or not interested in politics.	Go to Question 681
I would say I am right of centre.	Go to Question 687
The best description of me would be far right.	Go to Question 693

136 How do you feel about keeping pets?

I hate them (or am allergic to them).	Go to Question 670
I don't really like them.	Go to Question 676
Some I like, others I don't.	Go to Question 682
I enjoy them if it's practical and acceptable where I live.	Go to Question 688
I can't imagine life without having a pet.	Go to Question 694

137 How religious would you say you are?

I'm active and committed to my religion.	Go to Question 671
I go to church or a place of worship sometimes.	Go to Question 677
I worship in private.	Go to Question 683
I'm not really religious and never worship.	Go to Question 689
I'd say I was actively anti-religious.	Go to Question 695

138 How experienced are you sexually?

I am still a virgin.	Go to Question 672
To be honest I'm rather inexperienced.	Go to Question 678
I've had no complaints so far.	Go to Question 684
I would class myself as an experienced lover.	Go to Question 690
I'd say I'm really hot stuff.	Go to Question 696

139 **How would you say your IQ compares to other people's?**

I'd describe myself as bright.	Go to Question 697
I'm somewhat more intelligent than average.	Go to Question 703
My level of intelligence is about average.	Go to Question 709
I'd say I am a bit below average.	Go to Question 715
I think of myself as being a little dull, really.	Go to Question 721

140 **What job do you do (or plan to)?**

I'm a professional; eg doctor, teacher.	Go to Question 698
My role is managerial; eg business manager, police inspector.	Go to Question 704
My job is clerical, in admin or in customer service; eg secretary, chef.	Go to Question 710
I'm a skilled tradesperson; eg motor mechanic, decorator.	Go to Question 716
I work in a manual job; eg labourer, cleaner.	Go to Question 722

141 **How would you describe your political views?**

I'd describe myself as being far left.	Go to Question 699
You could label me left of centre.	Go to Question 705
I'm pretty neutral really, or not interested in politics.	Go to Question 711
I would say I am right of centre.	Go to Question 717
The best description of me would be far right.	Go to Question 723

142 **How do you feel about keeping pets?**

I hate them (or am allergic to them).	Go to Question 700
I don't really like them.	Go to Question 706
Some I like, others I don't.	Go to Question 712
I enjoy them if it's practical and acceptable where I live.	Go to Question 718
I can't imagine life without having a pet.	Go to Question 724

143 **How religious would you say you are?**

I'm active and committed to my religion.	Go to Question 701
I go to church or a place of worship sometimes.	Go to Question 707
I worship in private.	Go to Question 713
I'm not really religious and never worship.	Go to Question 719
I'd say I was actively anti-religious.	Go to Question 725

144 **How experienced are you sexually?**

I am still a virgin.	Go to Question 702
To be honest I'm rather inexperienced.	Go to Question 708
I've had no complaints so far.	Go to Question 714
I would class myself as an experienced lover.	Go to Question 720
I'd say I'm really hot stuff.	Go to Question 726

145 **How would you say your IQ compares to other people's?**

I'd describe myself as bright.	Go to Question 727
I'm somewhat more intelligent than average.	Go to Question 733
My level of intelligence is about average.	Go to Question 739
I'd say I am a bit below average.	Go to Question 745
I think of myself as being a little dull, really.	Go to Question 751

146 **What job do you do (or plan to)?**

I'm a professional; eg doctor, teacher.	Go to Question 728
My role is managerial; eg business manager, police inspector.	Go to Question 734
My job is clerical, in admin or in customer service; eg secretary, chef.	Go to Question 740
I'm a skilled tradesperson; eg motor mechanic, decorator.	Go to Question 746
I work in a manual job; eg labourer, cleaner.	Go to Question 752

147 **How would you describe your political views?**

I'd describe myself as being far left.	Go to Question 729
You could label me left of centre.	Go to Question 735
I'm pretty neutral really, or not interested in politics.	Go to Question 741
I would say I am right of centre.	Go to Question 747
The best description of me would be far right.	Go to Question 753

148 **How do you feel about keeping pets?**

I hate them (or am allergic to them).	Go to Question 730
I don't really like them.	Go to Question 736
Some I like, others I don't.	Go to Question 742
I enjoy them if it's practical and acceptable where I live.	Go to Question 748
I can't imagine life without having a pet.	Go to Question 754

149 **How religious would you say you are?**

I'm active and committed to my religion.	Go to Question 731
I go to church or a place of worship sometimes.	Go to Question 737
I worship in private.	Go to Question 743
I'm not really religious and never worship.	Go to Question 749
I'd say I was actively anti-religious.	Go to Question 755

150 **How experienced are you sexually?**

I am still a virgin.	Go to Question 732
To be honest I'm rather inexperienced.	Go to Question 738
I've had no complaints so far.	Go to Question 744
I would class myself as an experienced lover.	Go to Question 750
I'd say I'm really hot stuff.	Go to Question 756

151 **How would you say your IQ compares to other people's?**

I'd describe myself as bright.	Go to Question 757
I'm somewhat more intelligent than average.	Go to Question 763
My level of intelligence is about average.	Go to Question 769
I'd say I am a bit below average.	Go to Question 775
I think of myself as being a little dull, really.	Go to Question 781

152 **What job do you do (or plan to)?**

I'm a professional; eg doctor, teacher.	Go to Question 758
My role is managerial; eg business manager, police inspector.	Go to Question 764
My job is clerical, in admin or in customer service; eg secretary, chef.	Go to Question 770
I'm a skilled tradesperson; eg motor mechanic, decorator.	Go to Question 776
I work in a manual job; eg labourer, cleaner.	Go to Question 782

153 **How would you describe your political views?**

I'd describe myself as being far left.	Go to Question 759
You could label me left of centre.	Go to Question 765
I'm pretty neutral really, or not interested in politics.	Go to Question 771
I would say I am right of centre.	Go to Question 777
The best description of me would be far right.	Go to Question 783

154 **How do you feel about keeping pets?**

I hate them (or am allergic to them).	Go to Question 760
I don't really like them.	Go to Question 766
Some I like, others I don't.	Go to Question 772
I enjoy them if it's practical and acceptable where I live.	Go to Question 778
I can't imagine life without having a pet.	Go to Question 784

155 **How religious would you say you are?**

I'm active and committed to my religion.	Go to Question 761
I go to church or a place of worship sometimes.	Go to Question 767
I worship in private.	Go to Question 773
I'm not really religious and never worship.	Go to Question 779
I'd say I was actively anti-religious.	Go to Question 785

156 **How experienced are you sexually?**

I am still a virgin.	Go to Question 762
To be honest I'm rather inexperienced.	Go to Question 768
I've had no complaints so far.	Go to Question 774
I would class myself as an experienced lover.	Go to Question 780
I'd say I'm really hot stuff.	Go to Question 786

157 **How would you say your IQ compares to other people's?**

I'd describe myself as bright.	Go to Question 787
I'm somewhat more intelligent than average.	Go to Question 793
My level of intelligence is about average.	Go to Question 799
I'd say I am a bit below average.	Go to Question 805
I think of myself as being a little dull, really.	Go to Question 811

158 **What job do you do (or plan to)?**

I'm a professional; eg doctor, teacher.	Go to Question 788
My role is managerial; eg business manager, police inspector.	Go to Question 794
My job is clerical, in admin or in customer service; eg secretary, chef.	Go to Question 800
I'm a skilled tradesperson; eg motor mechanic, decorator.	Go to Question 806
I work in a manual job; eg labourer, cleaner.	Go to Question 812

159 **How would you describe your political views?**

I'd describe myself as being far left.	Go to Question 789
You could label me left of centre.	Go to Question 795
I'm pretty neutral really, or not interested in politics.	Go to Question 801
I would say I am right of centre.	Go to Question 807
The best description of me would be far right.	Go to Question 813

160 **How do you feel about keeping pets?**

I hate them (or am allergic to them).	Go to Question 790
I don't really like them.	Go to Question 796
Some I like, others I don't.	Go to Question 802
I enjoy them if it's practical and acceptable where I live.	Go to Question 808
I can't imagine life without having a pet.	Go to Question 814

161 **How religious would you say you are?**

I'm active and committed to my religion.	Go to Question 791
I go to church or a place of worship sometimes.	Go to Question 797
I worship in private.	Go to Question 803
I'm not really religious and never worship.	Go to Question 809
I'd say I was actively anti-religious.	Go to Question 815

162 **How experienced are you sexually?**

I am still a virgin.	Go to Question 792
To be honest I'm rather inexperienced.	Go to Question 798
I've had no complaints so far.	Go to Question 804
I would class myself as an experienced lover.	Go to Question 810
I'd say I'm really hot stuff.	Go to Question 816

163 How would you say your IQ compares to other people's?

I'd describe myself as bright.	Go to Question 817
I'm somewhat more intelligent than average.	Go to Question 823
My level of intelligence is about average.	Go to Question 829
I'd say I am a bit below average.	Go to Question 835
I think of myself as being a little dull, really.	Go to Question 841

164 What job do you do (or plan to)?

I'm a professional; eg doctor, teacher.	Go to Question 818
My role is managerial; eg business manager, police inspector.	Go to Question 824
My job is clerical, in admin or in customer service; eg secretary, chef.	Go to Question 830
I'm a skilled tradesperson; eg motor mechanic, decorator.	Go to Question 836
I work in a manual job; eg labourer, cleaner.	Go to Question 842

165 How would you describe your political views?

I'd describe myself as being far left.	Go to Question 819
You could label me left of centre.	Go to Question 825
I'm pretty neutral really, or not interested in politics.	Go to Question 831
I would say I am right of centre.	Go to Question 837
The best description of me would be far right.	Go to Question 843

166 How do you feel about keeping pets?

I hate them (or am allergic to them).	Go to Question 820
I don't really like them.	Go to Question 826
Some I like, others I don't.	Go to Question 832
I enjoy them if it's practical and acceptable where I live.	Go to Question 838
I can't imagine life without having a pet.	Go to Question 844

167 How religious would you say you are?

I'm active and committed to my religion.	Go to Question 821
I go to church or a place of worship sometimes.	Go to Question 827
I worship in private.	Go to Question 833
I'm not really religious and never worship.	Go to Question 839
I'd say I was actively anti-religious.	Go to Question 845

168 How experienced are you sexually?

I am still a virgin.	Go to Question 822
To be honest I'm rather inexperienced.	Go to Question 828
I've had no complaints so far.	Go to Question 834
I would class myself as an experienced lover.	Go to Question 840
I'd say I'm really hot stuff.	Go to Question 846

169 How would you say your IQ compares to other people's?

I'd describe myself as bright.	Go to Question 847
I'm somewhat more intelligent than average.	Go to Question 853
My level of intelligence is about average.	Go to Question 859
I'd say I am a bit below average.	Go to Question 865
I think of myself as being a little dull, really.	Go to Question 871

170 What job do you do (or plan to)?

I'm a professional; eg doctor, teacher.	Go to Question 848
My role is managerial; eg business manager, police inspector.	Go to Question 854
My job is clerical, in admin or in customer service; eg secretary, chef.	Go to Question 860
I'm a skilled tradesperson; eg motor mechanic, decorator.	Go to Question 866
I work in a manual job; eg labourer, cleaner.	Go to Question 872

171 How would you describe your political views?

I'd describe myself as being far left.	Go to Question 849
You could label me left of centre.	Go to Question 855
I'm pretty neutral really, or not interested in politics.	Go to Question 861
I would say I am right of centre.	Go to Question 867
The best description of me would be far right.	Go to Question 873

172 How do you feel about keeping pets?

I hate them (or am allergic to them).	Go to Question 850
I don't really like them.	Go to Question 856
Some I like, others I don't.	Go to Question 862
I enjoy them if it's practical and acceptable where I live.	Go to Question 868
I can't imagine life without having a pet.	Go to Question 874

173 How religious would you say you are?

I'm active and committed to my religion.	Go to Question 851
I go to church or a place of worship sometimes.	Go to Question 857
I worship in private.	Go to Question 863
I'm not really religious and never worship.	Go to Question 869
I'd say I was actively anti-religious.	Go to Question 875

174 How experienced are you sexually?

I am still a virgin.	Go to Question 852
To be honest I'm rather inexperienced.	Go to Question 858
I've had no complaints so far.	Go to Question 864
I would class myself as an experienced lover.	Go to Question 870
I'd say I'm really hot stuff.	Go to Question 876

175 **How would you say your IQ compares to other people's?**

I'd describe myself as bright.	Go to Question 877
I'm somewhat more intelligent than average.	Go to Question 883
My level of intelligence is about average.	Go to Question 889
I'd say I am a bit below average.	Go to Question 895
I think of myself as being a little dull, really.	Go to Question 901

176 **What job do you do (or plan to)?**

I'm a professional; eg doctor, teacher.	Go to Question 878
My role is managerial; eg business manager, police inspector.	Go to Question 884
My job is clerical, in admin or in customer service; eg secretary, chef.	Go to Question 890
I'm a skilled tradesperson; eg motor mechanic, decorator.	Go to Question 896
I work in a manual job; eg labourer, cleaner.	Go to Question 902

177 **How would you describe your political views?**

I'd describe myself as being far left.	Go to Question 879
You could label me left of centre.	Go to Question 885
I'm pretty neutral really, or not interested in politics.	Go to Question 891
I would say I am right of centre.	Go to Question 897
The best description of me would be far right.	Go to Question 903

178 **How do you feel about keeping pets?**

I hate them (or am allergic to them).	Go to Question 880
I don't really like them.	Go to Question 886
Some I like, others I don't.	Go to Question 892
I enjoy them if it's practical and acceptable where I live.	Go to Question 898
I can't imagine life without having a pet.	Go to Question 904

179 **How religious would you say you are?**

I'm active and committed to my religion.	Go to Question 881
I go to church or a place of worship sometimes.	Go to Question 887
I worship in private.	Go to Question 893
I'm not really religious and never worship.	Go to Question 899
I'd say I was actively anti-religious.	Go to Question 905

180 **How experienced are you sexually?**

I am still a virgin.	Go to Question 882
To be honest I'm rather inexperienced.	Go to Question 888
I've had no complaints so far.	Go to Question 894
I would class myself as an experienced lover.	Go to Question 900
I'd say I'm really hot stuff.	Go to Question 906

181 How would you say your IQ compares to other people's?

I'd describe myself as bright.	Go to Question 907
I'm somewhat more intelligent than average.	Go to Question 913
My level of intelligence is about average.	Go to Question 919
I'd say I am a bit below average.	Go to Question 925
I think of myself as being a little dull, really.	Go to Question 931

182 What job do you do (or plan to)?

I'm a professional; eg doctor, teacher.	Go to Question 908
My role is managerial; eg business manager, police inspector.	Go to Question 914
My job is clerical, in admin or in customer service; eg secretary, chef.	Go to Question 920
I'm a skilled tradesperson; eg motor mechanic, decorator.	Go to Question 926
I work in a manual job; eg labourer, cleaner.	Go to Question 932

183 How would you describe your political views?

I'd describe myself as being far left.	Go to Question 909
You could label me left of centre.	Go to Question 915
I'm pretty neutral really, or not interested in politics.	Go to Question 921
I would say I am right of centre.	Go to Question 927
The best description of me would be far right.	Go to Question 933

184 How do you feel about keeping pets?

I hate them (or am allergic to them).	Go to Question 910
I don't really like them.	Go to Question 916
Some I like, others I don't.	Go to Question 922
I enjoy them if it's practical and acceptable where I live.	Go to Question 928
I can't imagine life without having a pet.	Go to Question 934

185 How religious would you say you are?

I'm active and committed to my religion.	Go to Question 911
I go to church or a place of worship sometimes.	Go to Question 917
I worship in private.	Go to Question 923
I'm not really religious and never worship.	Go to Question 929
I'd say I was actively anti-religious.	Go to Question 935

186 How experienced are you sexually?

I am still a virgin.	Go to Question 912
To be honest I'm rather inexperienced.	Go to Question 918
I've had no complaints so far.	Go to Question 924
I would class myself as an experienced lover.	Go to Question 930
I'd say I'm really hot stuff.	Go to Question 936

187   **Which of these types of TV programmes do you like the most?**

Most of all I like game shows.	Result (i) I I
I couldn't do without soap operas.	Result (i) J I
I especially enjoy police dramas or comedies.	Result (i) X I
My preference is for serious dramas.	Result (i) R I
I enjoy news programmes and documentaries.	Result (i) Y I

188   **What is your view of chivalry?**

I think it's old-fashioned nonsense, to be quite honest.	Result (ii) I I
It's pretty undesirable.	Result (ii) W I
It depends; it's OK sometimes.	Result (ii) Q I
It's a desirable quality.	Result (ii) O I
I'd say it's an essential part of life.	Result (ii) T I

189   **If you had to choose just one, which of these is your favourite type of music?**

I prefer music such as heavy metal or rap.	Result (iii) I I
My favourite is rock or pop music; eg The Beatles.	Result (iii) J I
I particularly enjoy easy-listening music; eg Frank Sinatra.	Result (iii) X I
Jazz would be my number-one choice.	Result (iii) R I
My preference would be for classical music or opera.	Result (iii) Y I

190   **Which of these activities appeals most?**

I'd choose relaxing; sitting on the sofa, for example.	Result (iv) I I
My preference would be for some mild exercise, such as gardening.	Result (iv) W I
Moderate exercise, such as walking, would be my choice.	Result (iv) Q I
I would prefer more serious exercise, such as backpacking.	Result (iv) O I
Something strenuous like soccer or running would be my choice.	Result (iv) T I

191   **What sort of food do you like?**

I really just like traditional, plain food.	Result (v) I I
On the whole I prefer plain food.	Result (v) J I
I eat exotic food for a change.	Result (v) X I
I enjoy most foods, really.	Result (v) R I
I prefer foreign food.	Result (v) Y I

192   **What level of education have you reached (or do you expect to reach)?**

My education ended when I was 16.	Result (vi) I I
No further education after leaving school at 18.	Result (vi) W I
Some further education after leaving school at 18.	Result (vi) Q I
Graduate degree.	Result (vi) O I
Postgraduate degree.	Result (vi) T I

193 **Which of these types of TV programmes do you like the most?**

Most of all I like game shows.	Result (i) I J
I couldn't do without soap operas.	Result (i) J J
I especially enjoy police dramas or comedies.	Result (i) X J
My preference is for serious dramas.	Result (i) R J
I enjoy news programmes and documentaries.	Result (i) Y J

194 **What is your view of chivalry?**

I think it's old-fashioned nonsense, to be quite honest.	Result (ii) I W
It's pretty undesirable.	Result (ii) W W
It depends; it's OK sometimes.	Result (ii) Q W
It's a desirable quality.	Result (ii) O W
I'd say it's an essential part of life.	Result (ii) T W

195 **If you had to choose just one, which of these is your favourite type of music?**

I prefer music such as heavy metal or rap.	Result (iii) I J
My favourite is rock or pop music; eg The Beatles.	Result (iii) J J
I particularly enjoy easy-listening music; eg Frank Sinatra.	Result (iii) X J
Jazz would be my number one choice.	Result (iii) R J
My preference would be for classical music or opera.	Result (iii) Y J

196 **Which of these activities appeals most?**

I'd choose relaxing; sitting on the sofa, for example.	Result (iv) I J
My preference would be for some mild exercise, such as gardening.	Result (iv) W J
Moderate exercise, such as walking, would be my choice.	Result (iv) Q J
I would prefer more serious exercise, such as backpacking.	Result (iv) O J
Something strenuous like soccer or running would be my choice.	Result (iv) T J

197 **What do you think of foreign food?**

I really can't stand it.	Result (v) I W
On the whole I prefer plain food.	Result (v) J W
It's OK for a change.	Result (v) X W
I enjoy most foods really.	Result (v) R W
I prefer foreign food.	Result (v) Y W

198 **What level of education have you reached (or do you expect to reach)?**

My education ended when I was 16.	Result (vi) J I
No further education after leaving school at 18.	Result (vi) D I
Some further education after leaving school at 18.	Result (vi) U I
Graduate degree from college, university or polytechnic.	Result (vi) E I
Postgraduate degree.	Result (vi) A I

199 Which of these types of TV programmes do you like the most?

Most of all I like game shows.	Result (i) I X
I couldn't do without soap operas.	Result (i) J X
I especially enjoy police dramas or comedies.	Result (i) X X
My preference is for serious dramas.	Result (i) R X
I enjoy news programmes and documentaries.	Result (i) Y X

200 What is your view of chivalry?

I think it's old-fashioned nonsense, to be quite honest.	Result (ii) I Q
It's pretty undesirable.	Result (ii) W Q
It depends; it's OK sometimes.	Result (ii) Q Q
It's a desirable quality.	Result (ii) O Q
I'd say it's an essential part of life.	Result (ii) T Q

201 If you had to choose just one, which of these is your favourite type of music?

I prefer music such as heavy metal or rap.	Result (iii) I X
My favourite is rock or pop music; eg The Beatles.	Result (iii) J X
I particularly enjoy easy-listening music; eg Frank Sinatra.	Result (iii) X X
Jazz would be my number-one choice.	Result (iii) R X
My preference would be for classical music or opera.	Result (iii) Y X

202 Which of these activities appeals most?

I'd choose relaxing; sitting on the sofa, for example.	Result (iv) I X
My preference would be for some mild exercise, such as gardening.	Result (iv) W X
Moderate exercise, such as walking, would be my choice.	Result (iv) Q X
I would prefer more serious exercise, such as backpacking.	Result (iv) O X
Something strenuous like soccer or running would be my choice.	Result (iv) T X

203 What sort of food do you like?

I really just like traditional, plain food.	Result (v) I Q
On the whole I prefer traditional, plain food.	Result (v) J Q
I eat exotic food for a change.	Result (v) X Q
I enjoy most foods, really.	Result (v) R Q
I prefer a wide variety of dishes.	Result (v) Y Q

204 What level of education have you reached (or do you expect to reach)?

My education ended when I was 16.	Result (vi) X I
No further education after leaving school at 18.	Result (vi) G I
Some further education after leaving school at 18.	Result (vi) K I
Graduate degree.	Result (vi) V I
Postgraduate degree.	Result (vi) B I

205 **Which of these types of TV programmes do you like the most?**

Most of all I like game shows.	Result (i) I R
I couldn't do without soap operas.	Result (i) J R
I especially enjoy police dramas or comedies.	Result (i) X R
My preference is for serious dramas.	Result (i) R R
I enjoy news programmes and documentaries.	Result (i) Y R

206 **What is your view of chivalry?**

I think it's old-fashioned nonsense, to be quite honest.	Result (ii) I O
It's pretty undesirable.	Result (ii) W O
It depends; it's OK sometimes.	Result (ii) Q O
It's a desirable quality.	Result (ii) O O
I'd say it's an essential part of life.	Result (ii) T O

207 **If you had to choose just one, which of these is your favourite type of music?**

I prefer music such as heavy metal or rap.	Result (iii) I R
My favourite is rock or pop music; eg The Beatles.	Result (iii) J R
I particularly enjoy easy-listening music; eg Frank Sinatra.	Result (iii) X R
Jazz would be my number-one choice.	Result (iii) R R
My preference would be for classical music or opera.	Result (iii) Y R

208 **Which of these activities appeals most?**

I'd choose relaxing; sitting on the sofa, for example.	Result (iv) I R
My preference would be for some mild exercise, such as gardening.	Result (iv) W R
Moderate exercise, such as walking, would be my choice.	Result (iv) Q R
I would prefer more serious exercise, such as backpacking.	Result (iv) O R
Something strenuous like soccer or running would be my choice.	Result (iv) T R

209 **What sort of food do you like?**

I really just like traditional, plain food.	Result (v) I O
On the whole I prefer plain food.	Result (v) J O
I eat exotic food for a change.	Result (v) X O
I enjoy most foods, really.	Result (v) R O
I prefer a wide variety of dishes.	Result (v) Y O

210 **What level of education have you reached (or do you expect to reach)?**

My education ended when I was 16.	Result (vi) R I
No further education after leaving school at 18.	Result (vi) S I
Some further education after leaving school at 18.	Result (vi) H I
Graduate degree.	Result (vi) P I
Postgraduate degree.	Result (vi) N I

211 **Which of these types of TV programmes do you like the most?**

Most of all I like game shows.	Result (i) I Y
I couldn't do without soap operas.	Result (i) J Y
I especially enjoy police dramas or comedies.	Result (i) X Y
My preference is for serious dramas.	Result (i) R Y
I enjoy news programmes and documentaries.	Result (i) Y Y

212 **What is your view of chivalry?**

I think it's old-fashioned nonsense, to be quite honest.	Result (ii) I T
It's pretty undesirable.	Result (ii) W T
It depends; it's OK sometimes.	Result (ii) Q T
It's a desirable quality.	Result (ii) O T
I'd say it's an essential part of life.	Result (ii) T T

213 **If you had to choose just one, which of these is your favourite type of music?**

I prefer music such as heavy metal or rap.	Result (iii) I Y
My favourite is rock or pop music; eg The Beatles.	Result (iii) J Y
I particularly enjoy easy-listening music; eg Frank Sinatra.	Result (iii) X Y
Jazz would be my number-one choice.	Result (iii) R Y
My preference would be for classical music or opera.	Result (iii) Y Y

214 **Which of these activities appeals most?**

I'd choose relaxing; sitting on the sofa, for example.	Result (iv) I Y
My preference would be for some mild exercise, such as gardening.	Result (iv) W Y
Moderate exercise, such as walking, would be my choice.	Result (iv) Q Y
I would prefer more serious exercise, such as backpacking.	Result (iv) O Y
Something strenuous like soccer or running would be my choice.	Result (iv) T Y

215 **What sort of food do you like?**

I really just like traditional, plain food.	Result (v) I T
On the whole I prefer traditional, plain food.	Result (v) J T
I eat exotic food for a change.	Result (v) X T
I enjoy most foods, really.	Result (v) R T
I prefer a wide variety of dishes.	Result (v) Y T

216 **What level of education have you reached (or do you expect to reach)?**

My education ended when I was 16.	Result (vi) Y I
No further education after leaving school at 18.	Result (vi) F I
Some further education after leaving school at 18.	Result (vi) L I
Graduate degree.	Result (vi) C I
Postgraduate degree.	Result (vi) M I

217 **Which of these types of TV programmes do you like the most?**

Most of all I like game shows.	Result (i) W I
I couldn't do without soap operas.	Result (i) D I
I especially enjoy police dramas or comedies.	Result (i) G I
My preference is for serious dramas.	Result (i) S I
I enjoy news programmes and documentaries.	Result (i) F I

218 **What is your view of chivalry?**

I think it's old-fashioned nonsense, to be quite honest.	Result (ii) J I
It's pretty undesirable.	Result (ii) D I
It depends; it's OK sometimes.	Result (ii) U I
It's a desirable quality.	Result (ii) E I
I'd say it's an essential part of life.	Result (ii) A I

219 **If you had to choose just one, which of these is your favourite type of music?**

I prefer music such as heavy metal or rap.	Result (iii) W I
My favourite is rock or pop music; eg The Beatles.	Result (iii) D I
I particularly enjoy easy-listening music; eg Frank Sinatra.	Result (iii) G I
Jazz would be my number-one choice.	Result (iii) S I
My preference would be for classical music or opera.	Result (iii) F I

220 **Which of these activities appeals most?**

I'd choose relaxing; sitting on the sofa, for example.	Result (iv) J I
My preference would be for some mild exercise, such as gardening.	Result (iv) D I
Moderate exercise, such as walking, would be my choice.	Result (iv) U I
I would prefer more serious exercise, such as backpacking.	Result (iv) E !
Something strenuous like soccer or running would be my choice.	Result (iv) A I

221 **What sort of food do you like?**

I really just like traditional, plain food.	Result (v) I J
On the whole I prefer traditional, plain food.	Result (v) J J
I eat exotic food for a change.	Result (v) X J
I enjoy most foods, really.	Result (v) R J
I prefer a wide variety of dishes.	Result (v) Y J

222 **What level of education have you reached (or do you expect to reach)?**

My education ended when I was 16.	Result (vi) I W
No further education after leaving school at 18.	Result (vi) W W
Some further education after leaving school at 18.	Result (vi) Q W
Graduate degree.	Result (vi) O W
Postgraduate degree.	Result (vi) T W

223 Which of these types of TV programmes do you like the most?

Most of all I like game shows.	Result (i) W J
I couldn't do without soap operas.	Result (i) D J
I especially enjoy police dramas or comedies.	Result (i) G J
My preference is for serious dramas.	Result (i) S J
I enjoy news programmes and documentaries.	Result (i) F J

224 What is your view of chivalry?

I think it's old-fashioned nonsense, to be quite honest.	Result (ii) J W
It's pretty undesirable.	Result (ii) D W
It depends; it's OK sometimes.	Result (ii) U W
It's a desirable quality.	Result (ii) E W
I'd say it's an essential part of life.	Result (ii) A W

225 If you had to choose just one, which of these is your favourite type of music?

I prefer music such as heavy metal or rap.	Result (iii) W J
My favourite is rock or pop music; eg The Beatles.	Result (iii) D J
I particularly enjoy easy-listening music; eg Frank Sinatra.	Result (iii) G J
Jazz would be my number-one choice.	Result (iii) S J
My preference would be for classical music or opera.	Result (iii) F J

226 Which of these activities appeals most?

I'd choose relaxing; sitting on the sofa, for example.	Result (iv) J J
My preference would be for some mild exercise, such as gardening.	Result (iv) D J
Moderate exercise, such as walking, would be my choice.	Result (iv) U J
I would prefer more serious exercise, such as backpacking.	Result (iv) E J
Something strenuous like soccer or running would be my choice.	Result (iv) A J

227 What sort of food do you like?

I really just like traditional, plain food.	Result (v) I D
On the whole I prefer traditional, plain food.	Result (v) J D
I eat exotic food for a change.	Result (v) X D
I enjoy most foods, really.	Result (v) R D
I prefer a wide variety of dishes.	Result (v) Y D

228 What level of education have you reached (or do you expect to reach)?

My education ended when I was 16.	Result (vi) J W
No further education after leaving school at 18.	Result (vi) D W
Some further education after leaving school at 18.	Result (vi) U W
Graduate degree.	Result (vi) E W
Postgraduate degree.	Result (vi) A W

229 **Which of these types of TV programmes do you like the most?**

Most of all I like game shows.	Result (i) W X
I couldn't do without soap operas.	Result (i) D X
I especially enjoy police dramas or comedies.	Result (i) G X
My preference is for serious dramas.	Result (i) S X
I enjoy news programmes and documentaries.	Result (i) F X

230 **What is your view of chivalry?**

I think it's old-fashioned nonsense, to be quite honest.	Result (ii) J Q
It's pretty undesirable.	Result (ii) D Q
It depends; it's OK sometimes.	Result (ii) U Q
It's a desirable quality.	Result (ii) E Q
I'd say it's an essential part of life.	Result (ii) A Q

231 **If you had to choose just one, which of these is your favourite type of music?**

I prefer music such as heavy metal or rap.	Result (iii) W X
My favourite is rock or pop music; eg The Beatles.	Result (iii) D X
I particularly enjoy easy-listening music; eg Frank Sinatra.	Result (iii) G X
Jazz would be my number-one choice.	Result (iii) S X
My preference would be for classical music or opera.	Result (iii) F X

232 **Which of these activities appeals most?**

I'd choose relaxing; sitting on the sofa, for example.	Result (iv) J X
My preference would be for some mild exercise, such as gardening.	Result (iv) D X
Moderate exercise, such as walking, would be my choice.	Result (iv) U X
I would prefer more serious exercise, such as backpacking.	Result (iv) E X
Something strenuous like soccer or running would be my choice.	Result (iv) A X

233 **What sort of food do you like?**

I really just like traditional, plain food.	Result (v) I U
On the whole I prefer traditional, plain food.	Result (v) J U
I eat exotic food for a change.	Result (v) X U
I enjoy most foods, really.	Result (v) R U
I prefer a wide variety of dishes.	Result (v) Y U

234 **What level of education have you reached (or do you expect to reach)?**

My education ended when I was 16.	Result (vi) X W
No further education after leaving school at 18.	Result (vi) G W
Some further education after leaving school at 18.	Result (vi) K W
Graduate degree.	Result (vi) V W
Postgraduate degree.	Result (vi) B W

235 **Which of these types of TV programmes do you like the most?**

Most of all I like game shows.	Result (i) W R
I couldn't do without soap operas.	Result (i) D R
I especially enjoy police dramas or comedies.	Result (i) G R
My preference is for serious dramas.	Result (i) S R
I enjoy news programmes and documentaries.	Result (i) F R

236 **What is your view of chivalry?**

I think it's old-fashioned nonsense, to be quite honest.	Result (ii) J O
It's pretty undesirable.	Result (ii) D O
It depends; it's OK sometimes.	Result (ii) U O
It's a desirable quality.	Result (ii) E O
I'd say it's an essential part of life.	Result (ii) A O

237 **If you had to choose just one, which of these is your favourite type of music?**

I prefer music such as heavy metal or rap.	Result (iii) W R
My favourite is rock or pop music; eg The Beatles.	Result (iii) D R
I particularly enjoy easy-listening music; eg Frank Sinatra.	Result (iii) G R
Jazz would be my number-one choice.	Result (iii) S R
My preference would be for classical music or opera.	Result (iii) F R

238 **Which of these activities appeals most?**

I'd choose relaxing; sitting on the sofa, for example.	Result (iv) J R
My preference would be for some mild exercise, such as gardening.	Result (iv) D R
Moderate exercise, such as walking, would be my choice.	Result (iv) U R
I would prefer more serious exercise, such as backpacking.	Result (iv) E R
Something strenuous like soccer or running would be my choice.	Result (iv) A R

239 **What sort of food do you like?**

I really just like traditional, plain food.	Result (v) I E
On the whole I prefer traditional, plain food.	Result (v) J E
I eat exotic food for a change.	Result (v) X E
I enjoy most foods, really.	Result (v) R E
I prefer a wide variety of dishes.	Result (v) Y E

240 **What level of education have you reached (or do you expect to reach)?**

My education ended when I was 16.	Result (vi) R W
No further education after leaving school at 18.	Result (vi) S W
Some further education after leaving school at 18.	Result (vi) H W
Graduate degree.	Result (vi) P W
Postgraduate degree.	Result (vi) N W

241 **Which of these types of TV programmes do you like the most?**

Most of all I like game shows.	Result (i) W Y
I couldn't do without soap operas.	Result (i) D Y
I especially enjoy police dramas or comedies.	Result (i) G Y
My preference is for serious dramas.	Result (i) S Y
I enjoy news programmes and documentaries.	Result (i) F Y

242 **What is your view of chivalry?**

I think it's old-fashioned nonsense, to be quite honest.	Result (ii) J T
It's pretty undesirable.	Result (ii) D T
It depends; it's OK sometimes.	Result (ii) U T
It's a desirable quality.	Result (ii) E T
I'd say it's an essential part of life.	Result (ii) A T

243 **If you had to choose just one, which of these is your favourite type of music?**

I prefer music such as heavy metal or rap.	Result (iii) W Y
My favourite is rock or pop music; eg The Beatles.	Result (iii) D Y
I particularly enjoy easy-listening music; eg Frank Sinatra.	Result (iii) G Y
Jazz would be my number-one choice.	Result (iii) S Y
My preference would be for classical music or opera.	Result (iii) F Y

244 **Which of these activities appeals most?**

I'd choose relaxing; sitting on the sofa, for example.	Result (iv) J Y
My preference would be for some mild exercise, such as gardening.	Result (iv) D Y
Moderate exercise, such as walking, would be my choice.	Result (iv) U Y
I would prefer more serious exercise, such as backpacking.	Result (iv) E Y
Something strenuous like soccer or running would be my choice.	Result (iv) A Y

245 **What sort of food do you like?**

I really just like traditional, plain food.	Result (v) I A
On the whole I prefer traditional, plain food.	Result (v) J A
I eat exotic food for a change.	Result (v) X A
I enjoy most foods, really.	Result (v) R A
I prefer a wide variety of dishes.	Result (v) Y A

246 **What level of education have you reached (or do you expect to reach)?**

My education ended when I was 16.	Result (vi) Y W
No further education after leaving school at 18.	Result (vi) F W
Some further education after leaving school at 18.	Result (vi) L W
Graduate degree.	Result (vi) C W
Postgraduate degree.	Result (vi) M W

247 **Which of these types of TV programmes do you like the most?**

Most of all I like game shows.	Result (i) Q I
I couldn't do without soap operas.	Result (i) U I
I especially enjoy police dramas or comedies.	Result (i) K I
My preference is for serious dramas.	Result (i) H I
I enjoy news programmes and documentaries.	Result (i) L I

248 **What is your view of chivalry?**

I think it's old-fashioned nonsense, to be quite honest.	Result (ii) X I
It's pretty undesirable.	Result (ii) G I
It depends; it's OK sometimes.	Result (ii) K I
It's a desirable quality.	Result (ii) V I
I'd say it's an essential part of life.	Result (ii) B I

249 **If you had to choose just one, which of these is your favourite type of music?**

I prefer music such as heavy metal or rap.	Result (iii) Q I
My favourite is rock or pop music; eg The Beatles.	Result (iii) U I
I particularly enjoy easy-listening music; eg Frank Sinatra.	Result (iii) K I
Jazz would be my number-one choice.	Result (iii) H I
My preference would be for classical music or opera.	Result (iii) L I

250 **Which of these activities appeals most?**

I'd choose relaxing; sitting on the sofa, for example.	Result (iv) X I
My preference would be for some mild exercise, such as gardening.	Result (iv) G I
Moderate exercise, such as walking, would be my choice.	Result (iv) K I
I would prefer more serious exercise, such as backpacking.	Result (iv) V I
Something strenuous like soccer or running would be my choice.	Result (iv) B I

251 **What sort of food do you like?**

I really just like traditional, plain food.	Result (v) I X
On the whole I prefer traditional, plain food.	Result (v) J X
I eat exotic food for a change.	Result (v) X X
I enjoy most foods, really.	Result (v) R X
I prefer a wide variety of dishes.	Result (v) Y X

252 **What level of education have you reached (or do you expect to reach)?**

My education ended when I was 16.	Result (vi) I Q
No further education after leaving school at 18.	Result (vi) W Q
Some further education after leaving school at 18.	Result (vi) Q Q
Graduate degree.	Result (vi) O Q
Postgraduate degree.	Result (vi) T Q

253 **Which of these types of TV programmes do you like the most?**

Most of all I like game shows.	Result (i) Q J
I couldn't do without soap operas.	Result (i) U J
I especially enjoy police dramas or comedies.	Result (i) K J
My preference is for serious dramas.	Result (i) H J
I enjoy news programmes and documentaries.	Result (i) L J

254 **What is your view of chivalry?**

I think it's old-fashioned nonsense, to be quite honest.	Result (ii) X W
It's pretty undesirable.	Result (ii) G W
It depends; it's OK sometimes.	Result (ii) K W
It's a desirable quality.	Result (ii) V W
I'd say it's an essential part of life.	Result (ii) B W

255 **If you had to choose just one, which of these is your favourite type of music?**

I prefer music such as heavy metal or rap.	Result (iii) Q J
My favourite is rock or pop music; eg The Beatles.	Result (iii) U J
I particularly enjoy easy-listening music; eg Frank Sinatra.	Result (iii) K J
Jazz would be my number-one choice.	Result (iii) H J
My preference would be for classical music or opera.	Result (iii) L J

256 **Which of these activities appeals most?**

I'd choose relaxing; sitting on the sofa, for example.	Result (iv) X J
My preference would be for some mild exercise, such as gardening.	Result (iv) G J
Moderate exercise, such as walking, would be my choice.	Result (iv) K J
I would prefer more serious exercise, such as backpacking.	Result (iv) V J
Something strenuous like soccer or running would be my choice.	Result (iv) B J

257 **What sort of food do you like?**

I really just like traditional, plain food.	Result (v) I G
On the whole I prefer traditional, plain food.	Result (v) J G
I eat exotic food for a change.	Result (v) X G
I enjoy most foods, really.	Result (v) R G
I prefer a wide variety of dishes.	Result (v) Y G

258 **What level of education have you reached (or do you expect to reach)?**

My education ended when I was 16.	Result (vi) J Q
No further education after leaving school at 18.	Result (vi) D Q
Some further education after leaving school at 18.	Result (vi) U Q
Graduate degree.	Result (vi) E Q
Postgraduate degree.	Result (vi) A Q

259 Which of these types of TV programmes do you like the most?

Most of all I like game shows.	Result (i) Q X
I couldn't do without soap operas.	Result (i) U X
I especially enjoy police dramas or comedies.	Result (i) K X
My preference is for serious dramas.	Result (i) H X
I enjoy news programmes and documentaries.	Result (i) L X

260 What is your view of chivalry?

I think it's old-fashioned nonsense, to be quite honest.	Result (ii) X Q
It's pretty undesirable.	Result (ii) G Q
It depends; it's OK sometimes.	Result (ii) K Q
It's a desirable quality.	Result (ii) V Q
I'd say it's an essential part of life.	Result (ii) B Q

261 If you had to choose just one, which of these is your favourite type of music?

I prefer music such as heavy metal or rap.	Result (iii) Q X
My favourite is rock or pop music; eg The Beatles.	Result (iii) U X
I particularly enjoy easy-listening music; eg Frank Sinatra.	Result (iii) K X
Jazz would be my number-one choice.	Result (iii) H X
My preference would be for classical music or opera.	Result (iii) L X

262 Which of these activities appeals most?

I'd choose relaxing; sitting on the sofa, for example.	Result (iv) X X
My preference would be for some mild exercise, such as gardening.	Result (iv) G X
Moderate exercise, such as walking, would be my choice.	Result (iv) K X
I would prefer more serious exercise, such as backpacking.	Result (iv) V X
Something strenuous like soccer or running would be my choice.	Result (iv) B X

263 What sort of food do you like?

I really just like traditional, plain food.	Result (v) I K
On the whole I prefer traditional, plain food.	Result (v) J K
I eat exotic food for a change.	Result (v) X K
I enjoy most foods, really.	Result (v) R K
I prefer a wide variety of dishes.	Result (v) Y K

264 What level of education have you reached (or do you expect to reach)?

My education ended when I was 16.	Result (vi) X Q
No further education after leaving school at 18.	Result (vi) G Q
Some further education after leaving school at 18.	Result (vi) K Q
Graduate degree.	Result (vi) V Q
Postgraduate degree.	Result (vi) B Q

265 **Which of these types of TV programmes do you like the most?**

Most of all I like game shows.	Result (i) Q R
I couldn't do without soap operas.	Result (i) U R
I especially enjoy police dramas or comedies.	Result (i) K R
My preference is for serious dramas.	Result (i) H R
I enjoy news programmes and documentaries.	Result (i) L R

266 **What is your view of chivalry?**

I think it's old-fashioned nonsense, to be quite honest.	Result (ii) X O
It's pretty undesirable.	Result (ii) G O
It depends; it's OK sometimes.	Result (ii) K O
It's a desirable quality.	Result (ii) V O
I'd say it's an essential part of life.	Result (ii) B O

267 **If you had to choose just one, which of these is your favourite type of music?**

I prefer music such as heavy metal or rap.	Result (iii) Q R
My favourite is rock or pop music; eg The Beatles.	Result (iii) U R
I particularly enjoy easy-listening music; eg Frank Sinatra.	Result (iii) K R
Jazz would be my number-one choice.	Result (iii) H R
My preference would be for classical music or opera.	Result (iii) L R

268 **Which of these activities appeals most?**

I'd choose relaxing; sitting on the sofa, for example.	Result (iv) X R
My preference would be for some mild exercise, such as gardening.	Result (iv) G R
Moderate exercise, such as walking, would be my choice.	Result (iv) K R
I would prefer more serious exercise, such as backpacking.	Result (iv) V R
Something strenuous like soccer or running would be my choice.	Result (iv) B R

269 **What sort of food do you like?**

I really just like traditional, plain food.	Result (v) I V
On the whole I prefer traditional, plain food.	Result (v) J V
I eat exotic food for a change.	Result (v) X V
I enjoy most foods, really.	Result (v) R V
I prefer a wide variety of dishes.	Result (v) Y V

270 **What level of education have you reached (or do you expect to reach)?**

My education ended when I was 16.	Result (vi) R Q
No further education after leaving school at 18.	Result (vi) S Q
Some further education after leaving school at 18.	Result (vi) H Q
Graduate degree.	Result (vi) P Q
Postgraduate degree.	Result (vi) N Q

271 **Which of these types of TV programmes do you like the most?**

Most of all I like game shows.	Result (i) Q Y
I couldn't do without soap operas.	Result (i) U Y
I especially enjoy police dramas or comedies.	Result (i) K Y
My preference is for serious dramas.	Result (i) H Y
I enjoy news programmes and documentaries.	Result (i) L Y

272 **What is your view of chivalry?**

I think it's old-fashioned nonsense, to be quite honest.	Result (ii) X T
It's pretty undesirable.	Result (ii) G T
It depends; it's OK sometimes.	Result (ii) K T
It's a desirable quality.	Result (ii) V T
I'd say it's an essential part of life.	Result (ii) B T

273 **If you had to choose just one, which of these is your favourite type of music?**

I prefer music such as heavy metal or rap.	Result (iii) Q Y
My favourite is rock or pop music; eg The Beatles.	Result (iii) U Y
I particularly enjoy easy-listening music; eg Frank Sinatra.	Result (iii) K Y
Jazz would be my number-one choice.	Result (iii) H Y
My preference would be for classical music or opera.	Result (iii) L Y

274 **Which of these activities appeals most?**

I'd choose relaxing; sitting on the sofa, for example.	Result (iv) X Y
My preference would be for some mild exercise, such as gardening.	Result (iv) G Y
Moderate exercise, such as walking, would be my choice.	Result (iv) K Y
I would prefer more serious exercise, such as backpacking.	Result (iv) V Y
Something strenuous like soccer or running would be my choice.	Result (iv) B Y

275 **What sort of food do you like?**

I really just like traditional, plain food.	Result (v) I B
On the whole I prefer traditional, plain food.	Result (v) J B
I eat exotic food for a change.	Result (v) X B
I enjoy most foods, really.	Result (v) R B
I prefer a wide variety of dishes.	Result (v) Y B

276 **What level of education have you reached (or do you expect to reach)?**

My education ended when I was 16.	Result (vi) Y Q
No further education after leaving school at 18.	Result (vi) F Q
Some further education after leaving school at 18.	Result (vi) L Q
Graduate degree.	Result (vi) C Q
Postgraduate degree.	Result (vi) M Q

277 | **Which of these types of TV programmes do you like the most?**

Most of all I like game shows.	Result (i) O I
I couldn't do without soap operas.	Result (i) E I
I especially enjoy police dramas or comedies.	Result (i) V I
My preference is for serious dramas.	Result (i) P I
I enjoy news programmes and documentaries.	Result (i) C I

278 | **What is your view of chivalry?**

I think it's old-fashioned nonsense, to be quite honest.	Result (ii) R I
It's pretty undesirable.	Result (ii) S I
It depends; it's OK sometimes.	Result (ii) H I
It's a desirable quality.	Result (ii) P I
I'd say it's an essential part of life.	Result (ii) N I

279 | **If you had to choose just one, which of these is your favourite type of music?**

I prefer music such as heavy metal or rap.	Result (iii) O I
My favourite is rock or pop music; eg The Beatles.	Result (iii) E I
I particularly enjoy easy-listening music; eg Frank Sinatra.	Result (iii) V I
Jazz would be my number-one choice.	Result (iii) P I
My preference would be for classical music or opera.	Result (iii) C I

280 | **Which of these activities appeals most?**

I'd choose relaxing; sitting on the sofa, for example.	Result (iv) R I
My preference would be for some mild exercise, such as gardening.	Result (iv) S I
Moderate exercise, such as walking, would be my choice.	Result (iv) H I
I would prefer more serious exercise, such as backpacking.	Result (iv) P I
Something strenuous like soccer or running would be my choice.	Result (iv) N I

281 | **What sort of food do you like?**

I really just like traditional, plain food.	Result (v) I R
On the whole I prefer traditional, plain food.	Result (v) J R
I eat exotic food for a change.	Result (v) X R
I enjoy most foods, really.	Result (v) R R
I prefer a wide variety of dishes.	Result (v) Y R

282 | **What level of education have you reached (or do you expect to reach)?**

My education ended when I was 16.	Result (vi) I O
No further education after leaving school at 18.	Result (vi) W O
Some further education after leaving school at 18.	Result (vi) Q O
Graduate degree.	Result (vi) O O
Postgraduate degree.	Result (vi) T O

283 **Which of these types of TV programmes do you like the most?**

Most of all I like game shows.	Result (i) O J
I couldn't do without soap operas.	Result (i) E J
I especially enjoy police dramas or comedies.	Result (i) V J
My preference is for serious dramas.	Result (i) P J
I enjoy news programmes and documentaries.	Result (i) C J

284 **What is your view of chivalry?**

I think it's old-fashioned nonsense, to be quite honest.	Result (ii) R W
It's pretty undesirable.	Result (ii) S W
It depends; it's OK sometimes.	Result (ii) H W
It's a desirable quality.	Result (ii) P W
I'd say it's an essential part of life.	Result (ii) N W

285 **If you had to choose just one, which of these is your favourite type of music?**

I prefer music such as heavy metal or rap.	Result (iii) O J
My favourite is rock or pop music; eg The Beatles.	Result (iii) E J
I particularly enjoy easy-listening music; eg Frank Sinatra.	Result (iii) V J
Jazz would be my number-one choice.	Result (iii) P J
My preference would be for classical music or opera.	Result (iii) C J

286 **Which of these activities appeals most?**

I'd choose relaxing; sitting on the sofa, for example.	Result (iv) R J
My preference would be for some mild exercise, such as gardening.	Result (iv) S J
Moderate exercise, such as walking, would be my choice.	Result (iv) H J
I would prefer more serious exercise, such as backpacking.	Result (iv) P J
Something strenuous like soccer or running would be my choice.	Result (iv) N J

287 **What sort of food do you like?**

I really just like traditional, plain food.	Result (v) I S
On the whole I prefer traditional, plain food.	Result (v) J S
I eat exotic food for a change.	Result (v) X S
I enjoy most foods, really.	Result (v) R S
I prefer a wide variety of dishes.	Result (v) Y S

288 **What level of education have you reached (or do you expect to reach)?**

My education ended when I was 16.	Result (vi) J O
No further education after leaving school at 18.	Result (vi) D O
Some further education after leaving school at 18.	Result (vi) U O
Graduate degree.	Result (vi) E O
Postgraduate degree.	Result (vi) A O

289 **Which of these types of TV programmes do you like the most?**

Most of all I like game shows.	Result (i) O X
I couldn't do without soap operas.	Result (i) E X
I especially enjoy police dramas or comedies.	Result (i) V X
My preference is for serious dramas.	Result (i) P X
I enjoy news programmes and documentaries.	Result (i) C X

290 **What is your view of chivalry?**

I think it's old-fashioned nonsense, to be quite honest.	Result (ii) R Q
It's pretty undesirable.	Result (ii) S Q
It depends; it's OK sometimes.	Result (ii) H Q
It's a desirable quality.	Result (ii) P Q
I'd say it's an essential part of life.	Result (ii) N Q

291 **If you had to choose just one, which of these is your favourite type of music?**

I prefer music such as heavy metal or rap.	Result (iii) O X
My favourite is rock or pop music; eg The Beatles.	Result (iii) E X
I particularly enjoy easy-listening music; eg Frank Sinatra.	Result (iii) V X
Jazz would be my number-one choice.	Result (iii) P X
My preference would be for classical music or opera.	Result (iii) C X

292 **Which of these activities appeals most?**

I'd choose relaxing; sitting on the sofa, for example.	Result (iv) R X
My preference would be for some mild exercise, such as gardening.	Result (iv) S X
Moderate exercise, such as walking, would be my choice.	Result (iv) H X
I would prefer more serious exercise, such as backpacking.	Result (iv) P X
Something strenuous like soccer or running would be my choice.	Result (iv) N X

293 **What sort of food do you like?**

I really just like traditional, plain food.	Result (v) I H
On the whole I prefer traditional, plain food.	Result (v) J H
I eat exotic food for a change.	Result (v) X H
I enjoy most foods, really.	Result (v) R H
I prefer a wide variety of dishes.	Result (v) Y H

294 **What level of education have you reached (or do you expect to reach)?**

My education ended when I was 16.	Result (vi) X O
No further education after leaving school at 18.	Result (vi) G O
Some further education after leaving school at 18.	Result (vi) K O
Graduate degree.	Result (vi) V O
Postgraduate degree.	Result (vi) B O

295 Which of these types of TV programmes do you like the most?

Most of all I like game shows.	Result (i) O R
I couldn't do without soap operas.	Result (i) E R
I especially enjoy police dramas or comedies.	Result (i) V R
My preference is for serious dramas.	Result (i) P R
I enjoy news programmes and documentaries.	Result (i) C R

296 What is your view of chivalry?

I think it's old-fashioned nonsense, to be quite honest.	Result (ii) R O
It's pretty undesirable.	Result (ii) S O
It depends; it's OK sometimes.	Result (ii) H O
It's a desirable quality.	Result (ii) P O
I'd say it's an essential part of life.	Result (ii) N O

297 If you had to choose just one, which of these is your favourite type of music?

I prefer music such as heavy metal or rap.	Result (iii) O R
My favourite is rock or pop music; eg The Beatles.	Result (iii) E R
I particularly enjoy easy-listening music; eg Frank Sinatra.	Result (iii) V R
Jazz would be my number-one choice.	Result (iii) P R
My preference would be for classical music or opera.	Result (iii) C R

298 Which of these activities appeals most?

I'd choose relaxing; sitting on the sofa, for example.	Result (iv) R R
My preference would be for some mild exercise, such as gardening.	Result (iv) S R
Moderate exercise, such as walking, would be my choice.	Result (iv) H R
I would prefer more serious exercise, such as backpacking.	Result (iv) P R
Something strenuous like soccer or running would be my choice.	Result (iv) N R

299 What sort of food do you like?

I really just like traditional, plain food.	Result (v) I P
On the whole I prefer traditional, plain food.	Result (v) J P
I eat exotic food for a change.	Result (v) X P
I enjoy most foods, really.	Result (v) R P
I prefer a wide variety of dishes.	Result (v) Y P

300 What level of education have you reached (or do you expect to reach)?

My education ended when I was 16.	Result (vi) R O
No further education after leaving school at 18.	Result (vi) S O
Some further education after leaving school at 18.	Result (vi) H O
Graduate degree.	Result (vi) P O
Postgraduate degree.	Result (vi) N O

301 Which of these types of TV programmes do you like the most?

Most of all I like game shows.	Result (i) O Y
I couldn't do without soap operas.	Result (i) E Y
I especially enjoy police dramas or comedies.	Result (i) V Y
My preference is for serious dramas.	Result (i) P Y
I enjoy news programmes and documentaries.	Result (i) C Y

302 What is your view of chivalry?

I think it's old-fashioned nonsense, to be quite honest.	Result (ii) R T
It's pretty undesirable.	Result (ii) S T
It depends; it's OK sometimes.	Result (ii) H T
It's a desirable quality.	Result (ii) P T
I'd say it's an essential part of life.	Result (ii) N T

303 If you had to choose just one, which of these is your favourite type of music?

I prefer music such as heavy metal or rap.	Result (iii) O Y
My favourite is rock or pop music; eg The Beatles.	Result (iii) E Y
I particularly enjoy easy-listening music; eg Frank Sinatra.	Result (iii) V Y
Jazz would be my number-one choice.	Result (iii) P Y
My preference would be for classical music or opera.	Result (iii) C Y

304 Which of these activities appeals most?

I'd choose relaxing; sitting on the sofa, for example.	Result (iv) R Y
My preference would be for some mild exercise, such as gardening.	Result (iv) S Y
Moderate exercise, such as walking, would be my choice.	Result (iv) H Y
I would prefer more serious exercise, such as backpacking.	Result (iv) P Y
Something strenuous like soccer or running would be my choice.	Result (iv) N Y

305 What sort of food do you like?

I really just like traditional, plain food.	Result (v) I N
On the whole I prefer traditional, plain food.	Result (v) J N
I eat exotic food for a change.	Result (v) X N
I enjoy most foods, really.	Result (v) R N
I prefer a wide variety of dishes.	Result (v) Y N

306 What level of education have you reached (or do you expect to reach)?

My education ended when I was 16.	Result (vi) Y O
No further education after leaving school at 18.	Result (vi) F O
Some further education after leaving school at 18.	Result (vi) L O
Graduate degree.	Result (vi) C O
Postgraduate degree.	Result (vi) M O

307 Which of these types of TV programmes do you like the most?

Most of all I like game shows.	Result (i) T I
I couldn't do without soap operas.	Result (i) A I
I especially enjoy police dramas or comedies.	Result (i) B I
My preference is for serious dramas.	Result (i) N I
I enjoy news programmes and documentaries.	Result (i) M I

308 What is your view of chivalry?

I think it's old-fashioned nonsense, to be quite honest.	Result (ii) Y I
It's pretty undesirable.	Result (ii) F I
It depends; it's OK sometimes.	Result (ii) L I
It's a desirable quality.	Result (ii) C I
I'd say it's an essential part of life.	Result (ii) M I

309 If you had to choose just one, which of these is your favourite type of music?

I prefer music such as heavy metal or rap.	Result (iii) T I
My favourite is rock or pop music; eg The Beatles.	Result (iii) A I
I particularly enjoy easy-listening music; eg Frank Sinatra.	Result (iii) B I
Jazz would be my number-one choice.	Result (iii) N I
My preference would be for classical music or opera.	Result (iii) M I

310 Which of these activities appeals most?

I'd choose relaxing; sitting on the sofa, for example.	Result (iv) Y I
My preference would be for some mild exercise, such as gardening.	Result (iv) F I
Moderate exercise, such as walking, would be my choice.	Result (iv) L I
I would prefer more serious exercise, such as backpacking.	Result (iv) C I
Something strenuous like soccer or running would be my choice.	Result (iv) M I

311 What sort of food do you like?

I really just like traditional, plain food.	Result (v) I Y
On the whole I prefer traditional, plain food.	Result (v) J Y
I eat exotic food for a change.	Result (v) X Y
I enjoy most foods, really.	Result (v) R Y
I prefer a wide variety of dishes.	Result (v) Y Y

312 What level of education have you reached (or do you expect to reach)?

My education ended when I was 16.	Result (vi) I T
No further education after leaving school at 18.	Result (vi) W T
Some further education after leaving school at 18.	Result (vi) Q T
Graduate degree.	Result (vi) O T
Postgraduate degree.	Result (vi) T T

313 Which of these types of TV programmes do you like the most?

Most of all I like game shows.	Result (i) T J
I couldn't do without soap operas.	Result (i) A J
I especially enjoy police dramas or comedies.	Result (i) B J
My preference is for serious dramas.	Result (i) N J
I enjoy news programmes and documentaries.	Result (i) M J

314 What is your view of chivalry?

I think it's old-fashioned nonsense, to be quite honest.	Result (ii) Y W
It's pretty undesirable.	Result (ii) F W
It depends; it's OK sometimes.	Result (ii) L W
It's a desirable quality.	Result (ii) C W
I'd say it's an essential part of life.	Result (ii) M W

315 If you had to choose just one, which of these is your favourite type of music?

I prefer music such as heavy metal or rap.	Result (iii) T J
My favourite is rock or pop music; eg The Beatles.	Result (iii) A J
I particularly enjoy easy-listening music; eg Frank Sinatra.	Result (iii) B J
Jazz would be my number-one choice.	Result (iii) N J
My preference would be for classical music or opera.	Result (iii) M J

316 Which of these activities appeals most?

I'd choose relaxing; sitting on the sofa, for example.	Result (iv) Y J
My preference would be for some mild exercise, such as gardening.	Result (iv) F J
Moderate exercise, such as walking, would be my choice.	Result (iv) L J
I would prefer more serious exercise, such as backpacking.	Result (iv) C J
Something strenuous like soccer or running would be my choice.	Result (iv) M J

317 What sort of food do you like?

I really just like traditional, plain food.	Result (v) I F
On the whole I prefer traditional, plain food.	Result (v) J F
I eat exotic food for a change.	Result (v) X F
I enjoy most foods, really.	Result (v) R F
I prefer a wide variety of dishes.	Result (v) Y F

318 What level of education have you reached (or do you expect to reach)?

My education ended when I was 16.	Result (vi) J T
No further education after leaving school at 18.	Result (vi) D T
Some further education after leaving school at 18.	Result (vi) U T
Graduate degree.	Result (vi) E T
Postgraduate degree.	Result (vi) A T

319 Which of these types of TV programmes do you like the most?

Most of all I like game shows.	Result (i) T X
I couldn't do without soap operas.	Result (i) A X
I especially enjoy police dramas or comedies.	Result (i) B X
My preference is for serious dramas.	Result (i) N X
I enjoy news programmes and documentaries.	Result (i) M X

320 What is your view of chivalry?

I think it's old-fashioned nonsense, to be quite honest.	Result (ii) Y Q
It's pretty undesirable.	Result (ii) F Q
It depends; it's OK sometimes.	Result (ii) L Q
It's a desirable quality.	Result (ii) C Q
I'd say it's an essential part of life.	Result (ii) M Q

321 If you had to choose just one, which of these is your favourite type of music?

I prefer music such as heavy metal or rap.	Result (iii) T X
My favourite is rock or pop music; eg The Beatles.	Result (iii) A X
I particularly enjoy easy-listening music; eg Frank Sinatra.	Result (iii) B X
Jazz would be my number-one choice.	Result (iii) N X
My preference would be for classical music or opera.	Result (iii) M X

322 Which of these activities appeals most?

I'd choose relaxing; sitting on the sofa, for example.	Result (iv) Y X
My preference would be for some mild exercise, such as gardening.	Result (iv) F X
Moderate exercise, such as walking, would be my choice.	Result (iv) L X
I would prefer more serious exercise, such as backpacking.	Result (iv) C X
Something strenuous like soccer or running would be my choice.	Result (iv) M X

323 What sort of food do you like?

I really just like traditional, plain food.	Result (v) I L
On the whole I prefer traditional, plain food.	Result (v) J L
I eat exotic food for a change.	Result (v) X L
I enjoy most foods, really.	Result (v) R L
I prefer a wide variety of dishes.	Result (v) Y L

324 What level of education have you reached (or do you expect to reach)?

My education ended when I was 16.	Result (vi) X T
No further education after leaving school at 18.	Result (vi) G T
Some further education after leaving school at 18.	Result (vi) K T
Graduate degree.	Result (vi) V T
Postgraduate degree.	Result (vi) B T

325 **Which of these types of TV programmes do you like the most?**

Most of all I like game shows.	Result (i) T R
I couldn't do without soap operas.	Result (i) A R
I especially enjoy police dramas or comedies.	Result (i) B R
My preference is for serious dramas.	Result (i) N R
I enjoy news programmes and documentaries.	Result (i) M R

326 **What is your view of chivalry?**

I think it's old-fashioned nonsense, to be quite honest.	Result (ii) Y O
It's pretty undesirable.	Result (ii) F O
It depends; it's OK sometimes.	Result (ii) L O
It's a desirable quality.	Result (ii) C O
I'd say it's an essential part of life.	Result (ii) M O

327 **If you had to choose just one, which of these is your favourite type of music?**

I prefer music such as heavy metal or rap.	Result (iii) T R
My favourite is rock or pop music; eg The Beatles.	Result (iii) A R
I particularly enjoy easy-listening music; eg Frank Sinatra.	Result (iii) B R
Jazz would be my number-one choice.	Result (iii) N R
My preference would be for classical music or opera.	Result (iii) M R

328 **Which of these activities appeals most?**

I'd choose relaxing; sitting on the sofa, for example.	Result (iv) Y R
My preference would be for some mild exercise, such as gardening.	Result (iv) F R
Moderate exercise, such as walking, would be my choice.	Result (iv) L R
I would prefer more serious exercise, such as backpacking.	Result (iv) C R
Something strenuous like soccer or running would be my choice.	Result (iv) M R

329 **What sort of food do you like?**

I really just like traditional, plain food.	Result (v) I C
On the whole I prefer traditional, plain food.	Result (v) J C
I eat exotic food for a change.	Result (v) X C
I enjoy most foods, really.	Result (v) R C
I prefer a wide variety of dishes.	Result (v) Y C

330 **What level of education have you reached (or do you expect to reach)?**

My education ended when I was 16.	Result (vi) R T
No further education after leaving school at 18.	Result (vi) S T
Some further education after leaving school at 18.	Result (vi) H T
Graduate degree.	Result (vi) P T
Postgraduate degree.	Result (vi) N T

331   **Which of these types of TV programmes do you like the most?**

Most of all I like game shows.	Result (i) T Y
I couldn't do without soap operas.	Result (i) A Y
I especially enjoy police dramas or comedies.	Result (i) B Y
My preference is for serious dramas.	Result (i) N Y
I enjoy news programmes and documentaries.	Result (i) M Y

332   **What is your view of chivalry?**

I think it's old-fashioned nonsense, to be quite honest.	Result (ii) Y T
It's pretty undesirable.	Result (ii) F T
It depends; it's OK sometimes.	Result (ii) L T
It's a desirable quality.	Result (ii) C T
I'd say it's an essential part of life.	Result (ii) M T

333   **If you had to choose just one, which of these is your favourite type of music?**

I prefer music such as heavy metal or rap.	Result (iii) T Y
My favourite is rock or pop music; eg The Beatles.	Result (iii) A Y
I particularly enjoy easy-listening music; eg Frank Sinatra.	Result (iii) B Y
Jazz would be my number-one choice.	Result (iii) N Y
My preference would be for classical music or opera.	Result (iii) M Y

334   **Which of these activities appeals most?**

I'd choose relaxing; sitting on the sofa, for example.	Result (iv) Y Y
My preference would be for some mild exercise, such as gardening.	Result (iv) F Y
Moderate exercise, such as walking, would be my choice.	Result (iv) L Y
I would prefer more serious exercise, such as backpacking.	Result (iv) C Y
Something strenuous like soccer or running would be my choice.	Result (iv) M Y

335   **What sort of food do you like?**

I really just like traditional, plain food.	Result (v) I M
On the whole I prefer traditional, plain food.	Result (v) J M
I eat exotic food for a change.	Result (v) X M
I enjoy most foods, really.	Result (v) R M
I prefer a wide variety of dishes.	Result (v) Y M

336   **What level of education have you reached (or do you expect to reach)?**

My education ended when I was 16.	Result (vi) Y T
No further education after leaving school at 18.	Result (vi) F T
Some further education after leaving school at 18.	Result (vi) L T
Graduate degree.	Result (vi) C T
Postgraduate degree.	Result (vi) M T

337 Which of these types of TV programmes do you like the most?

Most of all I like game shows.	Result (i) I W
I couldn't do without soap operas.	Result (i) J W
I especially enjoy police dramas or comedies.	Result (i) X W
My preference is for serious dramas.	Result (i) R W
I enjoy news programmes and documentaries.	Result (i) Y W

338 What is your view of chivalry?

I think it's old-fashioned nonsense, to be quite honest.	Result (ii) I J
It's pretty undesirable.	Result (ii) W J
It depends; it's OK sometimes.	Result (ii) Q J
It's a desirable quality.	Result (ii) O J
I'd say it's an essential part of life.	Result (ii) T J

339 If you had to choose just one, which of these is your favourite type of music?

I prefer music such as heavy metal or rap.	Result (iii) I W
My favourite is rock or pop music; eg The Beatles.	Result (iii) J W
I particularly enjoy easy-listening music; eg Frank Sinatra.	Result (iii) X W
Jazz would be my number-one choice.	Result (iii) R W
My preference would be for classical music or opera.	Result (iii) Y W

340 Which of these activities appeals most?

I'd choose relaxing; sitting on the sofa, for example.	Result (iv) I W
My preference would be for some mild exercise, such as gardening.	Result (iv) W W
Moderate exercise, such as walking, would be my choice.	Result (iv) Q W
I would prefer more serious exercise, such as backpacking.	Result (iv) O W
Something strenuous like soccer or running would be my choice.	Result (iv) T W

341 What sort of food do you like?

I really just like traditional, plain food.	Result (v) W I
On the whole I prefer traditional, plain food.	Result (v) D I
I eat exotic food for a change.	Result (v) G I
I enjoy most foods, really.	Result (v) S I
I prefer a wide variety of dishes.	Result (v) F I

342 What level of education have you reached (or do you expect to reach)?

My education ended when I was 16.	Result (vi) I J
No further education after leaving school at 18.	Result (vi) W J
Some further education after leaving school at 18.	Result (vi) Q J
Graduate degree.	Result (vi) O J
Postgraduate degree.	Result (vi) T J

343 **Which of these types of TV programmes do you like the most?**

Most of all I like game shows.	Result (i) I D
I couldn't do without soap operas.	Result (i) J D
I especially enjoy police dramas or comedies.	Result (i) X D
My preference is for serious dramas.	Result (i) R D
I enjoy news programmes and documentaries.	Result (i) Y D ✓

344 **What is your view of chivalry?**

I think it's old-fashioned nonsense, to be quite honest.	Result (ii) I D
It's pretty undesirable.	Result (ii) W D
It depends; it's OK sometimes.	Result (ii) Q D
It's a desirable quality.	Result (ii) O D
I'd say it's an essential part of life.	Result (ii) T D

345 **If you had to choose just one, which of these is your favourite type of music?**

I prefer music such as heavy metal or rap.	Result (iii) I D
My favourite is rock or pop music; eg The Beatles.	Result (iii) J D
I particularly enjoy easy-listening music; eg Frank Sinatra.	Result (iii) X D
Jazz would be my number-one choice.	Result (iii) R D
My preference would be for classical music or opera.	Result (iii) Y D

346 **Which of these activities appeals most?**

I'd choose relaxing; sitting on the sofa, for example.	Result (iv) I D
My preference would be for some mild exercise, such as gardening.	Result (iv) W D
Moderate exercise, such as walking, would be my choice.	Result (iv) Q D
I would prefer more serious exercise, such as backpacking.	Result (iv) O D
Something strenuous like soccer or running would be my choice.	Result (iv) T D

347 **What sort of food do you like?**

I really just like traditional, plain food.	Result (v) W W
On the whole I prefer traditional, plain food.	Result (v) D W
I eat exotic food for a change.	Result (v) G W
I enjoy most foods, really.	Result (v) S W
I prefer a wide variety of dishes.	Result (v) F W

348 **What level of education have you reached (or do you expect to reach)?**

My education ended when I was 16.	Result (vi) J J
No further education after leaving school at 18.	Result (vi) D J
Some further education after leaving school at 18.	Result (vi) U J
Graduate degree.	Result (vi) E J
Postgraduate degree.	Result (vi) A J

349 **Which of these types of TV programmes do you like the most?**

Most of all I like game shows.	Result (i) I G
I couldn't do without soap operas.	Result (i) J G
I especially enjoy police dramas or comedies.	Result (i) X G
My preference is for serious dramas.	Result (i) R G
I enjoy news programmes and documentaries.	Result (i) Y G

350 **What is your view of chivalry?**

I think it's old-fashioned nonsense, to be quite honest.	Result (ii) I U
It's pretty undesirable.	Result (ii) W U
It depends; it's OK sometimes.	Result (ii) Q U
It's a desirable quality.	Result (ii) O U
I'd say it's an essential part of life.	Result (ii) T U

351 **If you had to choose just one, which of these is your favourite type of music?**

I prefer music such as heavy metal or rap.	Result (iii) I G
My favourite is rock or pop music; eg The Beatles.	Result (iii) J G
I particularly enjoy easy-listening music; eg Frank Sinatra.	Result (iii) X G
Jazz would be my number-one choice.	Result (iii) R G
My preference would be for classical music or opera.	Result (iii) Y G

352 **Which of these activities appeals most?**

I'd choose relaxing; sitting on the sofa, for example.	Result (iv) I G
My preference would be for some mild exercise, such as gardening.	Result (iv) W G
Moderate exercise, such as walking, would be my choice.	Result (iv) Q G
I would prefer more serious exercise, such as backpacking.	Result (iv) O G
Something strenuous like soccer or running would be my choice.	Result (iv) T G

353 **What sort of food do you like?**

I really just like traditional, plain food.	Result (v) W Q
On the whole I prefer traditional, plain food.	Result (v) D Q
I eat exotic food for a change.	Result (v) G Q
I enjoy most foods, really.	Result (v) S Q
I prefer a wide variety of dishes.	Result (v) F Q

354 **What level of education have you reached (or do you expect to reach)?**

My education ended when I was 16.	Result (vi) X J
No further education after leaving school at 18.	Result (vi) G J
Some further education after leaving school at 18.	Result (vi) K J
Graduate degree.	Result (vi) V J
Postgraduate degree.	Result (vi) B J

355 Which of these types of TV programmes do you like the most?

Most of all I like game shows.	Result (i) I S
I couldn't do without soap operas.	Result (i) J S
I especially enjoy police dramas or comedies.	Result (i) X S
My preference is for serious dramas.	Result (i) R S
I enjoy news programmes and documentaries.	Result (i) Y S

356 What is your view of chivalry?

I think it's old-fashioned nonsense, to be quite honest.	Result (ii) I E
It's pretty undesirable.	Result (ii) W E
It depends; it's OK sometimes.	Result (ii) Q E
It's a desirable quality.	Result (ii) O E
I'd say it's an essential part of life.	Result (ii) T E

357 If you had to choose just one, which of these is your favourite type of music?

I prefer music such as heavy metal or rap.	Result (iii) I S
My favourite is rock or pop music; eg The Beatles.	Result (iii) J S
I particularly enjoy easy-listening music; eg Frank Sinatra.	Result (iii) X S
Jazz would be my number-one choice.	Result (iii) R S
My preference would be for classical music or opera.	Result (iii) Y S

358 Which of these activities appeals most?

I'd choose relaxing; sitting on the sofa, for example.	Result (iv) I S
My preference would be for some mild exercise, such as gardening.	Result (iv) W S
Moderate exercise, such as walking, would be my choice.	Result (iv) Q S
I would prefer more serious exercise, such as backpacking.	Result (iv) O S
Something strenuous like soccer or running would be my choice.	Result (iv) T S

359 What sort of food do you like?

I really just like traditional, plain food.	Result (v) W O
On the whole I prefer traditional, plain food.	Result (v) D O
I eat exotic food for a change.	Result (v) G O
I enjoy most foods, really.	Result (v) S O
I prefer a wide variety of dishes.	Result (v) F O

360 What level of education have you reached (or do you expect to reach)?

My education ended when I was 16.	Result (vi) R J
No further education after leaving school at 18.	Result (vi) S J
Some further education after leaving school at 18.	Result (vi) H J
Graduate degree.	Result (vi) P J
Postgraduate degree.	Result (vi) N J

361 **Which of these types of TV programmes do you like the most?**

Most of all I like game shows.	Result (i) I F
I couldn't do without soap operas.	Result (i) J F
I especially enjoy police dramas or comedies.	Result (i) X F
My preference is for serious dramas.	Result (i) R F
I enjoy news programmes and documentaries.	Result (i) Y F

362 **What is your view of chivalry?**

I think it's old-fashioned nonsense, to be quite honest.	Result (ii) I A
It's pretty undesirable.	Result (ii) W A
It depends; it's OK sometimes.	Result (ii) Q A
It's a desirable quality.	Result (ii) O A
I'd say it's an essential part of life.	Result (ii) T A

363 **If you had to choose just one, which of these is your favourite type of music?**

I prefer music such as heavy metal or rap.	Result (iii) I F
My favourite is rock or pop music; eg The Beatles.	Result (iii) J F
I particularly enjoy easy-listening music; eg Frank Sinatra.	Result (iii) X F
Jazz would be my number-one choice.	Result (iii) R F
My preference would be for classical music or opera.	Result (iii) Y F

364 **Which of these activities appeals most?**

I'd choose relaxing; sitting on the sofa, for example.	Result (iv) I F
My preference would be for some mild exercise, such as gardening.	Result (iv) W F
Moderate exercise, such as walking, would be my choice.	Result (iv) Q F
I would prefer more serious exercise, such as backpacking.	Result (iv) O F
Something strenuous like soccer or running would be my choice.	Result (iv) T F

365 **What sort of food do you like?**

I really just like traditional, plain food.	Result (v) W T
On the whole I prefer traditional, plain food.	Result (v) D T
I eat exotic food for a change.	Result (v) G T
I enjoy most foods, really.	Result (v) S T
I prefer a wide variety of dishes.	Result (v) F T

366 **What level of education have you reached (or do you expect to reach)?**

My education ended when I was 16.	Result (vi) Y J
No further education after leaving school at 18.	Result (vi) F J
Some further education after leaving school at 18.	Result (vi) L J
Graduate degree.	Result (vi) C J
Postgraduate degree.	Result (vi) M J

367   **Which of these types of TV programmes do you like the most?**

Most of all I like game shows.	Result (i) W W
I couldn't do without soap operas.	Result (i) D W
I especially enjoy police dramas or comedies.	Result (i) G W
My preference is for serious dramas.	Result (i) S W
I enjoy news programmes and documentaries.	Result (i) F W

368   **What is your view of chivalry?**

I think it's old-fashioned nonsense, to be quite honest.	Result (ii) J J
It's pretty undesirable.	Result (ii) D J
It depends; it's OK sometimes.	Result (ii) U J
It's a desirable quality.	Result (ii) E J
I'd say it's an essential part of life.	Result (ii) A J

369   **If you had to choose just one, which of these is your favourite type of music?**

I prefer music such as heavy metal or rap.	Result (iii) W W
My favourite is rock or pop music; eg The Beatles.	Result (iii) D W
I particularly enjoy easy-listening music; eg Frank Sinatra.	Result (iii) G W
Jazz would be my number-one choice.	Result (iii) S W
My preference would be for classical music or opera.	Result (iii) F W

370   **Which of these activities appeals most?**

I'd choose relaxing; sitting on the sofa, for example.	Result (iv) J W
My preference would be for some mild exercise, such as gardening.	Result (iv) D W
Moderate exercise, such as walking, would be my choice.	Result (iv) U W
I would prefer more serious exercise, such as backpacking.	Result (iv) E W
Something strenuous like soccer or running would be my choice.	Result (iv) A W

371   **What sort of food do you like?**

I really just like traditional, plain food.	Result (v) W J
On the whole I prefer traditional, plain food.	Result (v) D J
I eat exotic food for a change.	Result (v) G J
I enjoy most foods, really.	Result (v) S J
I prefer a wide variety of dishes.	Result (v) F J

372   **What level of education have you reached (or do you expect to reach)?**

My education ended when I was 16.	Result (vi) I D
No further education after leaving school at 18.	Result (vi) W D
Some further education after leaving school at 18.	Result (vi) Q D
Graduate degree.	Result (vi) O D
Postgraduate degree.	Result (vi) T D

373 **Which of these types of TV programmes do you like the most?**

Most of all I like game shows.	Result (i) W D
I couldn't do without soap operas.	Result (i) D D
I especially enjoy police dramas or comedies.	Result (i) G D
My preference is for serious dramas.	Result (i) S D
I enjoy news programmes and documentaries.	Result (i) F D

374 **What is your view of chivalry?**

I think it's old-fashioned nonsense, to be quite honest.	Result (ii) J D
It's pretty undesirable.	Result (ii) D D
It depends; it's OK sometimes.	Result (ii) U D
It's a desirable quality.	Result (ii) E D
I'd say it's an essential part of life.	Result (ii) A D

375 **If you had to choose just one, which of these is your favourite type of music?**

I prefer music such as heavy metal or rap.	Result (iii) W D
My favourite is rock or pop music; eg The Beatles.	Result (iii) D D
I particularly enjoy easy-listening music; eg Frank Sinatra.	Result (iii) G D
Jazz would be my number-one choice.	Result (iii) S D
My preference would be for classical music or opera.	Result (iii) F D

376 **Which of these activities appeals most?**

I'd choose relaxing; sitting on the sofa, for example.	Result (iv) J D
My preference would be for some mild exercise, such as gardening.	Result (iv) D D
Moderate exercise, such as walking, would be my choice.	Result (iv) U D
I would prefer more serious exercise, such as backpacking.	Result (iv) E D
Something strenuous like soccer or running would be my choice.	Result (iv) A D

377 **What sort of food do you like?**

I really just like traditional, plain food.	Result (v) W D
On the whole I prefer traditional, plain food.	Result (v) D D
I eat exotic food for a change.	Result (v) G D
I enjoy most foods, really.	Result (v) S D
I prefer a wide variety of dishes.	Result (v) F D

378 **What level of education have you reached (or do you expect to reach)?**

My education ended when I was 16.	Result (vi) J D
No further education after leaving school at 18.	Result (vi) D D
Some further education after leaving school at 18.	Result (vi) U D
Graduate degree.	Result (vi) E D
Postgraduate degree.	Result (vi) A D

379 **Which of these types of TV programmes do you like the most?**

Most of all I like game shows.	Result (i) W G
I couldn't do without soap operas.	Result (i) D G
I especially enjoy police dramas or comedies.	Result (i) G G
My preference is for serious dramas.	Result (i) S G
I enjoy news programmes and documentaries.	Result (i) F G

380 **What is your view of chivalry?**

I think it's old-fashioned nonsense, to be quite honest.	Result (ii) J U
It's pretty undesirable.	Result (ii) D U
It depends; it's OK sometimes.	Result (ii) U U
It's a desirable quality.	Result (ii) E U
I'd say it's an essential part of life.	Result (ii) A U

381 **If you had to choose just one, which of these is your favourite type of music?**

I prefer music such as heavy metal or rap.	Result (iii) W G
My favourite is rock or pop music; eg The Beatles.	Result (iii) D G
I particularly enjoy easy-listening music; eg Frank Sinatra.	Result (iii) G G
Jazz would be my number-one choice.	Result (iii) S G
My preference would be for classical music or opera.	Result (iii) F G

382 **Which of these activities appeals most?**

I'd choose relaxing; sitting on the sofa, for example.	Result (iv) J G
My preference would be for some mild exercise, such as gardening.	Result (iv) D G
Moderate exercise, such as walking, would be my choice.	Result (iv) U G
I would prefer more serious exercise, such as backpacking.	Result (iv) E G
Something strenuous like soccer or running would be my choice.	Result (iv) A G

383 **What sort of food do you like?**

I really just like traditional, plain food.	Result (v) W U
On the whole I prefer traditional, plain food.	Result (v) D U
I eat exotic food for a change.	Result (v) G U
I enjoy most foods, really.	Result (v) S U
I prefer a wide variety of dishes.	Result (v) F U

384 **What level of education have you reached (or do you expect to reach)?**

My education ended when I was 16.	Result (vi) X D
No further education after leaving school at 18.	Result (vi) G D
Some further education after leaving school at 18.	Result (vi) K D
Graduate degree.	Result (vi) V D
Postgraduate degree.	Result (vi) B D

385 Which of these types of TV programmes do you like the most?

Most of all I like game shows.	Result (i) W S
I couldn't do without soap operas.	Result (i) D S
I especially enjoy police dramas or comedies.	Result (i) G S
My preference is for serious dramas.	Result (i) S S
I enjoy news programmes and documentaries.	Result (i) F S

386 What is your view of chivalry?

I think it's old-fashioned nonsense, to be quite honest.	Result (ii) J E
It's pretty undesirable.	Result (ii) D E
It depends; it's OK sometimes.	Result (ii) U E
It's a desirable quality.	Result (ii) E E
I'd say it's an essential part of life.	Result (ii) A E

387 If you had to choose just one, which of these is your favourite type of music?

I prefer music such as heavy metal or rap.	Result (iii) W S
My favourite is rock or pop music; eg The Beatles.	Result (iii) D S
I particularly enjoy easy-listening music; eg Frank Sinatra.	Result (iii) G S
Jazz would be my number-one choice.	Result (iii) S S
My preference would be for classical music or opera.	Result (iii) F S

388 Which of these activities appeals most?

I'd choose relaxing; sitting on the sofa, for example.	Result (iv) J S
My preference would be for some mild exercise, such as gardening.	Result (iv) D S
Moderate exercise, such as walking, would be my choice.	Result (iv) U S
I would prefer more serious exercise, such as backpacking.	Result (iv) E S
Something strenuous like soccer or running would be my choice.	Result (iv) A S

389 What sort of food do you like?

I really just like traditional, plain food.	Result (v) W E
On the whole I prefer traditional, plain food.	Result (v) D E
I eat exotic food for a change.	Result (v) G E
I enjoy most foods, really.	Result (v) S E
I prefer a wide variety of dishes.	Result (v) F E

390 What level of education have you reached (or do you expect to reach)?

My education ended when I was 16.	Result (vi) R D
No further education after leaving school at 18.	Result (vi) S D
Some further education after leaving school at 18.	Result (vi) H D
Graduate degree.	Result (vi) P D
Postgraduate degree.	Result (vi) N D

391 **Which of these types of TV programmes do you like the most?**

Most of all I like game shows.	Result (i) W F
I couldn't do without soap operas.	Result (i) D F
I especially enjoy police dramas or comedies.	Result (i) G F
My preference is for serious dramas.	Result (i) S F
I enjoy news programmes and documentaries.	Result (i) F F

392 **What is your view of chivalry?**

I think it's old-fashioned nonsense, to be quite honest.	Result (ii) J A
It's pretty undesirable.	Result (ii) D A
It depends; it's OK sometimes.	Result (ii) U A
It's a desirable quality.	Result (ii) E A
I'd say it's an essential part of life.	Result (ii) A A

393 **If you had to choose just one, which of these is your favourite type of music?**

I prefer music such as heavy metal or rap.	Result (iii) W F
My favourite is rock or pop music; eg The Beatles.	Result (iii) D F
I particularly enjoy easy-listening music; eg Frank Sinatra.	Result (iii) G F
Jazz would be my number-one choice.	Result (iii) S F
My preference would be for classical music or opera.	Result (iii) F F

394 **Which of these activities appeals most?**

I'd choose relaxing; sitting on the sofa, for example.	Result (iv) J F
My preference would be for some mild exercise, such as gardening.	Result (iv) D F
Moderate exercise, such as walking, would be my choice.	Result (iv) U F
I would prefer more serious exercise, such as backpacking.	Result (iv) E F
Something strenuous like soccer or running would be my choice.	Result (iv) A F

395 **What sort of food do you like?**

I really just like traditional, plain food.	Result (v) W A
On the whole I prefer traditional, plain food.	Result (v) D A
I eat exotic food for a change.	Result (v) G A
I enjoy most foods, really.	Result (v) S A
I prefer a wide variety of dishes.	Result (v) F A

396 **What level of education have you reached (or do you expect to reach)?**

My education ended when I was 16.	Result (vi) Y D
No further education after leaving school at 18.	Result (vi) F D
Some further education after leaving school at 18.	Result (vi) L D
Graduate degree.	Result (vi) C D
Postgraduate degree.	Result (vi) M D

397 **Which of these types of TV programmes do you like the most?**

Most of all I like game shows.	Result (i) Q W
I couldn't do without soap operas.	Result (i) U W
I especially enjoy police dramas or comedies.	Result (i) K W
My preference is for serious dramas.	Result (i) H W
I enjoy news programmes and documentaries.	Result (i) L W

398 **What is your view of chivalry?**

I think it's old-fashioned nonsense, to be quite honest.	Result (ii) X J
It's pretty undesirable.	Result (ii) G J
It depends; it's OK sometimes.	Result (ii) K J
It's a desirable quality.	Result (ii) V J
I'd say it's an essential part of life.	Result (ii) B J

399 **If you had to choose just one, which of these is your favourite type of music?**

I prefer music such as heavy metal or rap.	Result (iii) Q W
My favourite is rock or pop music; eg The Beatles.	Result (iii) U W
I particularly enjoy easy-listening music; eg Frank Sinatra.	Result (iii) K W
Jazz would be my number-one choice.	Result (iii) H W
My preference would be for classical music or opera.	Result (iii) L W

400 **Which of these activities appeals most?**

I'd choose relaxing; sitting on the sofa, for example.	Result (iv) X W
My preference would be for some mild exercise, such as gardening.	Result (iv) G W
Moderate exercise, such as walking, would be my choice.	Result (iv) K W
I would prefer more serious exercise, such as backpacking.	Result (iv) V W
Something strenuous like soccer or running would be my choice.	Result (iv) B W

401 **What sort of food do you like?**

I really just like traditional, plain food.	Result (v) W X
On the whole I prefer traditional, plain food.	Result (v) D X
I eat exotic food for a change.	Result (v) G X
I enjoy most foods, really.	Result (v) S X
I prefer a wide variety of dishes.	Result (v) F X

402 **What level of education have you reached (or do you expect to reach)?**

My education ended when I was 16.	Result (vi) I U
No further education after leaving school at 18.	Result (vi) W U
Some further education after leaving school at 18.	Result (vi) Q U
Graduate degree.	Result (vi) O U
Postgraduate degree.	Result (vi) T U

403 **Which of these types of TV programmes do you like the most?**

Most of all I like game shows.	Result (i) Q D
I couldn't do without soap operas.	Result (i) U D
I especially enjoy police dramas or comedies.	Result (i) K D
My preference is for serious dramas.	Result (i) H D
I enjoy news programmes and documentaries.	Result (i) L D

404 **What is your view of chivalry?**

I think it's old-fashioned nonsense, to be quite honest.	Result (ii) X D
It's pretty undesirable.	Result (ii) G D
It depends; it's OK sometimes.	Result (ii) K D
It's a desirable quality.	Result (ii) V D
I'd say it's an essential part of life.	Result (ii) B D

405 **If you had to choose just one, which of these is your favourite type of music?**

I prefer music such as heavy metal or rap.	Result (iii) Q D
My favourite is rock or pop music; eg The Beatles.	Result (iii) U D
I particularly enjoy easy-listening music; eg Frank Sinatra.	Result (iii) K D
Jazz would be my number-one choice.	Result (iii) H D
My preference would be for classical music or opera.	Result (iii) L D

406 **Which of these activities appeals most?**

I'd choose relaxing; sitting on the sofa, for example.	Result (iv) X D
My preference would be for some mild exercise, such as gardening.	Result (iv) G D
Moderate exercise, such as walking, would be my choice.	Result (iv) K D
I would prefer more serious exercise, such as backpacking.	Result (iv) V D
Something strenuous like soccer or running would be my choice.	Result (iv) B D

407 **What sort of food do you like?**

I really just like traditional, plain food.	Result (v) W G
On the whole I prefer traditional, plain food.	Result (v) D G
I eat exotic food for a change.	Result (v) G G
I enjoy most foods, really.	Result (v) S G
I prefer a wide variety of dishes.	Result (v) F G

408 **What level of education have you reached (or do you expect to reach)?**

My education ended when I was 16.	Result (vi) J U
No further education after leaving school at 18.	Result (vi) D U
Some further education after leaving school at 18.	Result (vi) U U
Graduate degree.	Result (vi) E U
Postgraduate degree.	Result (vi) A U

409 **Which of these types of TV programmes do you like the most?**

Most of all I like game shows.	Result (i) Q G
I couldn't do without soap operas.	Result (i) U G
I especially enjoy police dramas or comedies.	Result (i) K G
My preference is for serious dramas.	Result (i) H G
I enjoy news programmes and documentaries.	Result (i) L G

410 **What is your view of chivalry?**

I think it's old-fashioned nonsense, to be quite honest.	Result (ii) X U
It's pretty undesirable.	Result (ii) G U
It depends; it's OK sometimes.	Result (ii) K U
It's a desirable quality.	Result (ii) V U
I'd say it's an essential part of life.	Result (ii) B U

411 **If you had to choose just one, which of these is your favourite type of music?**

I prefer music such as heavy metal or rap.	Result (iii) Q G
My favourite is rock or pop music; eg The Beatles.	Result (iii) U G
I particularly enjoy easy-listening music; eg Frank Sinatra.	Result (iii) K G
Jazz would be my number-one choice.	Result (iii) H G
My preference would be for classical music or opera.	Result (iii) L G

412 **Which of these activities appeals most?**

I'd choose relaxing; sitting on the sofa, for example.	Result (iv) X G
My preference would be for some mild exercise, such as gardening.	Result (iv) G G
Moderate exercise, such as walking, would be my choice.	Result (iv) K G
I would prefer more serious exercise, such as backpacking.	Result (iv) V G
Something strenuous like soccer or running would be my choice.	Result (iv) B G

413 **What sort of food do you like?**

I really just like traditional, plain food.	Result (v) W K
On the whole I prefer traditional, plain food.	Result (v) D K
I eat exotic food for a change.	Result (v) G K
I enjoy most foods, really.	Result (v) S K
I prefer a wide variety of dishes.	Result (v) F K

414 **What level of education have you reached (or do you expect to reach)?**

My education ended when I was 16.	Result (vi) X U
No further education after leaving school at 18.	Result (vi) G U
Some further education after leaving school at 18.	Result (vi) K U
Graduate degree.	Result (vi) V U
Postgraduate degree.	Result (vi) B U

415 **Which of these types of TV programmes do you like the most?**

Most of all I like game shows.	Result (i) Q S
I couldn't do without soap operas.	Result (i) U S
I especially enjoy police dramas or comedies.	Result (i) K S
My preference is for serious dramas.	Result (i) H S
I enjoy news programmes and documentaries.	Result (i) L S

416 **What is your view of chivalry?**

I think it's old-fashioned nonsense, to be quite honest.	Result (ii) X E
It's pretty undesirable.	Result (ii) G E
It depends; it's OK sometimes.	Result (ii) K E
It's a desirable quality.	Result (ii) V E
I'd say it's an essential part of life.	Result (ii) B E

417 **If you had to choose just one, which of these is your favourite type of music?**

I prefer music such as heavy metal or rap.	Result (iii) Q S
My favourite is rock or pop music; eg The Beatles.	Result (iii) U S
I particularly enjoy easy-listening music; eg Frank Sinatra.	Result (iii) K S
Jazz would be my number-one choice.	Result (iii) H S
My preference would be for classical music or opera.	Result (iii) L S

418 **Which of these activities appeals most?**

I'd choose relaxing; sitting on the sofa, for example.	Result (iv) X S
My preference would be for some mild exercise, such as gardening.	Result (iv) G S
Moderate exercise, such as walking, would be my choice.	Result (iv) K S
I would prefer more serious exercise, such as backpacking.	Result (iv) V S
Something strenuous like soccer or running would be my choice.	Result (iv) B S

419 **What sort of food do you like?**

I really just like traditional, plain food.	Result (v) W V
On the whole I prefer traditional, plain food.	Result (v) D V
I eat exotic food for a change.	Result (v) G V
I enjoy most foods, really.	Result (v) S V
I prefer a wide variety of dishes.	Result (v) F V

420 **What level of education have you reached (or do you expect to reach)?**

My education ended when I was 16.	Result (vi) R U
No further education after leaving school at 18.	Result (vi) S U
Some further education after leaving school at 18.	Result (vi) H U
Graduate degree.	Result (vi) P U
Postgraduate degree.	Result (vi) N U

421	**Which of these types of TV programmes do you like the most?**
Most of all I like game shows.	Result (i) Q F
I couldn't do without soap operas.	Result (i) U F
I especially enjoy police dramas or comedies.	Result (i) K F
My preference is for serious dramas.	Result (i) H F
I enjoy news programmes and documentaries.	Result (i) L F

422	**What is your view of chivalry?**
I think it's old-fashioned nonsense, to be quite honest.	Result (ii) X A
It's pretty undesirable.	Result (ii) G A
It depends; it's OK sometimes.	Result (ii) K A
It's a desirable quality.	Result (ii) V A
I'd say it's an essential part of life.	Result (ii) B A

423	**If you had to choose just one, which of these is your favourite type of music?**
I prefer music such as heavy metal or rap.	Result (iii) Q F
My favourite is rock or pop music; eg The Beatles.	Result (iii) U F
I particularly enjoy easy-listening music; eg Frank Sinatra.	Result (iii) K F
Jazz would be my number-one choice.	Result (iii) H F
My preference would be for classical music or opera.	Result (iii) L F

424	**Which of these activities appeals most?**
I'd choose relaxing; sitting on the sofa, for example.	Result (iv) X F
My preference would be for some mild exercise, such as gardening.	Result (iv) G F
Moderate exercise, such as walking, would be my choice.	Result (iv) K F
I would prefer more serious exercise, such as backpacking.	Result (iv) V F
Something strenuous like soccer or running would be my choice.	Result (iv) B F

425	**What sort of food do you like?**
I really just like traditional, plain food.	Result (v) W B
On the whole I prefer traditional, plain food.	Result (v) D B
I eat exotic food for a change.	Result (v) G B
I enjoy most foods, really.	Result (v) S B
I prefer a wide variety of dishes.	Result (v) F B

426	**What level of education have you reached (or do you expect to reach)?**
My education ended when I was 16.	Result (vi) Y U
No further education after leaving school at 18.	Result (vi) F U
Some further education after leaving school at 18.	Result (vi) L U
Graduate degree.	Result (vi) C U
Postgraduate degree.	Result (vi) M U

427 **Which of these types of TV programmes do you like the most?**

Most of all I like game shows.	Result (i) O W
I couldn't do without soap operas.	Result (i) E W
I especially enjoy police dramas or comedies.	Result (i) V W
My preference is for serious dramas.	Result (i) P W
I enjoy news programmes and documentaries.	Result (i) C W

428 **What is your view of chivalry?**

I think it's old-fashioned nonsense, to be quite honest.	Result (ii) R J
It's pretty undesirable.	Result (ii) S J
It depends; it's OK sometimes.	Result (ii) H J
It's a desirable quality.	Result (ii) P J
I'd say it's an essential part of life.	Result (ii) N J

429 **If you had to choose just one, which of these is your favourite type of music?**

I prefer music such as heavy metal or rap.	Result (iii) O W
My favourite is rock or pop music; eg The Beatles.	Result (iii) E W
I particularly enjoy easy-listening music; eg Frank Sinatra.	Result (iii) V W
Jazz would be my number-one choice.	Result (iii) P W
My preference would be for classical music or opera.	Result (iii) C W

430 **Which of these activities appeals most?**

I'd choose relaxing; sitting on the sofa, for example.	Result (iv) R W
My preference would be for some mild exercise, such as gardening.	Result (iv) S W
Moderate exercise, such as walking, would be my choice.	Result (iv) H W
I would prefer more serious exercise, such as backpacking.	Result (iv) P W
Something strenuous like soccer or running would be my choice.	Result (iv) N W

431 **What sort of food do you like?**

I really just like traditional, plain food.	Result (v) W R
On the whole I prefer traditional, plain food.	Result (v) D R
I eat exotic food for a change.	Result (v) G R
I enjoy most foods, really.	Result (v) S R
I prefer a wide variety of dishes.	Result (v) F R

432 **What level of education have you reached (or do you expect to reach)?**

My education ended when I was 16.	Result (vi) I E
No further education after leaving school at 18.	Result (vi) W E
Some further education after leaving school at 18.	Result (vi) Q E
Graduate degree.	Result (vi) O E
Postgraduate degree.	Result (vi) T E

433 **Which of these types of TV programmes do you like the most?**

Most of all I like game shows.	Result (i) O D
I couldn't do without soap operas.	Result (i) E D
I especially enjoy police dramas or comedies.	Result (i) V D
My preference is for serious dramas.	Result (i) P D
I enjoy news programmes and documentaries.	Result (i) C D

434 **What is your view of chivalry?**

I think it's old-fashioned nonsense, to be quite honest.	Result (ii) R D
It's pretty undesirable.	Result (ii) S D
It depends; it's OK sometimes.	Result (ii) H D
It's a desirable quality.	Result (ii) P D
I'd say it's an essential part of life.	Result (ii) N D

435 **If you had to choose just one, which of these is your favourite type of music?**

I prefer music such as heavy metal or rap.	Result (iii) O D
My favourite is rock or pop music; eg The Beatles.	Result (iii) E D
I particularly enjoy easy-listening music; eg Frank Sinatra.	Result (iii) V D
Jazz would be my number-one choice.	Result (iii) P D
My preference would be for classical music or opera.	Result (iii) C D

436 **Which of these activities appeals most?**

I'd choose relaxing; sitting on the sofa, for example.	Result (iv) R D
My preference would be for some mild exercise, such as gardening.	Result (iv) S D
Moderate exercise, such as walking, would be my choice.	Result (iv) H D
I would prefer more serious exercise, such as backpacking.	Result (iv) P D
Something strenuous like soccer or running would be my choice.	Result (iv) N D

437 **What sort of food do you like?**

I really just like traditional, plain food.	Result (v) W S
On the whole I prefer traditional, plain food.	Result (v) D S
I eat exotic food for a change.	Result (v) G S
I enjoy most foods, really.	Result (v) S S
I prefer a wide variety of dishes.	Result (v) F S

438 **What level of education have you reached (or do you expect to reach)?**

My education ended when I was 16.	Result (vi) J E
No further education after leaving school at 18.	Result (vi) D E
Some further education after leaving school at 18.	Result (vi) U E
Graduate degree.	Result (vi) E E
Postgraduate degree.	Result (vi) A E

439 **Which of these types of TV programmes do you like the most?**

Most of all I like game shows.	Result (i) O G
I couldn't do without soap operas.	Result (i) E G
I especially enjoy police dramas or comedies.	Result (i) V G
My preference is for serious dramas.	Result (i) P G
I enjoy news programmes and documentaries.	Result (i) C G

440 **What is your view of chivalry?**

I think it's old-fashioned nonsense, to be quite honest.	Result (ii) R U
It's pretty undesirable.	Result (ii) S U
It depends; it's OK sometimes.	Result (ii) H U
It's a desirable quality.	Result (ii) P U
I'd say it's an essential part of life.	Result (ii) N U

441 **If you had to choose just one, which of these is your favourite type of music?**

I prefer music such as heavy metal or rap.	Result (iii) O G
My favourite is rock or pop music; eg The Beatles.	Result (iii) E G
I particularly enjoy easy-listening music; eg Frank Sinatra.	Result (iii) V G
Jazz would be my number-one choice.	Result (iii) P G
My preference would be for classical music or opera.	Result (iii) C G

442 **Which of these activities appeals most?**

I'd choose relaxing; sitting on the sofa, for example.	Result (iv) R G
My preference would be for some mild exercise, such as gardening.	Result (iv) S G
Moderate exercise, such as walking, would be my choice.	Result (iv) H G
I would prefer more serious exercise, such as backpacking.	Result (iv) P G
Something strenuous like soccer or running would be my choice.	Result (iv) N G

443 **What sort of food do you like?**

I really just like traditional, plain food.	Result (v) W H
On the whole I prefer traditional, plain food.	Result (v) D H
I eat exotic food for a change.	Result (v) G H
I enjoy most foods, really.	Result (v) S H
I prefer a wide variety of dishes.	Result (v) F H

444 **What level of education have you reached (or do you expect to reach)?**

My education ended when I was 16.	Result (vi) X E
No further education after leaving school at 18.	Result (vi) G E
Some further education after leaving school at 18.	Result (vi) K E
Graduate degree.	Result (vi) V E
Postgraduate degree.	Result (vi) B E

445 **Which of these types of TV programmes do you like the most?**

Most of all I like game shows.	Result (i) O S
I couldn't do without soap operas.	Result (i) E S
I especially enjoy police dramas or comedies.	Result (i) V S
My preference is for serious dramas.	Result (i) P S
I enjoy news programmes and documentaries.	Result (i) C S

446 **What is your view of chivalry?**

I think it's old-fashioned nonsense, to be quite honest.	Result (ii) R E
It's pretty undesirable.	Result (ii) S E
It depends; it's OK sometimes.	Result (ii) H E
It's a desirable quality.	Result (ii) P E
I'd say it's an essential part of life.	Result (ii) N E

447 **If you had to choose just one, which of these is your favourite type of music?**

I prefer music such as heavy metal or rap.	Result (iii) O S
My favourite is rock or pop music; eg The Beatles.	Result (iii) E S
I particularly enjoy easy-listening music; eg Frank Sinatra.	Result (iii) V S
Jazz would be my number-one choice.	Result (iii) P S
My preference would be for classical music or opera.	Result (iii) C S

448 **Which of these activities appeals most?**

I'd choose relaxing; sitting on the sofa, for example.	Result (iv) R S
My preference would be for some mild exercise, such as gardening.	Result (iv) S S
Moderate exercise, such as walking, would be my choice.	Result (iv) H S
I would prefer more serious exercise, such as backpacking.	Result (iv) P S
Something strenuous like soccer or running would be my choice.	Result (iv) N S

449 **What sort of food do you like?**

I really just like traditional, plain food.	Result (v) W P
On the whole I prefer traditional, plain food.	Result (v) D P
I eat exotic food for a change.	Result (v) G P
I enjoy most foods, really.	Result (v) S P
I prefer a wide variety of dishes.	Result (v) F P

450 **What level of education have you reached (or do you expect to reach)?**

My education ended when I was 16.	Result (vi) R E
No further education after leaving school at 18.	Result (vi) S E
Some further education after leaving school at 18.	Result (vi) H E
Graduate degree.	Result (vi) P E
Postgraduate degree.	Result (vi) N E

451 **Which of these types of TV programmes do you like the most?**

Most of all I like game shows.	Result (i) O F
I couldn't do without soap operas.	Result (i) E F
I especially enjoy police dramas or comedies.	Result (i) V F
My preference is for serious dramas.	Result (i) P F
I enjoy news programmes and documentaries.	Result (i) C F

452 **What is your view of chivalry?**

I think it's old-fashioned nonsense, to be quite honest.	Result (ii) R A
It's pretty undesirable.	Result (ii) S A
It depends; it's OK sometimes.	Result (ii) H A
It's a desirable quality.	Result (ii) P A
I'd say it's an essential part of life.	Result (ii) N A

453 **If you had to choose just one, which of these is your favourite type of music?**

I prefer music such as heavy metal or rap.	Result (iii) O F
My favourite is rock or pop music; eg The Beatles.	Result (iii) E F
I particularly enjoy easy-listening music; eg Frank Sinatra.	Result (iii) V F
Jazz would be my number-one choice.	Result (iii) P F
My preference would be for classical music or opera.	Result (iii) C F

454 **Which of these activities appeals most?**

I'd choose relaxing; sitting on the sofa, for example.	Result (iv) R F
My preference would be for some mild exercise, such as gardening.	Result (iv) S F
Moderate exercise, such as walking, would be my choice.	Result (iv) H F
I would prefer more serious exercise, such as backpacking.	Result (iv) P F
Something strenuous like soccer or running would be my choice.	Result (iv) N F

455 **What sort of food do you like?**

I really just like traditional, plain food.	Result (v) W N
On the whole I prefer traditional, plain food.	Result (v) D N
I eat exotic food for a change.	Result (v) G N
I enjoy most foods, really.	Result (v) S N
I prefer a wide variety of dishes.	Result (v) F N

456 **What level of education have you reached (or do you expect to reach)?**

My education ended when I was 16.	Result (vi) Y E
No further education after leaving school at 18.	Result (vi) F E
Some further education after leaving school at 18.	Result (vi) L E
Graduate degree.	Result (vi) C E
Postgraduate degree.	Result (vi) M E

457 Which of these types of TV programmes do you like the most?

Most of all I like game shows.	Result (i) T W
I couldn't do without soap operas.	Result (i) A W
I especially enjoy police dramas or comedies.	Result (i) B W
My preference is for serious dramas.	Result (i) N W
I enjoy news programmes and documentaries.	Result (i) M W

458 What is your view of chivalry?

I think it's old-fashioned nonsense, to be quite honest.	Result (ii) Y J
It's pretty undesirable.	Result (ii) F J
It depends; it's OK sometimes.	Result (ii) L J
It's a desirable quality.	Result (ii) C J
I'd say it's an essential part of life.	Result (ii) M J

459 If you had to choose just one, which of these is your favourite type of music?

I prefer music such as heavy metal or rap.	Result (iii) T W
My favourite is rock or pop music; eg The Beatles.	Result (iii) A W
I particularly enjoy easy-listening music; eg Frank Sinatra.	Result (iii) B W
Jazz would be my number-one choice.	Result (iii) N W
My preference would be for classical music or opera.	Result (iii) M W

460 Which of these activities appeals most?

I'd choose relaxing; sitting on the sofa, for example.	Result (iv) Y W
My preference would be for some mild exercise, such as gardening.	Result (iv) F W
Moderate exercise, such as walking, would be my choice.	Result (iv) L W
I would prefer more serious exercise, such as backpacking.	Result (iv) C W
Something strenuous like soccer or running would be my choice.	Result (iv) M W

461 What sort of food do you like?

I really just like traditional, plain food.	Result (v) W Y
On the whole I prefer traditional, plain food.	Result (v) D Y
I eat exotic food for a change.	Result (v) G Y
I enjoy most foods, really.	Result (v) S Y
I prefer a wide variety of dishes.	Result (v) F Y

462 What level of education have you reached (or do you expect to reach)?

My education ended when I was 16.	Result (vi) I A
No further education after leaving school at 18.	Result (vi) W A
Some further education after leaving school at 18.	Result (vi) Q A
Graduate degree.	Result (vi) O A
Postgraduate degree.	Result (vi) T A

463 Which of these types of TV programmes do you like the most?

Most of all I like game shows.	Result (i) T D
I couldn't do without soap operas.	Result (i) A D
I especially enjoy police dramas or comedies.	Result (i) B D
My preference is for serious dramas.	Result (i) N D
I enjoy news programmes and documentaries.	Result (i) M D

464 What is your view of chivalry?

I think it's old-fashioned nonsense, to be quite honest.	Result (ii) Y D
It's pretty undesirable.	Result (ii) F D
It depends; it's OK sometimes.	Result (ii) L D
It's a desirable quality.	Result (ii) C D
I'd say it's an essential part of life.	Result (ii) M D

465 If you had to choose just one, which of these is your favourite type of music?

I prefer music such as heavy metal or rap.	Result (iii) T D
My favourite is rock or pop music; eg The Beatles.	Result (iii) A D
I particularly enjoy easy-listening music; eg Frank Sinatra.	Result (iii) B D
Jazz would be my number-one choice.	Result (iii) N D
My preference would be for classical music or opera.	Result (iii) M D

466 Which of these activities appeals most?

I'd choose relaxing; sitting on the sofa, for example.	Result (iv) Y D
My preference would be for some mild exercise, such as gardening.	Result (iv) F D
Moderate exercise, such as walking, would be my choice.	Result (iv) L D
I would prefer more serious exercise, such as backpacking.	Result (iv) C D
Something strenuous like soccer or running would be my choice.	Result (iv) M D

467 What sort of food do you like?

I really just like traditional, plain food.	Result (v) W F
On the whole I prefer traditional, plain food.	Result (v) D F
I eat exotic food for a change.	Result (v) G F
I enjoy most foods, really.	Result (v) S F
I prefer a wide variety of dishes.	Result (v) F F

468 What level of education have you reached (or do you expect to reach)?

My education ended when I was 16.	Result (vi) J A
No further education after leaving school at 18.	Result (vi) D A
Some further education after leaving school at 18.	Result (vi) U A
Graduate degree.	Result (vi) E A
Postgraduate degree.	Result (vi) A A

469 **Which of these types of TV programmes do you like the most?**

Most of all I like game shows.	Result (i) T G
I couldn't do without soap operas.	Result (i) A G
I especially enjoy police dramas or comedies.	Result (i) B G
My preference is for serious dramas.	Result (i) N G
I enjoy news programmes and documentaries.	Result (i) M G

470 **What is your view of chivalry?**

I think it's old-fashioned nonsense, to be quite honest.	Result (ii) Y U
It's pretty undesirable.	Result (ii) F U
It depends; it's OK sometimes.	Result (ii) L U
It's a desirable quality.	Result (ii) C U
I'd say it's an essential part of life.	Result (ii) M U

471 **If you had to choose just one, which of these is your favourite type of music?**

I prefer music such as heavy metal or rap.	Result (iii) T G
My favourite is rock or pop music; eg The Beatles.	Result (iii) A G
I particularly enjoy easy-listening music; eg Frank Sinatra.	Result (iii) B G
Jazz would be my number-one choice.	Result (iii) N G
My preference would be for classical music or opera.	Result (iii) M G

472 **Which of these activities appeals most?**

I'd choose relaxing; sitting on the sofa, for example.	Result (iv) Y G
My preference would be for some mild exercise, such as gardening.	Result (iv) F G
Moderate exercise, such as walking, would be my choice.	Result (iv) L G
I would prefer more serious exercise, such as backpacking.	Result (iv) C G
Something strenuous like soccer or running would be my choice.	Result (iv) M G

473 **What sort of food do you like?**

I really just like traditional, plain food.	Result (v) W L
On the whole I prefer traditional, plain food.	Result (v) D L
I eat exotic food for a change.	Result (v) G L
I enjoy most foods, really.	Result (v) S L
I prefer a wide variety of dishes.	Result (v) F L

474 **What level of education have you reached (or do you expect to reach)?**

My education ended when I was 16.	Result (vi) X A
No further education after leaving school at 18.	Result (vi) G A
Some further education after leaving school at 18.	Result (vi) K A
Graduate degree.	Result (vi) V A
Postgraduate degree.	Result (vi) B A

475 **Which of these types of TV programmes do you like the most?**

Most of all I like game shows.	Result (i) T S
I couldn't do without soap operas.	Result (i) A S
I especially enjoy police dramas or comedies.	Result (i) B S
My preference is for serious dramas.	Result (i) N S
I enjoy news programmes and documentaries.	Result (i) M S

476 **What is your view of chivalry?**

I think it's old-fashioned nonsense, to be quite honest.	Result (ii) Y E
It's pretty undesirable.	Result (ii) F E
It depends; it's OK sometimes.	Result (ii) L E
It's a desirable quality.	Result (ii) C E
I'd say it's an essential part of life.	Result (ii) M E

477 **If you had to choose just one, which of these is your favourite type of music?**

I prefer music such as heavy metal or rap.	Result (iii) T S
My favourite is rock or pop music; eg The Beatles.	Result (iii) A S
I particularly enjoy easy-listening music; eg Frank Sinatra.	Result (iii) B S
Jazz would be my number-one choice.	Result (iii) N S
My preference would be for classical music or opera.	Result (iii) M S

478 **Which of these activities appeals most?**

I'd choose relaxing; sitting on the sofa, for example.	Result (iv) Y S
My preference would be for some mild exercise, such as gardening.	Result (iv) F S
Moderate exercise, such as walking, would be my choice.	Result (iv) L S
I would prefer more serious exercise, such as backpacking.	Result (iv) C S
Something strenuous like soccer or running would be my choice.	Result (iv) M S

479 **What sort of food do you like?**

I really just like traditional, plain food.	Result (v) W C
On the whole I prefer traditional, plain food.	Result (v) D C
I eat exotic food for a change.	Result (v) G C
I enjoy most foods, really.	Result (v) S C
I prefer a wide variety of dishes.	Result (v) F C

480 **What level of education have you reached (or do you expect to reach)?**

My education ended when I was 16.	Result (vi) R A
No further education after leaving school at 18.	Result (vi) S A
Some further education after leaving school at 18.	Result (vi) H A
Graduate degree.	Result (vi) P A
Postgraduate degree.	Result (vi) N A

Take the CQ Test

481 **Which of these types of TV programmes do you like the most?**

Most of all I like game shows.	Result (i) T F
I couldn't do without soap operas.	Result (i) A F
I especially enjoy police dramas or comedies.	Result (i) B F
My preference is for serious dramas.	Result (i) N F
I enjoy news programmes and documentaries.	Result (i) M F

482 **What is your view of chivalry?**

I think it's old-fashioned nonsense, to be quite honest.	Result (ii) Y A
It's pretty undesirable.	Result (ii) F A
It depends; it's OK sometimes.	Result (ii) L A
It's a desirable quality.	Result (ii) C A
I'd say it's an essential part of life.	Result (ii) M A

483 **If you had to choose just one, which of these is your favourite type of music?**

I prefer music such as heavy metal or rap.	Result (iii) T F
My favourite is rock or pop music; eg The Beatles.	Result (iii) A F
I particularly enjoy easy-listening music; eg Frank Sinatra.	Result (iii) B F
Jazz would be my number-one choice.	Result (iii) N F
My preference would be for classical music or opera.	Result (iii) M F

484 **Which of these activities appeals most?**

I'd choose relaxing; sitting on the sofa, for example.	Result (iv) Y F
My preference would be for some mild exercise, such as gardening.	Result (iv) F F
Moderate exercise, such as walking, would be my choice.	Result (iv) L F
I would prefer more serious exercise, such as backpacking.	Result (iv) C F
Something strenuous like soccer or running would be my choice.	Result (iv) M F

485 **What sort of food do you like?**

I really just like traditional, plain food.	Result (v) W M
On the whole I prefer traditional, plain food.	Result (v) D M
I eat exotic food for a change.	Result (v) G M
I enjoy most foods, really.	Result (v) S M
I prefer a wide variety of dishes.	Result (v) F M

486 **What level of education have you reached (or do you expect to reach)?**

My education ended when I was 16.	Result (vi) Y A
No further education after leaving school at 18.	Result (vi) F A
Some further education after leaving school at 18.	Result (vi) L A
Graduate degree.	Result (vi) C A
Postgraduate degree.	Result (vi) M A

487 Which of these types of TV programmes do you like the most?

Most of all I like game shows.	Result (i) I Q
I couldn't do without soap operas.	Result (i) J Q
I especially enjoy police dramas or comedies.	Result (i) X Q
My preference is for serious dramas.	Result (i) R Q
I enjoy news programmes and documentaries.	Result (i) Y Q

488 What is your view of chivalry?

I think it's old-fashioned nonsense, to be quite honest.	Result (ii) I X
It's pretty undesirable.	Result (ii) W X
It depends; it's OK sometimes.	Result (ii) Q X
It's a desirable quality.	Result (ii) O X
I'd say it's an essential part of life.	Result (ii) T X

489 If you had to choose just one, which of these is your favourite type of music?

I prefer music such as heavy metal or rap.	Result (iii) I Q
My favourite is rock or pop music; eg The Beatles.	Result (iii) J Q
I particularly enjoy easy-listening music; eg Frank Sinatra.	Result (iii) X Q
Jazz would be my number-one choice.	Result (iii) R Q
My preference would be for classical music or opera.	Result (iii) Y Q

490 Which of these activities appeals most?

I'd choose relaxing; sitting on the sofa, for example.	Result (iv) I Q
My preference would be for some mild exercise, such as gardening.	Result (iv) W Q
Moderate exercise, such as walking, would be my choice.	Result (iv) Q Q
I would prefer more serious exercise, such as backpacking.	Result (iv) O Q
Something strenuous like soccer or running would be my choice.	Result (iv) T Q

491 What sort of food do you like?

I really just like traditional, plain food.	Result (v) Q I
On the whole I prefer traditional, plain food.	Result (v) U I
I eat exotic food for a change.	Result (v) K I
I enjoy most foods, really.	Result (v) H I
I prefer a wide variety of dishes.	Result (v) L I

492 What level of education have you reached (or do you expect to reach)?

My education ended when I was 16.	Result (vi) I X
No further education after leaving school at 18.	Result (vi) W X
Some further education after leaving school at 18.	Result (vi) Q X
Graduate degree.	Result (vi) O X
Postgraduate degree.	Result (vi) T X

493 **Which of these types of TV programmes do you like the most?**

Most of all I like game shows.	Result (i) I U
I couldn't do without soap operas.	Result (i) J U
I especially enjoy police dramas or comedies.	Result (i) X U
My preference is for serious dramas.	Result (i) R U
I enjoy news programmes and documentaries.	Result (i) Y U

494 **What is your view of chivalry?**

I think it's old-fashioned nonsense, to be quite honest.	Result (ii) I G
It's pretty undesirable.	Result (ii) W G
It depends; it's OK sometimes.	Result (ii) Q G
It's a desirable quality.	Result (ii) O G
I'd say it's an essential part of life.	Result (ii) T G

495 **If you had to choose just one, which of these is your favourite type of music?**

I prefer music such as heavy metal or rap.	Result (iii) I U
My favourite is rock or pop music; eg The Beatles.	Result (iii) J U
I particularly enjoy easy-listening music; eg Frank Sinatra.	Result (iii) X U
Jazz would be my number-one choice.	Result (iii) R U
My preference would be for classical music or opera.	Result (iii) Y U

496 **Which of these activities appeals most?**

I'd choose relaxing; sitting on the sofa, for example.	Result (iv) I U
My preference would be for some mild exercise, such as gardening.	Result (iv) W U
Moderate exercise, such as walking, would be my choice.	Result (iv) Q U
I would prefer more serious exercise, such as backpacking.	Result (iv) O U
Something strenuous like soccer or running would be my choice.	Result (iv) T U

497 **What sort of food do you like?**

I really just like traditional, plain food.	Result (v) Q W
On the whole I prefer traditional, plain food.	Result (v) U W
I eat exotic food for a change.	Result (v) K W
I enjoy most foods, really.	Result (v) H W
I prefer a wide variety of dishes.	Result (v) L W

498 **What level of education have you reached (or do you expect to reach)?**

My education ended when I was 16.	Result (vi) J X
No further education after leaving school at 18.	Result (vi) D X
Some further education after leaving school at 18.	Result (vi) U X
Graduate degree.	Result (vi) E X
Postgraduate degree.	Result (vi) A X

499 **Which of these types of TV programmes do you like the most?**

Most of all I like game shows.	Result (i) I K
I couldn't do without soap operas.	Result (i) J K
I especially enjoy police dramas or comedies.	Result (i) X K
My preference is for serious dramas.	Result (i) R K
I enjoy news programmes and documentaries.	Result (i) Y K

500 **What is your view of chivalry?**

I think it's old-fashioned nonsense, to be quite honest.	Result (ii) I K
It's pretty undesirable.	Result (ii) W K
It depends; it's OK sometimes.	Result (ii) Q K
It's a desirable quality.	Result (ii) O K
I'd say it's an essential part of life.	Result (ii) T K

501 **If you had to choose just one, which of these is your favourite type of music?**

I prefer music such as heavy metal or rap.	Result (iii) I K
My favourite is rock or pop music; eg The Beatles.	Result (iii) J K
I particularly enjoy easy-listening music; eg Frank Sinatra.	Result (iii) X K
Jazz would be my number-one choice.	Result (iii) R K
My preference would be for classical music or opera.	Result (iii) Y K

502 **Which of these activities appeals most?**

I'd choose relaxing; sitting on the sofa, for example.	Result (iv) I K
My preference would be for some mild exercise, such as gardening.	Result (iv) W K
Moderate exercise, such as walking, would be my choice.	Result (iv) Q K
I would prefer more serious exercise, such as backpacking.	Result (iv) O K
Something strenuous like soccer or running would be my choice.	Result (iv) T K

503 **What sort of food do you like?**

I really just like traditional, plain food.	Result (v) Q Q
On the whole I prefer traditional, plain food.	Result (v) U Q
I eat exotic food for a change.	Result (v) K Q
I enjoy most foods, really.	Result (v) H Q
I prefer a wide variety of dishes.	Result (v) L Q

504 **What level of education have you reached (or do you expect to reach)?**

My education ended when I was 16.	Result (vi) X X
No further education after leaving school at 18.	Result (vi) G X
Some further education after leaving school at 18.	Result (vi) K X
Graduate degree.	Result (vi) V X
Postgraduate degree.	Result (vi) B X

505 **Which of these types of TV programmes do you like the most?**

Most of all I like game shows.	Result (i) I H
I couldn't do without soap operas.	Result (i) J H
I especially enjoy police dramas or comedies.	Result (i) X H
My preference is for serious dramas.	Result (i) R H
I enjoy news programmes and documentaries.	Result (i) Y H

506 **What is your view of chivalry?**

I think it's old-fashioned nonsense, to be quite honest.	Result (ii) I V
It's pretty undesirable.	Result (ii) W V
It depends; it's OK sometimes.	Result (ii) Q V
It's a desirable quality.	Result (ii) O V
I'd say it's an essential part of life.	Result (ii) T V

507 **If you had to choose just one, which of these is your favourite type of music?**

I prefer music such as heavy metal or rap.	Result (iii) I H
My favourite is rock or pop music; eg The Beatles.	Result (iii) J H
I particularly enjoy easy-listening music; eg Frank Sinatra.	Result (iii) X H
Jazz would be my number-one choice.	Result (iii) R H
My preference would be for classical music or opera.	Result (iii) Y H

508 **Which of these activities appeals most?**

I'd choose relaxing; sitting on the sofa, for example.	Result (iv) I H
My preference would be for some mild exercise, such as gardening.	Result (iv) W H
Moderate exercise, such as walking, would be my choice.	Result (iv) Q H
I would prefer more serious exercise, such as backpacking.	Result (iv) O H
Something strenuous like soccer or running would be my choice.	Result (iv) T H

509 **What sort of food do you like?**

I really just like traditional, plain food.	Result (v) Q O
On the whole I prefer traditional, plain food.	Result (v) U O
I eat exotic food for a change.	Result (v) K O
I enjoy most foods, really.	Result (v) H O
I prefer a wide variety of dishes.	Result (v) L O

510 **What level of education have you reached (or do you expect to reach)?**

My education ended when I was 16.	Result (vi) R X
No further education after leaving school at 18.	Result (vi) S X
Some further education after leaving school at 18.	Result (vi) H X
Graduate degree.	Result (vi) P X
Postgraduate degree.	Result (vi) N X

511 **Which of these types of TV programmes do you like the most?**

Most of all I like game shows.	Result (i) I L
I couldn't do without soap operas.	Result (i) J L
I especially enjoy police dramas or comedies.	Result (i) X L
My preference is for serious dramas.	Result (i) R L
I enjoy news programmes and documentaries.	Result (i) Y L

512 **What is your view of chivalry?**

I think it's old-fashioned nonsense, to be quite honest.	Result (ii) I B
It's pretty undesirable.	Result (ii) W B
It depends; it's OK sometimes.	Result (ii) Q B
It's a desirable quality.	Result (ii) O B
I'd say it's an essential part of life.	Result (ii) T B

513 **If you had to choose just one, which of these is your favourite type of music?**

I prefer music such as heavy metal or rap.	Result (iii) I L
My favourite is rock or pop music; eg The Beatles.	Result (iii) J L
I particularly enjoy easy-listening music; eg Frank Sinatra.	Result (iii) X L
Jazz would be my number-one choice.	Result (iii) R L
My preference would be for classical music or opera.	Result (iii) Y L

514 **Which of these activities appeals most?**

I'd choose relaxing; sitting on the sofa, for example.	Result (iv) I L
My preference would be for some mild exercise, such as gardening.	Result (iv) W L
Moderate exercise, such as walking, would be my choice.	Result (iv) Q L
I would prefer more serious exercise, such as backpacking.	Result (iv) O L
Something strenuous like soccer or running would be my choice.	Result (iv) T L

515 **What sort of food do you like?**

I really just like traditional, plain food.	Result (v) Q T
On the whole I prefer traditional, plain food.	Result (v) U T
I eat exotic food for a change.	Result (v) K T
I enjoy most foods, really.	Result (v) H T
I prefer a wide variety of dishes.	Result (v) L T

516 **What level of education have you reached (or do you expect to reach)?**

My education ended when I was 16.	Result (vi) Y X
No further education after leaving school at 18.	Result (vi) F X
Some further education after leaving school at 18.	Result (vi) L X
Graduate degree.	Result (vi) C X
Postgraduate degree.	Result (vi) M X

517 **Which of these types of TV programmes do you like the most?**

Most of all I like game shows.	Result (i) W Q
I couldn't do without soap operas.	Result (i) D Q
I especially enjoy police dramas or comedies.	Result (i) G Q
My preference is for serious dramas.	Result (i) S Q
I enjoy news programmes and documentaries.	Result (i) F Q

518 **What is your view of chivalry?**

I think it's old-fashioned nonsense, to be quite honest.	Result (ii) J X
It's pretty undesirable.	Result (ii) D X
It depends; it's OK sometimes.	Result (ii) U X
It's a desirable quality.	Result (ii) E X
I'd say it's an essential part of life.	Result (ii) A X

519 **If you had to choose just one, which of these is your favourite type of music?**

I prefer music such as heavy metal or rap.	Result (iii) W Q
My favourite is rock or pop music; eg The Beatles.	Result (iii) D Q
I particularly enjoy easy-listening music; eg Frank Sinatra.	Result (iii) G Q
Jazz would be my number-one choice.	Result (iii) S Q
My preference would be for classical music or opera.	Result (iii) F Q

520 **Which of these activities appeals most?**

I'd choose relaxing; sitting on the sofa, for example.	Result (iv) J Q
My preference would be for some mild exercise, such as gardening.	Result (iv) D Q
Moderate exercise, such as walking, would be my choice.	Result (iv) U Q
I would prefer more serious exercise, such as backpacking.	Result (iv) E Q
Something strenuous like soccer or running would be my choice.	Result (iv) A Q

521 **What sort of food do you like?**

I really just like traditional, plain food.	Result (v) Q J
On the whole I prefer traditional, plain food.	Result (v) U J
I eat exotic food for a change.	Result (v) K J
I enjoy most foods, really.	Result (v) H J
I prefer a wide variety of dishes.	Result (v) L J

522 **What level of education have you reached (or do you expect to reach)?**

My education ended when I was 16.	Result (vi) I G
No further education after leaving school at 18.	Result (vi) W G
Some further education after leaving school at 18.	Result (vi) Q G
Graduate degree.	Result (vi) O G
Postgraduate degree.	Result (vi) T G

523 **Which of these types of TV programmes do you like the most?**

Most of all I like game shows.	Result (i) W U
I couldn't do without soap operas.	Result (i) D U
I especially enjoy police dramas or comedies.	Result (i) G U
My preference is for serious dramas.	Result (i) S U
I enjoy news programmes and documentaries.	Result (i) F U

524 **What is your view of chivalry?**

I think it's old-fashioned nonsense, to be quite honest.	Result (ii) J G
It's pretty undesirable.	Result (ii) D G
It depends; it's OK sometimes.	Result (ii) U G
It's a desirable quality.	Result (ii) E G
I'd say it's an essential part of life.	Result (ii) A G

525 **If you had to choose just one, which of these is your favourite type of music?**

I prefer music such as heavy metal or rap.	Result (iii) W U
My favourite is rock or pop music; eg The Beatles.	Result (iii) D U
I particularly enjoy easy-listening music; eg Frank Sinatra.	Result (iii) G U
Jazz would be my number-one choice.	Result (iii) S U
My preference would be for classical music or opera.	Result (iii) F U

526 **Which of these activities appeals most?**

I'd choose relaxing; sitting on the sofa, for example.	Result (iv) J U
My preference would be for some mild exercise, such as gardening.	Result (iv) D U
Moderate exercise, such as walking, would be my choice.	Result (iv) U U
I would prefer more serious exercise, such as backpacking.	Result (iv) E U
Something strenuous like soccer or running would be my choice.	Result (iv) A U

527 **What sort of food do you like?**

I really just like traditional, plain food.	Result (v) Q D
On the whole I prefer traditional, plain food.	Result (v) U D
I eat exotic food for a change.	Result (v) K D
I enjoy most foods, really.	Result (v) H D
I prefer a wide variety of dishes.	Result (v) L D

528 **What level of education have you reached (or do you expect to reach)?**

My education ended when I was 16.	Result (vi) J G
No further education after leaving school at 18.	Result (vi) D G
Some further education after leaving school at 18.	Result (vi) U G
Graduate degree.	Result (vi) E G
Postgraduate degree.	Result (vi) A G

529 **Which of these types of TV programmes do you like the most?**

Most of all I like game shows.	Result (i) W K
I couldn't do without soap operas.	Result (i) D K
I especially enjoy police dramas or comedies.	Result (i) G K
My preference is for serious dramas.	Result (i) S K
I enjoy news programmes and documentaries.	Result (i) F K

530 **What is your view of chivalry?**

I think it's old-fashioned nonsense, to be quite honest.	Result (ii) J K
It's pretty undesirable.	Result (ii) D K
It depends; it's OK sometimes.	Result (ii) U K
It's a desirable quality.	Result (ii) E K
I'd say it's an essential part of life.	Result (ii) A K

531 **If you had to choose just one, which of these is your favourite type of music?**

I prefer music such as heavy metal or rap.	Result (iii) W K
My favourite is rock or pop music; eg The Beatles.	Result (iii) D K
I particularly enjoy easy-listening music; eg Frank Sinatra.	Result (iii) G K
Jazz would be my number-one choice.	Result (iii) S K
My preference would be for classical music or opera.	Result (iii) F K

532 **Which of these activities appeals most?**

I'd choose relaxing; sitting on the sofa, for example.	Result (iv) J K
My preference would be for some mild exercise, such as gardening.	Result (iv) D K
Moderate exercise, such as walking, would be my choice.	Result (iv) U K
I would prefer more serious exercise, such as backpacking.	Result (iv) E K
Something strenuous like soccer or running would be my choice.	Result (iv) A K

533 **What sort of food do you like?**

I really just like traditional, plain food.	Result (v) Q U
On the whole I prefer traditional, plain food.	Result (v) U U
I eat exotic food for a change.	Result (v) K U
I enjoy most foods, really.	Result (v) H U
I prefer a wide variety of dishes.	Result (v) L U

534 **What level of education have you reached (or do you expect to reach)?**

My education ended when I was 16.	Result (vi) X G
No further education after leaving school at 18.	Result (vi) G G
Some further education after leaving school at 18.	Result (vi) K G
Graduate degree.	Result (vi) V G
Postgraduate degree.	Result (vi) B G

535 **Which of these types of TV programmes do you like the most?**

Most of all I like game shows.	Result (i) W H
I couldn't do without soap operas.	Result (i) D H
I especially enjoy police dramas or comedies.	Result (i) G H
My preference is for serious dramas.	Result (i) S H
I enjoy news programmes and documentaries.	Result (i) F H

536 **What is your view of chivalry?**

I think it's old-fashioned nonsense, to be quite honest.	Result (ii) J V
It's pretty undesirable.	Result (ii) D V
It depends; it's OK sometimes.	Result (ii) U V
It's a desirable quality.	Result (ii) E V
I'd say it's an essential part of life.	Result (ii) A V

537 **If you had to choose just one, which of these is your favourite type of music?**

I prefer music such as heavy metal or rap.	Result (iii) W H
My favourite is rock or pop music; eg The Beatles.	Result (iii) D H
I particularly enjoy easy-listening music; eg Frank Sinatra.	Result (iii) G H
Jazz would be my number-one choice.	Result (iii) S H
My preference would be for classical music or opera.	Result (iii) F H

538 **Which of these activities appeals most?**

I'd choose relaxing; sitting on the sofa, for example.	Result (iv) J H
My preference would be for some mild exercise, such as gardening.	Result (iv) D H
Moderate exercise, such as walking, would be my choice.	Result (iv) U H
I would prefer more serious exercise, such as backpacking.	Result (iv) E H
Something strenuous like soccer or running would be my choice.	Result (iv) A H

539 **What sort of food do you like?**

I really just like traditional, plain food.	Result (v) Q E
On the whole I prefer traditional, plain food.	Result (v) U E
I eat exotic food for a change.	Result (v) K E
I enjoy most foods, really.	Result (v) H E
I prefer a wide variety of dishes.	Result (v) L E

540 **What level of education have you reached (or do you expect to reach)?**

My education ended when I was 16.	Result (vi) R G
No further education after leaving school at 18.	Result (vi) S G
Some further education after leaving school at 18.	Result (vi) H G
Graduate degree.	Result (vi) P G
Postgraduate degree.	Result (vi) N G

541 **Which of these types of TV programmes do you like the most?**

Most of all I like game shows.	Result (i) W L
I couldn't do without soap operas.	Result (i) D L
I especially enjoy police dramas or comedies.	Result (i) G L
My preference is for serious dramas.	Result (i) S L
I enjoy news programmes and documentaries.	Result (i) F L

542 **What is your view of chivalry?**

I think it's old-fashioned nonsense, to be quite honest.	Result (ii) J B
It's pretty undesirable.	Result (ii) D B
It depends; it's OK sometimes.	Result (ii) U B
It's a desirable quality.	Result (ii) E B
I'd say it's an essential part of life.	Result (ii) A B

543 **If you had to choose just one, which of these is your favourite type of music?**

I prefer music such as heavy metal or rap.	Result (iii) W L
My favourite is rock or pop music; eg The Beatles.	Result (iii) D L
I particularly enjoy easy-listening music; eg Frank Sinatra.	Result (iii) G L
Jazz would be my number-one choice.	Result (iii) S L
My preference would be for classical music or opera.	Result (iii) F L

544 **Which of these activities appeals most?**

I'd choose relaxing; sitting on the sofa, for example.	Result (iv) J L
My preference would be for some mild exercise, such as gardening.	Result (iv) D L
Moderate exercise, such as walking, would be my choice.	Result (iv) U L
I would prefer more serious exercise, such as backpacking.	Result (iv) E L
Something strenuous like soccer or running would be my choice.	Result (iv) A L

545 **What sort of food do you like?**

I really just like traditional, plain food.	Result (v) Q A
On the whole I prefer traditional, plain food.	Result (v) U A
I eat exotic food for a change.	Result (v) K A
I enjoy most foods, really.	Result (v) H A
I prefer a wide variety of dishes.	Result (v) L A

546 **What level of education have you reached (or do you expect to reach)?**

My education ended when I was 16.	Result (vi) Y G
No further education after leaving school at 18.	Result (vi) F G
Some further education after leaving school at 18.	Result (vi) L G
Graduate degree.	Result (vi) C G
Postgraduate degree.	Result (vi) M G

547 Which of these types of TV programmes do you like the most?

Most of all I like game shows.	Result (i) Q Q
I couldn't do without soap operas.	Result (i) U Q
I especially enjoy police dramas or comedies.	Result (i) K Q
My preference is for serious dramas.	Result (i) H Q
I enjoy news programmes and documentaries.	Result (i) L Q

548 What is your view of chivalry?

I think it's old-fashioned nonsense, to be quite honest.	Result (ii) X X
It's pretty undesirable.	Result (ii) G X
It depends; it's OK sometimes.	Result (ii) K X
It's a desirable quality.	Result (ii) V X
I'd say it's an essential part of life.	Result (ii) B X

549 If you had to choose just one, which of these is your favourite type of music?

I prefer music such as heavy metal or rap.	Result (iii) Q Q
My favourite is rock or pop music; eg The Beatles.	Result (iii) U Q
I particularly enjoy easy-listening music; eg Frank Sinatra.	Result (iii) K Q
Jazz would be my number-one choice.	Result (iii) H Q
My preference would be for classical music or opera.	Result (iii) L Q

550 Which of these activities appeals most?

I'd choose relaxing; sitting on the sofa, for example.	Result (iv) X Q
My preference would be for some mild exercise, such as gardening.	Result (iv) G Q
Moderate exercise, such as walking, would be my choice.	Result (iv) K Q
I would prefer more serious exercise, such as backpacking.	Result (iv) V Q
Something strenuous like soccer or running would be my choice.	Result (iv) B Q

551 What sort of food do you like?

I really just like traditional, plain food.	Result (v) Q X
On the whole I prefer traditional, plain food.	Result (v) U X
I eat exotic food for a change.	Result (v) K X
I enjoy most foods, really.	Result (v) H X
I prefer a wide variety of dishes.	Result (v) L X

552 What level of education have you reached (or do you expect to reach)?

My education ended when I was 16.	Result (vi) I K
No further education after leaving school at 18.	Result (vi) W K
Some further education after leaving school at 18.	Result (vi) Q K
Graduate degree.	Result (vi) O K
Postgraduate degree.	Result (vi) T K

553 **Which of these types of TV programmes do you like the most?**

Most of all I like game shows.	Result (i) Q U
I couldn't do without soap operas.	Result (i) U U
I especially enjoy police dramas or comedies.	Result (i) K U
My preference is for serious dramas.	Result (i) H U
I enjoy news programmes and documentaries.	Result (i) L U

554 **What is your view of chivalry?**

I think it's old-fashioned nonsense, to be quite honest.	Result (ii) X G
It's pretty undesirable.	Result (ii) G G
It depends; it's OK sometimes.	Result (ii) K G
It's a desirable quality.	Result (ii) V G
I'd say it's an essential part of life.	Result (ii) B G

555 **If you had to choose just one, which of these is your favourite type of music?**

I prefer music such as heavy metal or rap.	Result (iii) Q U
My favourite is rock or pop music; eg The Beatles.	Result (iii) U U
I particularly enjoy easy-listening music; eg Frank Sinatra.	Result (iii) K U
Jazz would be my number-one choice.	Result (iii) H U
My preference would be for classical music or opera.	Result (iii) L U

556 **Which of these activities appeals most?**

I'd choose relaxing; sitting on the sofa, for example.	Result (iv) X U
My preference would be for some mild exercise, such as gardening.	Result (iv) G U
Moderate exercise, such as walking, would be my choice.	Result (iv) K U
I would prefer more serious exercise, such as backpacking.	Result (iv) V U
Something strenuous like soccer or running would be my choice.	Result (iv) B U

557 **What sort of food do you like?**

I really just like traditional, plain food.	Result (v) Q G
On the whole I prefer traditional, plain food.	Result (v) U G
I eat exotic food for a change.	Result (v) K G
I enjoy most foods, really.	Result (v) H G
I prefer a wide variety of dishes.	Result (v) L G

558 **What level of education have you reached (or do you expect to reach)?**

My education ended when I was 16.	Result (vi) J K
No further education after leaving school at 18.	Result (vi) D K
Some further education after leaving school at 18.	Result (vi) U K
Graduate degree.	Result (vi) E K
Postgraduate degree.	Result (vi) A K

559 **Which of these types of TV programmes do you like the most?**

Most of all I like game shows.	Result (i) Q K
I couldn't do without soap operas.	Result (i) U K
I especially enjoy police dramas or comedies.	Result (i) K K
My preference is for serious dramas.	Result (i) H K
I enjoy news programmes and documentaries.	Result (i) L K

560 **What is your view of chivalry?**

I think it's old-fashioned nonsense, to be quite honest.	Result (ii) X K
It's pretty undesirable.	Result (ii) G K
It depends; it's OK sometimes.	Result (ii) K K
It's a desirable quality.	Result (ii) V K
I'd say it's an essential part of life.	Result (ii) B K

561 **If you had to choose just one, which of these is your favourite type of music?**

I prefer music such as heavy metal or rap.	Result (iii) Q K
My favourite is rock or pop music; eg The Beatles.	Result (iii) U K
I particularly enjoy easy-listening music; eg Frank Sinatra.	Result (iii) K K
Jazz would be my number-one choice.	Result (iii) H K
My preference would be for classical music or opera.	Result (iii) L K

562 **Which of these activities appeals most?**

I'd choose relaxing; sitting on the sofa, for example.	Result (iv) X K
My preference would be for some mild exercise, such as gardening.	Result (iv) G K
Moderate exercise, such as walking, would be my choice.	Result (iv) K K
I would prefer more serious exercise, such as backpacking.	Result (iv) V K
Something strenuous like soccer or running would be my choice.	Result (iv) B K

563 **What sort of food do you like?**

I really just like traditional, plain food.	Result (v) Q K
On the whole I prefer traditional, plain food.	Result (v) U K
I eat exotic food for a change.	Result (v) K K
I enjoy most foods, really.	Result (v) H K
I prefer a wide variety of dishes.	Result (v) L K

564 **What level of education have you reached (or do you expect to reach)?**

My education ended when I was 16.	Result (vi) X K
No further education after leaving school at 18.	Result (vi) G K
Some further education after leaving school at 18.	Result (vi) K K
Graduate degree.	Result (vi) V K
Postgraduate degree.	Result (vi) B K

565 Which of these types of TV programmes do you like the most?

Most of all I like game shows.	Result (i) Q H
I couldn't do without soap operas.	Result (i) U H
I especially enjoy police dramas or comedies.	Result (i) K H
My preference is for serious dramas.	Result (i) H H
I enjoy news programmes and documentaries.	Result (i) L H

566 What is your view of chivalry?

I think it's old-fashioned nonsense, to be quite honest.	Result (ii) X V
It's pretty undesirable.	Result (ii) G V
It depends; it's OK sometimes.	Result (ii) K V
It's a desirable quality.	Result (ii) V V
I'd say it's an essential part of life.	Result (ii) B V

567 If you had to choose just one, which of these is your favourite type of music?

I prefer music such as heavy metal or rap.	Result (iii) Q H
My favourite is rock or pop music; eg The Beatles.	Result (iii) U H
I particularly enjoy easy-listening music; eg Frank Sinatra.	Result (iii) K H
Jazz would be my number-one choice.	Result (iii) H H
My preference would be for classical music or opera.	Result (iii) L H

568 Which of these activities appeals most?

I'd choose relaxing; sitting on the sofa, for example.	Result (iv) X H
My preference would be for some mild exercise, such as gardening.	Result (iv) G H
Moderate exercise, such as walking, would be my choice.	Result (iv) K H
I would prefer more serious exercise, such as backpacking.	Result (iv) V H
Something strenuous like soccer or running would be my choice.	Result (iv) B H

569 What sort of food do you like?

I really just like traditional, plain food.	Result (v) Q V
On the whole I prefer traditional, plain food.	Result (v) U V
I eat exotic food for a change.	Result (v) K V
I enjoy most foods, really.	Result (v) H V
I prefer a wide variety of dishes.	Result (v) L V

570 What level of education have you reached (or do you expect to reach)?

My education ended when I was 16.	Result (vi) R K
No further education after leaving school at 18.	Result (vi) S K
Some further education after leaving school at 18.	Result (vi) H K
Graduate degree.	Result (vi) P K
Postgraduate degree.	Result (vi) N K

571 **Which of these types of TV programmes do you like the most?**

Most of all I like game shows.	Result (i) Q L
I couldn't do without soap operas.	Result (i) U L
I especially enjoy police dramas or comedies.	Result (i) K L
My preference is for serious dramas.	Result (i) H L
I enjoy news programmes and documentaries.	Result (i) L L

572 **What is your view of chivalry?**

I think it's old-fashioned nonsense, to be quite honest.	Result (ii) X B
It's pretty undesirable.	Result (ii) G B
It depends; it's OK sometimes.	Result (ii) K B
It's a desirable quality.	Result (ii) V B
I'd say it's an essential part of life.	Result (ii) B B

573 **If you had to choose just one, which of these is your favourite type of music?**

I prefer music such as heavy metal or rap.	Result (iii) Q L
My favourite is rock or pop music; eg The Beatles.	Result (iii) U L
I particularly enjoy easy-listening music; eg Frank Sinatra.	Result (iii) K L
Jazz would be my number-one choice.	Result (iii) H L
My preference would be for classical music or opera.	Result (iii) L L

574 **Which of these activities appeals most?**

I'd choose relaxing; sitting on the sofa, for example.	Result (iv) X L
My preference would be for some mild exercise, such as gardening.	Result (iv) G L
Moderate exercise, such as walking, would be my choice.	Result (iv) K L
I would prefer more serious exercise, such as backpacking.	Result (iv) V L
Something strenuous like soccer or running would be my choice.	Result (iv) B L

575 **What sort of food do you like?**

I really just like traditional, plain food.	Result (v) Q B
On the whole I prefer traditional, plain food.	Result (v) U B
I eat exotic food for a change.	Result (v) K B
I enjoy most foods, really.	Result (v) H B
I prefer a wide variety of dishes.	Result (v) L B

576 **What level of education have you reached (or do you expect to reach)?**

My education ended when I was 16.	Result (vi) Y K
No further education after leaving school at 18.	Result (vi) F K
Some further education after leaving school at 18.	Result (vi) L K
Graduate degree.	Result (vi) C K
Postgraduate degree.	Result (vi) M K

577 **Which of these types of TV programmes do you like the most?**

Most of all I like game shows.	Result (i) O Q
I couldn't do without soap operas.	Result (i) E Q
I especially enjoy police dramas or comedies.	Result (i) V Q
My preference is for serious dramas.	Result (i) P Q
I enjoy news programmes and documentaries.	Result (i) C Q

578 **What is your view of chivalry?**

I think it's old-fashioned nonsense, to be quite honest.	Result (ii) R X
It's pretty undesirable.	Result (ii) S X
It depends; it's OK sometimes.	Result (ii) H X
It's a desirable quality.	Result (ii) P X
I'd say it's an essential part of life.	Result (ii) N X

579 **If you had to choose just one, which of these is your favourite type of music?**

I prefer music such as heavy metal or rap.	Result (iii) O Q
My favourite is rock or pop music; eg The Beatles.	Result (iii) E Q
I particularly enjoy easy-listening music; eg Frank Sinatra.	Result (iii) V Q
Jazz would be my number-one choice.	Result (iii) P Q
My preference would be for classical music or opera.	Result (iii) C Q

580 **Which of these activities appeals most?**

I'd choose relaxing; sitting on the sofa, for example.	Result (iv) R Q
My preference would be for some mild exercise, such as gardening.	Result (iv) S Q
Moderate exercise, such as walking, would be my choice.	Result (iv) H Q
I would prefer more serious exercise, such as backpacking.	Result (iv) P Q
Something strenuous like soccer or running would be my choice.	Result (iv) N Q

581 **What sort of food do you like?**

I really just like traditional, plain food.	Result (v) Q R
On the whole I prefer traditional, plain food.	Result (v) U R
I eat exotic food for a change.	Result (v) K R
I enjoy most foods, really.	Result (v) H R
I prefer a wide variety of dishes.	Result (v) L R

582 **What level of education have you reached (or do you expect to reach)?**

My education ended when I was 16.	Result (vi) I V
No further education after leaving school at 18.	Result (vi) W V
Some further education after leaving school at 18.	Result (vi) Q V
Graduate degree.	Result (vi) O V
Postgraduate degree.	Result (vi) T V

583 **Which of these types of TV programmes do you like the most?**

Most of all I like game shows.	Result (i) O U
I couldn't do without soap operas.	Result (i) E U
I especially enjoy police dramas or comedies.	Result (i) V U
My preference is for serious dramas.	Result (i) P U
I enjoy news programmes and documentaries.	Result (i) C U

584 **What is your view of chivalry?**

I think it's old-fashioned nonsense, to be quite honest.	Result (ii) R G
It's pretty undesirable.	Result (ii) S G
It depends; it's OK sometimes.	Result (ii) H G
It's a desirable quality.	Result (ii) P G
I'd say it's an essential part of life.	Result (ii) N G

585 **If you had to choose just one, which of these is your favourite type of music?**

I prefer music such as heavy metal or rap.	Result (iii) O U
My favourite is rock or pop music; eg The Beatles.	Result (iii) E U
I particularly enjoy easy-listening music; eg Frank Sinatra.	Result (iii) V U
Jazz would be my number-one choice.	Result (iii) P U
My preference would be for classical music or opera.	Result (iii) C U

586 **Which of these activities appeals most?**

I'd choose relaxing; sitting on the sofa, for example.	Result (iv) R U
My preference would be for some mild exercise, such as gardening.	Result (iv) S U
Moderate exercise, such as walking, would be my choice.	Result (iv) H U
I would prefer more serious exercise, such as backpacking.	Result (iv) P U
Something strenuous like soccer or running would be my choice.	Result (iv) N U

587 **What sort of food do you like?**

I really just like traditional, plain food.	Result (v) Q S
On the whole I prefer traditional, plain food.	Result (v) U S
I eat exotic food for a change.	Result (v) K S
I enjoy most foods, really.	Result (v) H S
I prefer a wide variety of dishes.	Result (v) L S

588 **What level of education have you reached (or do you expect to reach)?**

My education ended when I was 16.	Result (vi) J V
No further education after leaving school at 18.	Result (vi) D V
Some further education after leaving school at 18.	Result (vi) U V
Graduate degree.	Result (vi) E V
Postgraduate degree.	Result (vi)A V

589 **Which of these types of TV programmes do you like the most?**

Most of all I like game shows.	Result (i) O K
I couldn't do without soap operas.	Result (i) E K
I especially enjoy police dramas or comedies.	Result (i) V K
My preference is for serious dramas.	Result (i) P K
I enjoy news programmes and documentaries.	Result (i) C K

590 **What is your view of chivalry?**

I think it's old-fashioned nonsense, to be quite honest.	Result (ii) R K
It's pretty undesirable.	Result (ii) S K
It depends; it's OK sometimes.	Result (ii) H K
It's a desirable quality.	Result (ii) P K
I'd say it's an essential part of life.	Result (ii) N K

591 **If you had to choose just one, which of these is your favourite type of music?**

I prefer music such as heavy metal or rap.	Result (iii) O K
My favourite is rock or pop music; eg The Beatles.	Result (iii) E K
I particularly enjoy easy-listening music; eg Frank Sinatra.	Result (iii) V K
Jazz would be my number-one choice.	Result (iii) P K
My preference would be for classical music or opera.	Result (iii) C K

592 **Which of these activities appeals most?**

I'd choose relaxing; sitting on the sofa, for example.	Result (iv) R K
My preference would be for some mild exercise, such as gardening.	Result (iv) S K
Moderate exercise, such as walking, would be my choice.	Result (iv) H K
I would prefer more serious exercise, such as backpacking.	Result (iv) P K
Something strenuous like soccer or running would be my choice.	Result (iv) N K

593 **What sort of food do you like?**

I really just like traditional, plain food.	Result (v) Q H
On the whole I prefer traditional, plain food.	Result (v) U H
I eat exotic food for a change.	Result (v) K H
I enjoy most foods, really.	Result (v) H H
I prefer a wide variety of dishes.	Result (v) L H

594 **What level of education have you reached (or do you expect to reach)?**

My education ended when I was 16.	Result (vi) X V
No further education after leaving school at 18.	Result (vi) G V
Some further education after leaving school at 18.	Result (vi) K V
Graduate degree.	Result (vi) V V
Postgraduate degree.	Result (vi) B V

595 **Which of these types of TV programmes do you like the most?**

Most of all I like game shows.	Result (i) O H
I couldn't do without soap operas.	Result (i) E H
I especially enjoy police dramas or comedies.	Result (i) V H
My preference is for serious dramas.	Result (i) P H
I enjoy news programmes and documentaries.	Result (i) CH

596 **What is your view of chivalry?**

I think it's old-fashioned nonsense, to be quite honest.	Result (ii) R V
It's pretty undesirable.	Result (ii) S V
It depends; it's OK sometimes.	Result (ii) H V
It's a desirable quality.	Result (ii) P V
I'd say it's an essential part of life.	Result (ii) N V

597 **If you had to choose just one, which of these is your favourite type of music?**

I prefer music such as heavy metal or rap.	Result (iii) O H
My favourite is rock or pop music; eg The Beatles.	Result (iii) E H
I particularly enjoy easy-listening music; eg Frank Sinatra.	Result (iii) V H
Jazz would be my number-one choice.	Result (iii) P H
My preference would be for classical music or opera.	Result (iii) C H

598 **Which of these activities appeals most?**

I'd choose relaxing; sitting on the sofa, for example.	Result (iv) R H
My preference would be for some mild exercise, such as gardening.	Result (iv) S H
Moderate exercise, such as walking, would be my choice.	Result (iv) H H
I would prefer more serious exercise, such as backpacking.	Result (iv) P H
Something strenuous like soccer or running would be my choice.	Result (iv) N H

599 **What sort of food do you like?**

I really just like traditional, plain food.	Result (v) Q P
On the whole I prefer traditional, plain food.	Result (v) U P
I eat exotic food for a change.	Result (v) K P
I enjoy most foods, really.	Result (v) H P
I prefer a wide variety of dishes.	Result (v) L P

600 **What level of education have you reached (or do you expect to reach)?**

My education ended when I was 16.	Result (vi) R V
No further education after leaving school at 18.	Result (vi) S V
Some further education after leaving school at 18.	Result (vi) H V
Graduate degree.	Result (vi) P V
Postgraduate degree.	Result (vi) N V

601 **Which of these types of TV programmes do you like the most?**

Most of all I like game shows.	Result (i) O L
I couldn't do without soap operas.	Result (i) E L
I especially enjoy police dramas or comedies.	Result (i) V L
My preference is for serious dramas.	Result (i) P L
I enjoy news programmes and documentaries.	Result (i) C L

602 **What is your view of chivalry?**

I think it's old-fashioned nonsense, to be quite honest.	Result (ii) R B
It's pretty undesirable.	Result (ii) S B
It depends; it's OK sometimes.	Result (ii) H B
It's a desirable quality.	Result (ii) P B
I'd say it's an essential part of life.	Result (ii) N B

603 **If you had to choose just one, which of these is your favourite type of music?**

I prefer music such as heavy metal or rap.	Result (iii) O L
My favourite is rock or pop music; eg The Beatles.	Result (iii) E L
I particularly enjoy easy-listening music; eg Frank Sinatra.	Result (iii) V L
Jazz would be my number-one choice.	Result (iii) P L
My preference would be for classical music or opera.	Result (iii) C L

604 **Which of these activities appeals most?**

I'd choose relaxing; sitting on the sofa, for example.	Result (iv) R L
My preference would be for some mild exercise, such as gardening.	Result (iv) S L
Moderate exercise, such as walking, would be my choice.	Result (iv) H L
I would prefer more serious exercise, such as backpacking.	Result (iv) P L
Something strenuous like soccer or running would be my choice.	Result (iv) N L

605 **What sort of food do you like?**

I really just like traditional, plain food.	Result (v) Q N
On the whole I prefer traditional, plain food.	Result (v) U N
I eat exotic food for a change.	Result (v) K N
I enjoy most foods, really.	Result (v) H N
I prefer a wide variety of dishes.	Result (v) L N

606 **What level of education have you reached (or do you expect to reach)?**

My education ended when I was 16.	Result (vi) Y V
No further education after leaving school at 18.	Result (vi) F V
Some further education after leaving school at 18.	Result (vi) L V
Graduate degree.	Result (vi) C V
Postgraduate degree.	Result (vi) M V

607 **Which of these types of TV programmes do you like the most?**

Most of all I like game shows.	Result (i) T Q
I couldn't do without soap operas.	Result (i) A Q
I especially enjoy police dramas or comedies.	Result (i) B Q
My preference is for serious dramas.	Result (i) N Q
I enjoy news programmes and documentaries.	Result (i) M Q

608 **What is your view of chivalry?**

I think it's old-fashioned nonsense, to be quite honest.	Result (ii) Y X
It's pretty undesirable.	Result (ii) F X
It depends; it's OK sometimes.	Result (ii) L X
It's a desirable quality.	Result (ii) C X
I'd say it's an essential part of life.	Result (ii) M X

609 **If you had to choose just one, which of these is your favourite type of music?**

I prefer music such as heavy metal or rap.	Result (iii) T Q
My favourite is rock or pop music; eg The Beatles.	Result (iii) A Q
I particularly enjoy easy-listening music; eg Frank Sinatra.	Result (iii) B Q
Jazz would be my number-one choice.	Result (iii) N Q
My preference would be for classical music or opera.	Result (iii) M Q

610 **Which of these activities appeals most?**

I'd choose relaxing; sitting on the sofa, for example.	Result (iv) Y Q
My preference would be for some mild exercise, such as gardening.	Result (iv) F Q
Moderate exercise, such as walking, would be my choice.	Result (iv) L Q
I would prefer more serious exercise, such as backpacking.	Result (iv) C Q
Something strenuous like soccer or running would be my choice.	Result (iv) M Q

611 **What sort of food do you like?**

I really just like traditional, plain food.	Result (v) Q Y
On the whole I prefer traditional, plain food.	Result (v) U Y
I eat exotic food for a change.	Result (v) K Y
I enjoy most foods, really.	Result (v) H L
I prefer a wide variety of dishes.	Result (v) L Y

612 **What level of education have you reached (or do you expect to reach)?**

My education ended when I was 16.	Result (vi) I B
No further education after leaving school at 18.	Result (vi) W B
Some further education after leaving school at 18.	Result (vi) Q B
Graduate degree.	Result (vi) O B
Postgraduate degree.	Result (vi) T B

Take the CQ Test

613 **Which of these types of TV programmes do you like the most?**

Most of all I like game shows.	Result (i) T U
I couldn't do without soap operas.	Result (i) A U
I especially enjoy police dramas or comedies.	Result (i) B U
My preference is for serious dramas.	Result (i) N U
I enjoy news programmes and documentaries.	Result (i) M U

614 **What is your view of chivalry?**

I think it's old-fashioned nonsense, to be quite honest.	Result (ii) Y G
It's pretty undesirable.	Result (ii) F G
It depends; it's OK sometimes.	Result (ii) L G
It's a desirable quality.	Result (ii) C G
I'd say it's an essential part of life.	Result (ii) M G

615 **If you had to choose just one, which of these is your favourite type of music?**

I prefer music such as heavy metal or rap.	Result (iii) T U
My favourite is rock or pop music; eg The Beatles.	Result (iii) A U
I particularly enjoy easy-listening music; eg Frank Sinatra.	Result (iii) B U
Jazz would be my number-one choice.	Result (iii) N U
My preference would be for classical music or opera.	Result (iii) M U

616 **Which of these activities appeals most?**

I'd choose relaxing; sitting on the sofa, for example.	Result (iv) Y U
My preference would be for some mild exercise, such as gardening.	Result (iv) F U
Moderate exercise, such as walking, would be my choice.	Result (iv) L U
I would prefer more serious exercise, such as backpacking.	Result (iv) C U
Something strenuous like soccer or running would be my choice.	Result (iv) M U

617 **What sort of food do you like?**

I really just like traditional, plain food.	Result (v) Q F
On the whole I prefer traditional, plain food.	Result (v) U F
I eat exotic food for a change.	Result (v) K F
I enjoy most foods, really.	Result (v) H F
I prefer a wide variety of dishes.	Result (v) L F

618 **What level of education have you reached (or do you expect to reach)?**

My education ended when I was 16.	Result (vi) J B
No further education after leaving school at 18.	Result (vi) D B
Some further education after leaving school at 18.	Result (vi) U B
Graduate degree.	Result (vi) E B
Postgraduate degree.	Result (vi) A B

619 **Which of these types of TV programmes do you like the most?**

Most of all I like game shows.	Result (i) T K
I couldn't do without soap operas.	Result (i) A K
I especially enjoy police dramas or comedies.	Result (i) B K
My preference is for serious dramas.	Result (i) N K
I enjoy news programmes and documentaries.	Result (i) M K

620 **What is your view of chivalry?**

I think it's old-fashioned nonsense, to be quite honest.	Result (ii) Y K
It's pretty undesirable.	Result (ii) F K
It depends; it's OK sometimes.	Result (ii) L K
It's a desirable quality.	Result (ii) C K
I'd say it's an essential part of life.	Result (ii) M K

621 **If you had to choose just one, which of these is your favourite type of music?**

I prefer music such as heavy metal or rap.	Result (iii) T K
My favourite is rock or pop music; eg The Beatles.	Result (iii) A K
I particularly enjoy easy-listening music; eg Frank Sinatra.	Result (iii) B K
Jazz would be my number-one choice.	Result (iii) N K
My preference would be for classical music or opera.	Result (iii) M K

622 **Which of these activities appeals most?**

I'd choose relaxing; sitting on the sofa, for example.	Result (iv) Y K
My preference would be for some mild exercise, such as gardening.	Result (iv) F K
Moderate exercise, such as walking, would be my choice.	Result (iv) L K
I would prefer more serious exercise, such as backpacking.	Result (iv) C K
Something strenuous like soccer or running would be my choice.	Result (iv) M K

623 **What sort of food do you like?**

I really just like traditional, plain food.	Result (v) Q L
On the whole I prefer traditional, plain food.	Result (v) U L
I eat exotic food for a change.	Result (v) K L
I enjoy most foods, really.	Result (v) H L
I prefer a wide variety of dishes.	Result (v) L L

624 **What level of education have you reached (or do you expect to reach)?**

My education ended when I was 16.	Result (vi) X B
No further education after leaving school at 18.	Result (vi) G B
Some further education after leaving school at 18.	Result (vi) K B
Graduate degree.	Result (vi) V B
Postgraduate degree.	Result (vi) B B

625   **Which of these types of TV programmes do you like the most?**

Most of all I like game shows.	Result (i) T H
I couldn't do without soap operas.	Result (i) A H
I especially enjoy police dramas or comedies.	Result (i) B H
My preference is for serious dramas.	Result (i) N H
I enjoy news programmes and documentaries.	Result (i) M H

626   **What is your view of chivalry?**

I think it's old-fashioned nonsense, to be quite honest.	Result (ii) Y V
It's pretty undesirable.	Result (ii) F V
It depends; it's OK sometimes.	Result (ii) L V
It's a desirable quality.	Result (ii) C V
I'd say it's an essential part of life.	Result (ii) M V

627   **If you had to choose just one, which of these is your favourite type of music?**

I prefer music such as heavy metal or rap.	Result (iii) T H
My favourite is rock or pop music; eg The Beatles.	Result (iii) A H
I particularly enjoy easy-listening music; eg Frank Sinatra.	Result (iii) B H
Jazz would be my number-one choice.	Result (iii) N H
My preference would be for classical music or opera.	Result (iii) M H

628   **Which of these activities appeals most?**

I'd choose relaxing; sitting on the sofa, for example.	Result (iv) Y H
My preference would be for some mild exercise, such as gardening.	Result (iv) F H
Moderate exercise, such as walking, would be my choice.	Result (iv) L H
I would prefer more serious exercise, such as backpacking.	Result (iv) C H
Something strenuous like soccer or running would be my choice.	Result (iv) M H

629   **What sort of food do you like?**

I really just like traditional, plain food.	Result (v) Q C
On the whole I prefer traditional, plain food.	Result (v) U C
I eat exotic food for a change.	Result (v) K C
I enjoy most foods, really.	Result (v) H C
I prefer a wide variety of dishes.	Result (v) L C

630   **What level of education have you reached (or do you expect to reach)?**

My education ended when I was 16.	Result (vi) R B
No further education after leaving school at 18.	Result (vi) S B
Some further education after leaving school at 18.	Result (vi) H B
Graduate degree.	Result (vi) P B
Postgraduate degree.	Result (vi) N B

631 **Which of these types of TV programmes do you like the most?**

Most of all I like game shows.	Result (i) T L
I couldn't do without soap operas.	Result (i) A L
I especially enjoy police dramas or comedies.	Result (i) B L
My preference is for serious dramas.	Result (i) N L
I enjoy news programmes and documentaries.	Result (i) M L

632 **What is your view of chivalry?**

I think it's old-fashioned nonsense, to be quite honest.	Result (i) Y B
It's pretty undesirable.	Result (ii) F B
It depends; it's OK sometimes.	Result (ii) L B
It's a desirable quality.	Result (ii) C B
I'd say it's an essential part of life.	Result (ii) M B

633 **If you had to choose just one, which of these is your favourite type of music?**

I prefer music such as heavy metal or rap.	Result (iii) T L
My favourite is rock or pop music; eg The Beatles.	Result (iii) A L
I particularly enjoy easy-listening music; eg Frank Sinatra.	Result (iii) B L
Jazz would be my number-one choice.	Result (iii) N L
My preference would be for classical music or opera.	Result (iii) M L

634 **Which of these activities appeals most?**

I'd choose relaxing; sitting on the sofa, for example.	Result (iv) Y L
My preference would be for some mild exercise, such as gardening.	Result (iv) F L
Moderate exercise, such as walking, would be my choice.	Result (iv) L L
I would prefer more serious exercise, such as backpacking.	Result (iv) C L
Something strenuous like soccer or running would be my choice.	Result (iv) M L

635 **What sort of food do you like?**

I really just like traditional, plain food.	Result (v) Q M
On the whole I prefer traditional, plain food.	Result (v) U M
I eat exotic food for a change.	Result (v) K M
I enjoy most foods, really.	Result (v) H M
I prefer a wide variety of dishes.	Result (v) L M

636 **What level of education have you reached (or do you expect to reach)?**

My education ended when I was 16.	Result (vi) Y B
No further education after leaving school at 18.	Result (vi) F B
Some further education after leaving school at 18.	Result (vi) L B
Graduate degree.	Result (vi) C B
Postgraduate degree.	Result (vi) M B

637 **Which of these types of TV programmes do you like the most?**

Most of all I like game shows.	Result (i) I O
I couldn't do without soap operas.	Result (i) J O
I especially enjoy police dramas or comedies.	Result (i) X O
My preference is for serious dramas.	Result (i) R O
I enjoy news programmes and documentaries.	Result (i) Y O

638 **What is your view of chivalry?**

I think it's old-fashioned nonsense, to be quite honest.	Result (ii) I R
It's pretty undesirable.	Result (ii) W R
It depends; it's OK sometimes.	Result (ii) Q R
It's a desirable quality.	Result (ii) O R
I'd say it's an essential part of life.	Result (ii) T R

639 **If you had to choose just one, which of these is your favourite type of music?**

I prefer music such as heavy metal or rap.	Result (iii) I O
My favourite is rock or pop music; eg The Beatles.	Result (iii) J O
I particularly enjoy easy-listening music; eg Frank Sinatra.	Result (iii) X O
Jazz would be my number-one choice.	Result (iii) R O
My preference would be for classical music or opera.	Result (iii) Y O

640 **Which of these activities appeals most?**

I'd choose relaxing; sitting on the sofa, for example.	Result (iv) I O
My preference would be for some mild exercise, such as gardening.	Result (iv) W O
Moderate exercise, such as walking, would be my choice.	Result (iv) Q O
I would prefer more serious exercise, such as backpacking.	Result (iv) O O
Something strenuous like soccer or running would be my choice.	Result (iv) T O

641 **What sort of food do you like?**

I really just like traditional, plain food.	Result (v) O I
On the whole I prefer traditional, plain food.	Result (v) E I
I eat exotic food for a change.	Result (v) V I
I enjoy most foods, really.	Result (v) P I
I prefer a wide variety of dishes.	Result (v) C I

642 **What level of education have you reached (or do you expect to reach)?**

My education ended when I was 16.	Result (vi) I R
No further education after leaving school at 18.	Result (vi) W R
Some further education after leaving school at 18.	Result (vi) Q R
Graduate degree.	Result (vi) O R
Postgraduate degree.	Result (vi) T R

643 **Which of these types of TV programmes do you like the most?**

Most of all I like game shows.	Result (i) I E
I couldn't do without soap operas.	Result (i) J E
I especially enjoy police dramas or comedies.	Result (i) X E
My preference is for serious dramas.	Result (i) R E
I enjoy news programmes and documentaries.	Result (i) Y E

644 **What is your view of chivalry?**

I think it's old-fashioned nonsense, to be quite honest.	Result (ii) I S
It's pretty undesirable.	Result (ii) W S
It depends; it's OK sometimes.	Result (ii) Q S
It's a desirable quality.	Result (ii) O S
I'd say it's an essential part of life.	Result (ii) T S

645 **If you had to choose just one, which of these is your favourite type of music?**

I prefer music such as heavy metal or rap.	Result (iii) I E
My favourite is rock or pop music; eg The Beatles.	Result (iii) J E
I particularly enjoy easy-listening music; eg Frank Sinatra.	Result (iii) X E
Jazz would be my number-one choice.	Result (iii) R E
My preference would be for classical music or opera.	Result (iii) Y E

646 **Which of these activities appeals most?**

I'd choose relaxing; sitting on the sofa, for example.	Result (iv) I E
My preference would be for some mild exercise, such as gardening.	Result (iv) W E
Moderate exercise, such as walking, would be my choice.	Result (iv) Q E
I would prefer more serious exercise, such as backpacking.	Result (iv) O E
Something strenuous like soccer or running would be my choice.	Result (iv) T E

647 **What sort of food do you like?**

I really just like traditional, plain food.	Result (v) O W
On the whole I prefer traditional, plain food.	Result (v) E W
I eat exotic food for a change.	Result (v) V W
I enjoy most foods, really.	Result (v) P W
I prefer a wide variety of dishes.	Result (v) C W

648 **What level of education have you reached (or do you expect to reach)?**

My education ended when I was 16.	Result (vi) J R
No further education after leaving school at 18.	Result (vi) D R
Some further education after leaving school at 18.	Result (vi) U R
Graduate degree.	Result (vi) E R
Postgraduate degree.	Result (vi) A R

649 **Which of these types of TV programmes do you like the most?**

Most of all I like game shows.	Result (i) I V
I couldn't do without soap operas.	Result (i) J V
I especially enjoy police dramas or comedies.	Result (i) X V
My preference is for serious dramas.	Result (i) R V
I enjoy news programmes and documentaries.	Result (i) Y V

650 **What is your view of chivalry?**

I think it's old-fashioned nonsense, to be quite honest.	Result (ii) I H
It's pretty undesirable.	Result (ii) W H
It depends; it's OK sometimes.	Result (ii) Q H
It's a desirable quality.	Result (ii) O H
I'd say it's an essential part of life.	Result (ii) T H

651 **If you had to choose just one, which of these is your favourite type of music?**

I prefer music such as heavy metal or rap.	Result (iii) I V
My favourite is rock or pop music; eg The Beatles.	Result (iii) J V
I particularly enjoy easy-listening music; eg Frank Sinatra.	Result (iii) X V
Jazz would be my number-one choice.	Result (iii) R V
My preference would be for classical music or opera.	Result (iii) Y V

652 **Which of these activities appeals most?**

I'd choose relaxing; sitting on the sofa, for example.	Result (iv) I V
My preference would be for some mild exercise, such as gardening.	Result (iv) W V
Moderate exercise, such as walking, would be my choice.	Result (iv) Q V
I would prefer more serious exercise, such as backpacking.	Result (iv) O V
Something strenuous like soccer or running would be my choice.	Result (iv) T V

653 **What sort of food do you like?**

I really just like traditional, plain food.	Result (v) O Q
On the whole I prefer traditional, plain food.	Result (v) E Q
I eat exotic food for a change.	Result (v) V Q
I enjoy most foods, really.	Result (v) P Q
I prefer a wide variety of dishes.	Result (v) C Q

654 **What level of education have you reached (or do you expect to reach)?**

My education ended when I was 16.	Result (vi) X R
No further education after leaving school at 18.	Result (vi) G R
Some further education after leaving school at 18.	Result (vi) K R
Graduate degree.	Result (vi) V R
Postgraduate degree.	Result (vi) B R

655 Which of these types of TV programmes do you like the most?

Most of all I like game shows.	Result (i) I P
I couldn't do without soap operas.	Result (i) J P
I especially enjoy police dramas or comedies.	Result (i) X P
My preference is for serious dramas.	Result (i) R P
I enjoy news programmes and documentaries.	Result (i) Y P

656 What is your view of chivalry?

I think it's old-fashioned nonsense, to be quite honest.	Result (ii) I P
It's pretty undesirable.	Result (ii) W P
It depends; it's OK sometimes.	Result (ii) Q P
It's a desirable quality.	Result (ii) O P
I'd say it's an essential part of life.	Result (ii) T P

657 If you had to choose just one, which of these is your favourite type of music?

I prefer music such as heavy metal or rap.	Result (iii) I P
My favourite is rock or pop music; eg The Beatles.	Result (iii) J P
I particularly enjoy easy-listening music; eg Frank Sinatra.	Result (iii) X P
Jazz would be my number-one choice.	Result (iii) R P
My preference would be for classical music or opera.	Result (iii) Y P

658 Which of these activities appeals most?

I'd choose relaxing; sitting on the sofa, for example.	Result (iv) I P
My preference would be for some mild exercise, such as gardening.	Result (iv) W P
Moderate exercise, such as walking, would be my choice.	Result (iv) Q P
I would prefer more serious exercise, such as backpacking.	Result (iv) O P
Something strenuous like soccer or running would be my choice.	Result (iv) T P

659 What sort of food do you like?

I really just like traditional, plain food.	Result (v) O O
On the whole I prefer traditional, plain food.	Result (v) E O
I eat exotic food for a change.	Result (v) V O
I enjoy most foods, really.	Result (v) P O
I prefer a wide variety of dishes.	Result (v) C O

660 What level of education have you reached (or do you expect to reach)?

My education ended when I was 16.	Result (vi) R R
No further education after leaving school at 18.	Result (vi) S R
Some further education after leaving school at 18.	Result (vi) H R
Graduate degree.	Result (vi) P R
Postgraduate degree.	Result (vi) N R

661 **Which of these types of TV programmes do you like the most?**

Most of all I like game shows.	Result (i) I C
I couldn't do without soap operas.	Result (i) J C
I especially enjoy police dramas or comedies.	Result (i) X C
My preference is for serious dramas.	Result (i) R C
I enjoy news programmes and documentaries.	Result (i) Y C

662 **What is your view of chivalry?**

I think it's old-fashioned nonsense, to be quite honest.	Result (ii) I N
It's pretty undesirable.	Result (ii) W N
It depends; it's OK sometimes.	Result (ii) Q N
It's a desirable quality.	Result (ii) O N
I'd say it's an essential part of life.	Result (ii) T N

663 **If you had to choose just one, which of these is your favourite type of music?**

I prefer music such as heavy metal or rap.	Result (iii) I C
My favourite is rock or pop music; eg The Beatles.	Result (iii) J C
I particularly enjoy easy-listening music; eg Frank Sinatra.	Result (iii) X C
Jazz would be my number-one choice.	Result (iii) R C
My preference would be for classical music or opera.	Result (iii) Y C

664 **Which of these activities appeals most?**

I'd choose relaxing; sitting on the sofa, for example.	Result (iv) I C
My preference would be for some mild exercise, such as gardening.	Result (iv) W C
Moderate exercise, such as walking, would be my choice.	Result (iv) Q C
I would prefer more serious exercise, such as backpacking.	Result (iv) O C
Something strenuous like soccer or running would be my choice.	Result (iv) T C

665 **What sort of food do you like?**

I really just like traditional, plain food.	Result (v) O T
On the whole I prefer traditional, plain food.	Result (v) E T
I eat exotic food for a change.	Result (v) V T
I enjoy most foods, really.	Result (v) P T
I prefer a wide variety of dishes.	Result (v) C T

666 **What level of education have you reached (or do you expect to reach)?**

My education ended when I was 16.	Result (vi) Y R
No further education after leaving school at 18.	Result (vi) F R
Some further education after leaving school at 18.	Result (vi) L R
Graduate degree.	Result (vi) C R
Postgraduate degree.	Result (vi) M R

667 **Which of these types of TV programmes do you like the most?**

Most of all I like game shows.	Result (i) W O
I couldn't do without soap operas.	Result (i) D O
I especially enjoy police dramas or comedies.	Result (i) G O
My preference is for serious dramas.	Result (i) S O
I enjoy news programmes and documentaries.	Result (i) F O

668 **What is your view of chivalry?**

I think it's old-fashioned nonsense, to be quite honest.	Result (ii) J R
It's pretty undesirable.	Result (ii) D R
It depends; it's OK sometimes.	Result (ii) U R
It's a desirable quality.	Result (ii) E R
I'd say it's an essential part of life.	Result (ii) A R

669 **If you had to choose just one, which of these is your favourite type of music?**

I prefer music such as heavy metal or rap.	Result (iii) W O
My favourite is rock or pop music; eg The Beatles.	Result (iii) D O
I particularly enjoy easy-listening music; eg Frank Sinatra.	Result (iii) G O
Jazz would be my number-one choice.	Result (iii) S O
My preference would be for classical music or opera.	Result (iii) F O

670 **Which of these activities appeals most?**

I'd choose relaxing; sitting on the sofa, for example.	Result (iv) J O
My preference would be for some mild exercise, such as gardening.	Result (iv) D O
Moderate exercise, such as walking, would be my choice.	Result (iv) U O
I would prefer more serious exercise, such as backpacking.	Result (iv) E O
Something strenuous like soccer or running would be my choice.	Result (iv) A O

671 **What sort of food do you like?**

I really just like traditional, plain food.	Result (v) O J
On the whole I prefer traditional, plain food.	Result (v) E J
I eat exotic food for a change.	Result (v) V J
I enjoy most foods, really.	Result (v) P J
I prefer a wide variety of dishes.	Result (v) C J

672 **What level of education have you reached (or do you expect to reach)?**

My education ended when I was 16.	Result (vi) I S
No further education after leaving school at 18.	Result (vi) W S
Some further education after leaving school at 18.	Result (vi) Q S
Graduate degree.	Result (vi) O S
Postgraduate degree.	Result (vi) T S

Take the CQ Test

673 Which of these types of TV programmes do you like the most?

Most of all I like game shows.	Result (i) W E
I couldn't do without soap operas.	Result (i) D E
I especially enjoy police dramas or comedies.	Result (i) G E
My preference is for serious dramas.	Result (i) S E
I enjoy news programmes and documentaries.	Result (i) F E

674 What is your view of chivalry?

I think it's old-fashioned nonsense, to be quite honest.	Result (ii) J S
It's pretty undesirable.	Result (ii) D S
It depends; it's OK sometimes.	Result (ii) U S
It's a desirable quality.	Result (ii) E S
I'd say it's an essential part of life.	Result (ii) A S

675 If you had to choose just one, which of these is your favourite type of music?

I prefer music such as heavy metal or rap.	Result (iii) W E
My favourite is rock or pop music; eg The Beatles.	Result (iii) D E
I particularly enjoy easy-listening music; eg Frank Sinatra.	Result (iii) G E
Jazz would be my number-one choice.	Result (iii) S E
My preference would be for classical music or opera.	Result (iii) F E

676 Which of these activities appeals most?

I'd choose relaxing; sitting on the sofa, for example.	Result (iv) J E
My preference would be for some mild exercise, such as gardening.	Result (iv) D E
Moderate exercise, such as walking, would be my choice.	Result (iv) U E
I would prefer more serious exercise, such as backpacking.	Result (iv) E E
Something strenuous like soccer or running would be my choice.	Result (iv) A E

677 What sort of food do you like?

I really just like traditional, plain food.	Result (v) O D
On the whole I prefer traditional, plain food.	Result (v) E D
I eat exotic food for a change.	Result (v) V D
I enjoy most foods, really.	Result (v) P D
I prefer a wide variety of dishes.	Result (v) C D

678 What level of education have you reached (or do you expect to reach)?

My education ended when I was 16.	Result (vi) J S
No further education after leaving school at 18.	Result (vi) D S
Some further education after leaving school at 18.	Result (vi) U S
Graduate degree.	Result (vi) E S
Postgraduate degree.	Result (vi) A S

679 **Which of these types of TV programmes do you like the most?**

Most of all I like game shows.	Result (i) W V
I couldn't do without soap operas.	Result (i) D V
I especially enjoy police dramas or comedies.	Result (i) G V
My preference is for serious dramas.	Result (i) S V
I enjoy news programmes and documentaries.	Result (i) F V

680 **What is your view of chivalry?**

I think it's old-fashioned nonsense, to be quite honest.	Result (ii) J H
It's pretty undesirable.	Result (ii) D H
It depends; it's OK sometimes.	Result (ii) U H
It's a desirable quality.	Result (ii) E H
I'd say it's an essential part of life.	Result (ii) A H

681 **If you had to choose just one, which of these is your favourite type of music?**

I prefer music such as heavy metal or rap.	Result (iii) W V
My favourite is rock or pop music; eg The Beatles.	Result (iii) D V
I particularly enjoy easy-listening music; eg Frank Sinatra.	Result (iii) G V
Jazz would be my number-one choice.	Result (iii) S V
My preference would be for classical music or opera.	Result (iii) F V

682 **Which of these activities appeals most?**

I'd choose relaxing; sitting on the sofa, for example.	Result (iv) J V
My preference would be for some mild exercise, such as gardening.	Result (iv) D V
Moderate exercise, such as walking, would be my choice.	Result (iv) U V
I would prefer more serious exercise, such as backpacking.	Result (iv) E V
Something strenuous like soccer or running would be my choice.	Result (iv) A V

683 **What sort of food do you like?**

I really just like traditional, plain food.	Result (v) O U
On the whole I prefer traditional, plain food.	Result (v) E U
I eat exotic food for a change.	Result (v) V U
I enjoy most foods, really.	Result (v) P U
I prefer a wide variety of dishes.	Result (v) C U

684 **What level of education have you reached (or do you expect to reach)?**

My education ended when I was 16.	Result (vi) X S
No further education after leaving school at 18.	Result (vi) G S
Some further education after leaving school at 18.	Result (vi) K S
Graduate degree.	Result (vi) V S
Postgraduate degree.	Result (vi) B S

685 **Which of these types of TV programmes do you like the most?**

Most of all I like game shows.	Result (i) W P
I couldn't do without soap operas.	Result (i) D P
I especially enjoy police dramas or comedies.	Result (i) G P
My preference is for serious dramas.	Result (i) S P
I enjoy news programmes and documentaries.	Result (i) F P

686 **What is your view of chivalry?**

I think it's old-fashioned nonsense, to be quite honest.	Result (ii) J P
It's pretty undesirable.	Result (ii) D P
It depends; it's OK sometimes.	Result (ii) U P
It's a desirable quality.	Result (ii) E P
I'd say it's an essential part of life.	Result (ii) A P

687 **If you had to choose just one, which of these is your favourite type of music?**

I prefer music such as heavy metal or rap.	Result (iii) W P
My favourite is rock or pop music; eg The Beatles.	Result (iii) D P
I particularly enjoy easy-listening music; eg Frank Sinatra.	Result (iii) G P
Jazz would be my number-one choice.	Result (iii) S P
My preference would be for classical music or opera.	Result (iii) F P

688 **Which of these activities appeals most?**

I'd choose relaxing; sitting on the sofa, for example.	Result (iv) J P
My preference would be for some mild exercise, such as gardening.	Result (iv) D P
Moderate exercise, such as walking, would be my choice.	Result (iv) U P
I would prefer more serious exercise, such as backpacking.	Result (iv) E P
Something strenuous like soccer or running would be my choice.	Result (iv) A P

689 **What sort of food do you like?**

I really just like traditional, plain food.	Result (v) O E
On the whole I prefer traditional, plain food.	Result (v) E E
I eat exotic food for a change.	Result (v) V E
I enjoy most foods, really.	Result (v) P E
I prefer a wide variety of dishes.	Result (v) C E

690 **What level of education have you reached (or do you expect to reach)?**

My education ended when I was 16.	Result (vi) R S
No further education after leaving school at 18.	Result (vi) S S
Some further education after leaving school at 18.	Result (vi) H S
Graduate degree.	Result (vi) P S
Postgraduate degree.	Result (vi) N S

691 **Which of these types of TV programmes do you like the most?**

Most of all I like game shows.	Result (i) W C
I couldn't do without soap operas.	Result (i) D C
I especially enjoy police dramas or comedies.	Result (i) G C
My preference is for serious dramas.	Result (i) S C
I enjoy news programmes and documentaries.	Result (i) F C

692 **What is your view of chivalry?**

I think it's old-fashioned nonsense, to be quite honest.	Result (ii) J N
It's pretty undesirable.	Result (ii) D N
It depends; it's OK sometimes.	Result (ii) U N
It's a desirable quality.	Result (ii) E N
I'd say it's an essential part of life.	Result (ii) A N

693 **If you had to choose just one, which of these is your favourite type of music?**

I prefer music such as heavy metal or rap.	Result (iii) W C
My favourite is rock or pop music; eg The Beatles.	Result (iii) D C
I particularly enjoy easy-listening music; eg Frank Sinatra.	Result (iii) G C
Jazz would be my number-one choice.	Result (iii) S C
My preference would be for classical music or opera.	Result (iii) F C

694 **Which of these activities appeals most?**

I'd choose relaxing; sitting on the sofa, for example.	Result (iv) J C
My preference would be for some mild exercise, such as gardening.	Result (iv) D C
Moderate exercise, such as walking, would be my choice.	Result (iv) U C
I would prefer more serious exercise, such as backpacking.	Result (iv) E C
Something strenuous like soccer or running would be my choice.	Result (iv) A C

695 **What sort of food do you like?**

I really just like traditional, plain food.	Result (v) O A
On the whole I prefer traditional, plain food.	Result (v) E A
I eat exotic food for a change.	Result (v) V A
I enjoy most foods, really.	Result (v) P A
I prefer a wide variety of dishes.	Result (v) C A

696 **What level of education have you reached (or do you expect to reach)?**

My education ended when I was 16.	Result (vi) Y S
No further education after leaving school at 18.	Result (vi) F S
Some further education after leaving school at 18.	Result (vi) L S
Graduate degree.	Result (vi) C S
Postgraduate degree.	Result (vi) M S

697 **Which of these types of TV programmes do you like the most?**

Most of all I like game shows.	Result (i) Q O
I couldn't do without soap operas.	Result (i) U O
I especially enjoy police dramas or comedies.	Result (i) K O
My preference is for serious dramas.	Result (i) H O
I enjoy news programmes and documentaries.	Result (i) L O

698 **What is your view of chivalry?**

I think it's old-fashioned nonsense, to be quite honest.	Result (ii) X R
It's pretty undesirable.	Result (ii) G R
It depends; it's OK sometimes.	Result (ii) K R
It's a desirable quality.	Result (ii) V R
I'd say it's an essential part of life.	Result (ii) B R

699 **If you had to choose just one, which of these is your favourite type of music?**

I prefer music such as heavy metal or rap.	Result (iii) Q O
My favourite is rock or pop music; eg The Beatles.	Result (iii) U O
I particularly enjoy easy-listening music; eg Frank Sinatra.	Result (iii) K O
Jazz would be my number-one choice.	Result (iii) H O
My preference would be for classical music or opera.	Result (iii) L O

700 **Which of these activities appeals most?**

I'd choose relaxing; sitting on the sofa, for example.	Result (iv) X O
My preference would be for some mild exercise, such as gardening.	Result (iv) G O
Moderate exercise, such as walking, would be my choice.	Result (iv) K O
I would prefer more serious exercise, such as backpacking.	Result (iv) V O
Something strenuous like soccer or running would be my choice.	Result (iv) B O

701 **What sort of food do you like?**

I really just like traditional, plain food.	Result (v) O X
On the whole I prefer traditional, plain food.	Result (v) E X
I eat exotic food for a change.	Result (v) V X
I enjoy most foods, really.	Result (v) P X
I prefer a wide variety of dishes.	Result (v) C X

702 **What level of education have you reached (or do you expect to reach)?**

My education ended when I was 16.	Result (vi) I H
No further education after leaving school at 18.	Result (vi) W H
Some further education after leaving school at 18.	Result (vi) Q H
Graduate degree.	Result (vi) O H
Postgraduate degree.	Result (vi) T H

703 **Which of these types of TV programmes do you like the most?**

Most of all I like game shows.	Result (i) Q E
I couldn't do without soap operas.	Result (i) U E
I especially enjoy police dramas or comedies.	Result (i) K E
My preference is for serious dramas.	Result (i) H E
I enjoy news programmes and documentaries.	Result (i) L E

704 **What is your view of chivalry?**

I think it's old-fashioned nonsense, to be quite honest.	Result (ii) X S
It's pretty undesirable.	Result (ii) G S
It depends; it's OK sometimes.	Result (ii) K S
It's a desirable quality.	Result (ii) V S
I'd say it's an essential part of life.	Result (ii) B S

705 **If you had to choose just one, which of these is your favourite type of music?**

I prefer music such as heavy metal or rap.	Result (iii) Q E
My favourite is rock or pop music; eg The Beatles.	Result (iii) U E
I particularly enjoy easy-listening music; eg Frank Sinatra.	Result (iii) K E
Jazz would be my number-one choice.	Result (iii) H E
My preference would be for classical music or opera.	Result (iii) L E

706 **Which of these activities appeals most?**

I'd choose relaxing; sitting on the sofa, for example.	Result (iv) X E
My preference would be for some mild exercise, such as gardening.	Result (iv) G E
Moderate exercise, such as walking, would be my choice.	Result (iv) K E
I would prefer more serious exercise, such as backpacking.	Result (iv) V E
Something strenuous like soccer or running would be my choice.	Result (iv) B E

707 **What sort of food do you like?**

I really just like traditional, plain food.	Result (v) O G
On the whole I prefer traditional, plain food.	Result (v) E G
I eat exotic food for a change.	Result (v) V G
I enjoy most foods, really.	Result (v) P G
I prefer a wide variety of dishes.	Result (v) C G

708 **What level of education have you reached (or do you expect to reach)?**

My education ended when I was 16.	Result (vi) J H
No further education after leaving school at 18.	Result (vi) D H
Some further education after leaving school at 18.	Result (vi) U H
Graduate degree.	Result (vi) E H
Postgraduate degree.	Result (vi) A H

709 **Which of these types of TV programmes do you like the most?**

Most of all I like game shows.	Result (i) Q V
I couldn't do without soap operas.	Result (i) U V
I especially enjoy police dramas or comedies.	Result (i) K V
My preference is for serious dramas.	Result (i) H V
I enjoy news programmes and documentaries.	Result (i) L V

710 **What is your view of chivalry?**

I think it's old-fashioned nonsense, to be quite honest.	Result (ii) X H
It's pretty undesirable.	Result (ii) G H
It depends; it's OK sometimes.	Result (ii) K H
It's a desirable quality.	Result (ii) V H
I'd say it's an essential part of life.	Result (ii) B H

711 **If you had to choose just one, which of these is your favourite type of music?**

I prefer music such as heavy metal or rap.	Result (iii) Q V
My favourite is rock or pop music; eg The Beatles.	Result (iii) U V
I particularly enjoy easy-listening music; eg Frank Sinatra.	Result (iii) K V
Jazz would be my number-one choice.	Result (iii) H V
My preference would be for classical music or opera.	Result (iii) L V

712 **Which of these activities appeals most?**

I'd choose relaxing; sitting on the sofa, for example.	Result (iv) X V
My preference would be for some mild exercise, such as gardening.	Result (iv) G V
Moderate exercise, such as walking, would be my choice.	Result (iv) K V
I would prefer more serious exercise, such as backpacking.	Result (iv) V V
Something strenuous like soccer or running would be my choice.	Result (iv) B V

713 **What sort of food do you like?**

I really just like traditional, plain food.	Result (v) O K
On the whole I prefer traditional, plain food.	Result (v) E K
I eat exotic food for a change.	Result (v) V K
I enjoy most foods, really.	Result (v) P K
I prefer a wide variety of dishes.	Result (v) C K

714 **What level of education have you reached (or do you expect to reach)?**

My education ended when I was 16.	Result (vi) X H
No further education after leaving school at 18.	Result (vi) G H
Some further education after leaving school at 18.	Result (vi) K H
Graduate degree.	Result (vi) V H
Postgraduate degree.	Result (vi) B H

715 Which of these types of TV programmes do you like the most?

Most of all I like game shows.	Result (i) Q P
I couldn't do without soap operas.	Result (i) U P
I especially enjoy police dramas or comedies.	Result (i) K P
My preference is for serious dramas.	Result (i) H P
I enjoy news programmes and documentaries.	Result (i) L P

716 What is your view of chivalry?

I think it's old-fashioned nonsense, to be quite honest.	Result (ii) X P
It's pretty undesirable.	Result (ii) G P
It depends; it's OK sometimes.	Result (ii) K P
It's a desirable quality.	Result (ii) V P
I'd say it's an essential part of life.	Result (ii) B P

717 If you had to choose just one, which of these is your favourite type of music?

I prefer music such as heavy metal or rap.	Result (iii) Q P
My favourite is rock or pop music; eg The Beatles.	Result (iii) U P
I particularly enjoy easy-listening music; eg Frank Sinatra.	Result (iii) K P
Jazz would be my number-one choice.	Result (iii) H P
My preference would be for classical music or opera.	Result (iii) L P

718 Which of these activities appeals most?

I'd choose relaxing; sitting on the sofa, for example.	Result (iv) X P
My preference would be for some mild exercise, such as gardening.	Result (iv) G P
Moderate exercise, such as walking, would be my choice.	Result (iv) K P
I would prefer more serious exercise, such as backpacking.	Result (iv) V P
Something strenuous like soccer or running would be my choice.	Result (iv) B P

719 What sort of food do you like?

I really just like traditional, plain food.	Result (v) O V
On the whole I prefer traditional, plain food.	Result (v) E V
I eat exotic food for a change.	Result (v) V V
I enjoy most foods, really.	Result (v) P V
I prefer a wide variety of dishes.	Result (v) C V

720 What level of education have you reached (or do you expect to reach)?

My education ended when I was 16.	Result (vi) R H
No further education after leaving school at 18.	Result (vi) S H
Some further education after leaving school at 18.	Result (vi) H H
Graduate degree.	Result (vi) P H
Postgraduate degree.	Result (vi) N H

Take the CQ Test

721 **Which of these types of TV programmes do you like the most?**

Most of all I like game shows.	Result (i) Q C
I couldn't do without soap operas.	Result (i) U C
I especially enjoy police dramas or comedies.	Result (i) K C
My preference is for serious dramas.	Result (i) H C
I enjoy news programmes and documentaries.	Result (i) L C

722 **What is your view of chivalry?**

I think it's old-fashioned nonsense, to be quite honest.	Result (ii) X N
It's pretty undesirable.	Result (ii) G N
It depends; it's OK sometimes.	Result (ii) K N
It's a desirable quality.	Result (ii) V N
I'd say it's an essential part of life.	Result (ii) B N

723 **If you had to choose just one, which of these is your favourite type of music?**

I prefer music such as heavy metal or rap.	Result (iii) Q C
My favourite is rock or pop music; eg The Beatles.	Result (iii) U C
I particularly enjoy easy-listening music; eg Frank Sinatra.	Result (iii) K C
Jazz would be my number-one choice.	Result (iii) H C
My preference would be for classical music or opera.	Result (iii) L C

724 **Which of these activities appeals most?**

I'd choose relaxing; sitting on the sofa, for example.	Result (iv) X C
My preference would be for some mild exercise, such as gardening.	Result (iv) G C
Moderate exercise, such as walking, would be my choice.	Result (iv) K C
I would prefer more serious exercise, such as backpacking.	Result (iv) V C
Something strenuous like soccer or running would be my choice.	Result (iv) B C

725 **What sort of food do you like?**

I really just like traditional, plain food.	Result (v) O B
On the whole I prefer traditional, plain food.	Result (v) E B
I eat exotic food for a change.	Result (v) V B
I enjoy most foods, really.	Result (v) P B
I prefer a wide variety of dishes.	Result (v) C B

726 **What level of education have you reached (or do you expect to reach)?**

My education ended when I was 16.	Result (vi) Y H
No further education after leaving school at 18.	Result (vi) F H
Some further education after leaving school at 18.	Result (vi) L H
Graduate degree.	Result (vi) C H
Postgraduate degree.	Result (vi) M H

727 Which of these types of TV programmes do you like the most?

Most of all I like game shows.	Result (i) O O
I couldn't do without soap operas.	Result (i) E O
I especially enjoy police dramas or comedies.	Result (i) V O
My preference is for serious dramas.	Result (i) P O
I enjoy news programmes and documentaries.	Result (i) C O

728 What is your view of chivalry?

I think it's old-fashioned nonsense, to be quite honest.	Result (ii) R R
It's pretty undesirable.	Result (ii) S R
It depends; it's OK sometimes.	Result (ii) H R
It's a desirable quality.	Result (ii) P R
I'd say it's an essential part of life.	Result (ii) N R

729 If you had to choose just one, which of these is your favourite type of music?

I prefer music such as heavy metal or rap.	Result (iii) O O
My favourite is rock or pop music; eg The Beatles.	Result (iii) E O
I particularly enjoy easy-listening music; eg Frank Sinatra.	Result (iii) V O
Jazz would be my number-one choice.	Result (iii) P O
My preference would be for classical music or opera.	Result (iii) C O

730 Which of these activities appeals most?

I'd choose relaxing; sitting on the sofa, for example.	Result (iv) R O
My preference would be for some mild exercise, such as gardening.	Result (iv) S O
Moderate exercise, such as walking, would be my choice.	Result (iv) H O
I would prefer more serious exercise, such as backpacking.	Result (iv) P O
Something strenuous like soccer or running would be my choice.	Result (iv) N O

731 What sort of food do you like?

I really just like traditional, plain food.	Result (v) O R
On the whole I prefer traditional, plain food.	Result (v) E R
I eat exotic food for a change.	Result (v) V R
I enjoy most foods, really.	Result (v) P R
I prefer a wide variety of dishes.	Result (v) C R

732 What level of education have you reached (or do you expect to reach)?

My education ended when I was 16.	Result (vi) I P
No further education after leaving school at 18.	Result (vi) W P
Some further education after leaving school at 18.	Result (vi) Q P
Graduate degree.	Result (vi) O P
Postgraduate degree.	Result (vi) T P

733 **Which of these types of TV programmes do you like the most?**

Most of all I like game shows.	Result (i) O E
I couldn't do without soap operas.	Result (i) E E
I especially enjoy police dramas or comedies.	Result (i) V E
My preference is for serious dramas.	Result (i) P E
I enjoy news programmes and documentaries.	Result (i) C E

734 **What is your view of chivalry?**

I think it's old-fashioned nonsense, to be quite honest.	Result (ii) R S
It's pretty undesirable.	Result (ii) S S
It depends; it's OK sometimes.	Result (ii) H S
It's a desirable quality.	Result (ii) P S
I'd say it's an essential part of life.	Result (ii) N S

735 **If you had to choose just one, which of these is your favourite type of music?**

I prefer music such as heavy metal or rap.	Result (iii) O E
My favourite is rock or pop music; eg The Beatles.	Result (iii) E E
I particularly enjoy easy-listening music; eg Frank Sinatra.	Result (iii) V E
Jazz would be my number-one choice.	Result (iii) P E
My preference would be for classical music or opera.	Result (iii) C E

736 **Which of these activities appeals most?**

I'd choose relaxing; sitting on the sofa, for example.	Result (iv) R E
My preference would be for some mild exercise, such as gardening.	Result (iv) S E
Moderate exercise, such as walking, would be my choice.	Result (iv) H E
I would prefer more serious exercise, such as backpacking.	Result (iv) P E
Something strenuous like soccer or running would be my choice.	Result (iv) N E

737 **What sort of food do you like?**

I really just like traditional, plain food.	Result (v) O S
On the whole I prefer traditional, plain food.	Result (v) E S
I eat exotic food for a change.	Result (v) V S
I enjoy most foods, really.	Result (v) P S
I prefer a wide variety of dishes.	Result (v) C S

738 **What level of education have you reached (or do you expect to reach)?**

My education ended when I was 16.	Result (vi) J P
No further education after leaving school at 18.	Result (vi) D P
Some further education after leaving school at 18.	Result (vi) U P
Graduate degree.	Result (vi) E P
Postgraduate degree.	Result (vi) A P

739 **Which of these types of TV programmes do you like the most?**

Most of all I like game shows.	Result (i) O V
I couldn't do without soap operas.	Result (i) E V
I especially enjoy police dramas or comedies.	Result (i) V V
My preference is for serious dramas.	Result (i) P V
I enjoy news programmes and documentaries.	Result (i) C V

740 **What is your view of chivalry?**

I think it's old-fashioned nonsense, to be quite honest.	Result (ii) R H
It's pretty undesirable.	Result (ii) S H
It depends; it's OK sometimes.	Result (ii) H H
It's a desirable quality.	Result (ii) P H
I'd say it's an essential part of life.	Result (ii) N H

741 **If you had to choose just one, which of these is your favourite type of music?**

I prefer music such as heavy metal or rap.	Result (iii) O V
My favourite is rock or pop music; eg The Beatles.	Result (iii) E V
I particularly enjoy easy-listening music; eg Frank Sinatra.	Result (iii) V V
Jazz would be my number-one choice.	Result (iii) P V
My preference would be for classical music or opera.	Result (iii) C V

742 **Which of these activities appeals most?**

I'd choose relaxing; sitting on the sofa, for example.	Result (iv) R V
My preference would be for some mild exercise, such as gardening.	Result (iv) S V
Moderate exercise, such as walking, would be my choice.	Result (iv) H V
I would prefer more serious exercise, such as backpacking.	Result (iv) P V
Something strenuous like soccer or running would be my choice.	Result (iv) N V

743 **What sort of food do you like?**

I really just like traditional, plain food.	Result (v) O H
On the whole I prefer traditional, plain food.	Result (v) E H
I eat exotic food for a change.	Result (v) V H
I enjoy most foods, really.	Result (v) P H
I prefer a wide variety of dishes.	Result (v) C H

744 **What level of education have you reached (or do you expect to reach)?**

My education ended when I was 16.	Result (vi) X P
No further education after leaving school at 18.	Result (vi) G P
Some further education after leaving school at 18.	Result (vi) K P
Graduate degree.	Result (vi) V P
Postgraduate degree.	Result (vi) B P

745 Which of these types of TV programmes do you like the most?

Most of all I like game shows.	Result (i) O P
I couldn't do without soap operas.	Result (i) E P
I especially enjoy police dramas or comedies.	Result (i) V P
My preference is for serious dramas.	Result (i) P P
I enjoy news programmes and documentaries.	Result (i) C P

746 What is your view of chivalry?

I think it's old-fashioned nonsense, to be quite honest.	Result (ii) R P
It's pretty undesirable.	Result (ii) S P
It depends; it's OK sometimes.	Result (ii) H P
It's a desirable quality.	Result (ii) P P
I'd say it's an essential part of life.	Result (ii) N P

747 If you had to choose just one, which of these is your favourite type of music?

I prefer music such as heavy metal or rap.	Result (iii) O P
My favourite is rock or pop music; eg The Beatles.	Result (iii) E P
I particularly enjoy easy-listening music; eg Frank Sinatra.	Result (iii) V P
Jazz would be my number-one choice.	Result (iii) P P
My preference would be for classical music or opera.	Result (iii) C P

748 Which of these activities appeals most?

I'd choose relaxing; sitting on the sofa, for example.	Result (iv) R P
My preference would be for some mild exercise, such as gardening.	Result (iv) S P
Moderate exercise, such as walking, would be my choice.	Result (iv) H P
I would prefer more serious exercise, such as backpacking.	Result (iv) P P
Something strenuous like soccer or running would be my choice.	Result (iv) N P

749 What sort of food do you like?

I really just like traditional, plain food.	Result (v) O P
On the whole I prefer traditional, plain food.	Result (v) E P
I eat exotic food for a change.	Result (v) V P
I enjoy most foods, really.	Result (v) P P
I prefer a wide variety of dishes.	Result (v) C P

750 What level of education have you reached (or do you expect to reach)?

My education ended when I was 16.	Result (vi) R P
No further education after leaving school at 18.	Result (vi) S P
Some further education after leaving school at 18.	Result (vi) H P
Graduate degree.	Result (vi) P P
Postgraduate degree.	Result (vi) N P

751 Which of these types of TV programmes do you like the most?

Most of all I like game shows.	Result (i) O C
I couldn't do without soap operas.	Result (i) E C
I especially enjoy police dramas or comedies.	Result (i) V C
My preference is for serious dramas.	Result (i) P C
I enjoy news programmes and documentaries.	Result (i) C C

752 What is your view of chivalry?

I think it's old-fashioned nonsense, to be quite honest.	Result (ii) R N
It's pretty undesirable.	Result (ii) S N
It depends; it's OK sometimes.	Result (ii) H N
It's a desirable quality.	Result (ii) P N
I'd say it's an essential part of life.	Result (ii) N N

753 If you had to choose just one, which of these is your favourite type of music?

I prefer music such as heavy metal or rap.	Result (iii) O C
My favourite is rock or pop music; eg The Beatles.	Result (iii) E C
I particularly enjoy easy-listening music; eg Frank Sinatra.	Result (iii) V C
Jazz would be my number-one choice.	Result (iii) P C
My preference would be for classical music or opera.	Result (iii) C C

754 Which of these activities appeals most?

I'd choose relaxing; sitting on the sofa, for example.	Result (iv) R C
My preference would be for some mild exercise, such as gardening.	Result (iv) S C
Moderate exercise, such as walking, would be my choice.	Result (iv) H C
I would prefer more serious exercise, such as backpacking.	Result (iv) P C
Something strenuous like soccer or running would be my choice.	Result (iv) N C

755 What sort of food do you like?

I really just like traditional, plain food.	Result (v) O N
On the whole I prefer traditional, plain food.	Result (v) E N
I eat exotic food for a change.	Result (v) V N
I enjoy most foods, really.	Result (v) P N
I prefer a wide variety of dishes.	Result (v) C N

756 What level of education have you reached (or do you expect to reach)?

My education ended when I was 16.	Result (vi) Y P
No further education after leaving school at 18.	Result (vi) F P
Some further education after leaving school at 18.	Result (vi) L P
Graduate degree.	Result (vi) C P
Postgraduate degree.	Result (vi) M P

757 **Which of these types of TV programmes do you like the most?**

Most of all I like game shows.	Result (i) T O
I couldn't do without soap operas.	Result (i) A O
I especially enjoy police dramas or comedies.	Result (i) B O
My preference is for serious dramas.	Result (i) N O
I enjoy news programmes and documentaries.	Result (i) M O

758 **What is your view of chivalry?**

I think it's old-fashioned nonsense, to be quite honest.	Result (ii) Y R
It's pretty undesirable.	Result (ii) F R
It depends; it's OK sometimes.	Result (ii) L R
It's a desirable quality.	Result (ii) C R
I'd say it's an essential part of life.	Result (ii) M R

759 **If you had to choose just one, which of these is your favourite type of music?**

I prefer music such as heavy metal or rap.	Result (iii) T O
My favourite is rock or pop music; eg The Beatles.	Result (iii) A O
I particularly enjoy easy-listening music; eg Frank Sinatra.	Result (iii) B O
Jazz would be my number-one choice.	Result (iii) N O
My preference would be for classical music or opera.	Result (iii) M O

760 **Which of these activities appeals most?**

I'd choose relaxing; sitting on the sofa, for example.	Result (iv) Y O
My preference would be for some mild exercise, such as gardening.	Result (iv) F O
Moderate exercise, such as walking, would be my choice.	Result (iv) L O
I would prefer more serious exercise, such as backpacking.	Result (iv) C O
Something strenuous like soccer or running would be my choice.	Result (iv) M O

761 **What sort of food do you like?**

I really just like traditional, plain food.	Result (v) O Y
On the whole I prefer traditional, plain food.	Result (v) E Y
I eat exotic food for a change.	Result (v) V Y
I enjoy most foods, really.	Result (v) P Y
I prefer a wide variety of dishes.	Result (v) C Y

762 **What level of education have you reached (or do you expect to reach)?**

My education ended when I was 16.	Result (vi) I N
No further education after leaving school at 18.	Result (vi) W N
Some further education after leaving school at 18.	Result (vi) Q N
Graduate degree.	Result (vi) O N
Postgraduate degree.	Result (vi) T N

763 **Which of these types of TV programmes do you like the most?**

Most of all I like game shows.	Result (i) T E
I couldn't do without soap operas.	Result (i) A E
I especially enjoy police dramas or comedies.	Result (i) B E
My preference is for serious dramas.	Result (i) N E
I enjoy news programmes and documentaries.	Result (i) M E

764 **What is your view of chivalry?**

I think it's old-fashioned nonsense, to be quite honest.	Result (ii) Y S
It's pretty undesirable.	Result (ii) F S
It depends; it's OK sometimes.	Result (ii) L S
It's a desirable quality.	Result (ii) C S
I'd say it's an essential part of life.	Result (ii) M S

765 **If you had to choose just one, which of these is your favourite type of music?**

I prefer music such as heavy metal or rap.	Result (iii) T E
My favourite is rock or pop music; eg The Beatles.	Result (iii) A E
I particularly enjoy easy-listening music; eg Frank Sinatra.	Result (iii) B E
Jazz would be my number-one choice.	Result (iii) N E
My preference would be for classical music or opera.	Result (iii) M E

766 **Which of these activities appeals most?**

I'd choose relaxing; sitting on the sofa, for example.	Result (iv) Y E
My preference would be for some mild exercise, such as gardening.	Result (iv) F E
Moderate exercise, such as walking, would be my choice.	Result (iv) L E
I would prefer more serious exercise, such as backpacking.	Result (iv) C E
Something strenuous like soccer or running would be my choice.	Result (iv) M E

767 **What sort of food do you like?**

I really just like traditional, plain food.	Result (v) O F
On the whole I prefer traditional, plain food.	Result (v) E F
I eat exotic food for a change.	Result (v) V F
I enjoy most foods, really.	Result (v) P F
I prefer a wide variety of dishes.	Result (v) C F

768 **What level of education have you reached (or do you expect to reach)?**

My education ended when I was 16.	Result (vi) J N
No further education after leaving school at 18.	Result (vi) D N
Some further education after leaving school at 18.	Result (vi) U N
Graduate degree.	Result (vi) E N
Postgraduate degree.	Result (vi) A N

769 **Which of these types of TV programmes do you like the most?**

Most of all I like game shows.	Result (i) T V
I couldn't do without soap operas.	Result (i) A V
I especially enjoy police dramas or comedies.	Result (i) B V
My preference is for serious dramas.	Result (i) N V
I enjoy news programmes and documentaries.	Result (i) M V

770 **What is your view of chivalry?**

I think it's old-fashioned nonsense, to be quite honest.	Result (ii) Y H
It's pretty undesirable.	Result (ii) F H
It depends; it's OK sometimes.	Result (ii) L H
It's a desirable quality.	Result (ii) C H
I'd say it's an essential part of life.	Result (ii) M H

771 **If you had to choose just one, which of these is your favourite type of music?**

I prefer music such as heavy metal or rap.	Result (iii) T V
My favourite is rock or pop music; eg The Beatles.	Result (iii) A V
I particularly enjoy easy-listening music; eg Frank Sinatra.	Result (iii) B V
Jazz would be my number-one choice.	Result (iii) N V
My preference would be for classical music or opera.	Result (iii) M V

772 **Which of these activities appeals most?**

I'd choose relaxing; sitting on the sofa, for example.	Result (iv) Y V
My preference would be for some mild exercise, such as gardening.	Result (iv) F V
Moderate exercise, such as walking, would be my choice.	Result (iv) L V
I would prefer more serious exercise, such as backpacking.	Result (iv) C V
Something strenuous like soccer or running would be my choice.	Result (iv) M V

773 **What sort of food do you like?**

I really just like traditional, plain food.	Result (v) O L
On the whole I prefer traditional, plain food.	Result (v) E L
I eat exotic food for a change.	Result (v) V L
I enjoy most foods, really.	Result (v) P L
I prefer a wide variety of dishes.	Result (v) C L

774 **What level of education have you reached (or do you expect to reach)?**

My education ended when I was 16.	Result (vi) X N
No further education after leaving school at 18.	Result (vi) G N
Some further education after leaving school at 18.	Result (vi) K N
Graduate degree.	Result (vi) V N
Postgraduate degree.	Result (vi) B N

775 **Which of these types of TV programmes do you like the most?**

Most of all I like game shows.	Result (i) T P
I couldn't do without soap operas.	Result (i) A P
I especially enjoy police dramas or comedies.	Result (i) B P
My preference is for serious dramas.	Result (i) N P
I enjoy news programmes and documentaries.	Result (i) M P

776 **What is your view of chivalry?**

I think it's old-fashioned nonsense, to be quite honest.	Result (ii) Y P
It's pretty undesirable.	Result (ii) F P
It depends; it's OK sometimes.	Result (ii) L P
It's a desirable quality.	Result (ii) C P
I'd say it's an essential part of life.	Result (ii) M P

777 **If you had to choose just one, which of these is your favourite type of music?**

I prefer music such as heavy metal or rap.	Result (iii) T P
My favourite is rock or pop music; eg The Beatles.	Result (iii) A P
I particularly enjoy easy-listening music; eg Frank Sinatra.	Result (iii) B P
Jazz would be my number-one choice.	Result (iii) N P
My preference would be for classical music or opera.	Result (iii) M P

778 **Which of these activities appeals most?**

I'd choose relaxing; sitting on the sofa, for example.	Result (iv) Y P
My preference would be for some mild exercise, such as gardening.	Result (iv) F P
Moderate exercise, such as walking, would be my choice.	Result (iv) L P
I would prefer more serious exercise, such as backpacking.	Result (iv) C P
Something strenuous like soccer or running would be my choice.	Result (iv) M P

779 **What sort of food do you like?**

I really just like traditional, plain food.	Result (v) O C
On the whole I prefer traditional, plain food.	Result (v) E C
I eat exotic food for a change.	Result (v) V C
I enjoy most foods, really.	Result (v) P C
I prefer a wide variety of dishes.	Result (v) C C

780 **What level of education have you reached (or do you expect to reach)?**

My education ended when I was 16.	Result (vi) R N
No further education after leaving school at 18.	Result (vi) S N
Some further education after leaving school at 18.	Result (vi) H N
Graduate degree.	Result (vi) P N
Postgraduate degree.	Result (vi) N N

781   **Which of these types of TV programmes do you like the most?**

Most of all I like game shows.	Result (i) T C
I couldn't do without soap operas.	Result (i) A C
I especially enjoy police dramas or comedies.	Result (i) B C
My preference is for serious dramas.	Result (i) N C
I enjoy news programmes and documentaries.	Result (i) M C

782   **What is your view of chivalry?**

I think it's old-fashioned nonsense, to be quite honest.	Result (ii) Y N
It's pretty undesirable.	Result (ii) F N
It depends; it's OK sometimes.	Result (ii) L N
It's a desirable quality.	Result (ii) C N
I'd say it's an essential part of life.	Result (ii) M N

783   **If you had to choose just one, which of these is your favourite type of music?**

I prefer music such as heavy metal or rap.	Result (iii) T C
My favourite is rock or pop music; eg The Beatles.	Result (iii) A C
I particularly enjoy easy-listening music; eg Frank Sinatra.	Result (iii) B C
Jazz would be my number-one choice.	Result (iii) N C
My preference would be for classical music or opera.	Result (iii) M C

784   **Which of these activities appeals most?**

I'd choose relaxing; sitting on the sofa, for example.	Result (iv) Y C
My preference would be for some mild exercise, such as gardening.	Result (iv) F C
Moderate exercise, such as walking, would be my choice.	Result (iv) L C
I would prefer more serious exercise, such as backpacking.	Result (iv) C C
Something strenuous like soccer or running would be my choice.	Result (iv) M C

785   **What sort of food do you like?**

I really just like traditional, plain food.	Result (v) O M
On the whole I prefer traditional, plain food.	Result (v) E M
I eat exotic food for a change.	Result (v) V M
I enjoy most foods, really.	Result (v) P M
I prefer a wide variety of dishes.	Result (v) C M

786   **What level of education have you reached (or do you expect to reach)?**

My education ended when I was 16.	Result (vi) Y N
No further education after leaving school at 18.	Result (vi) F N
Some further education after leaving school at 18.	Result (vi) L N
Graduate degree.	Result (vi) C N
Postgraduate degree.	Result (vi) M N

787 **Which of these types of TV programmes do you like the most?**

Most of all I like game shows.	Result (i) I T
I couldn't do without soap operas.	Result (i) J T
I especially enjoy police dramas or comedies.	Result (i) X T
My preference is for serious dramas.	Result (i) R T
I enjoy news programmes and documentaries.	Result (i) Y T

788 **What is your view of chivalry?**

I think it's old-fashioned nonsense, to be quite honest.	Result (ii) I Y
It's pretty undesirable.	Result (ii) W Y
It depends; it's OK sometimes.	Result (ii) Q Y
It's a desirable quality.	Result (ii) O Y
I'd say it's an essential part of life.	Result (ii) T Y

789 **If you had to choose just one, which of these is your favourite type of music?**

I prefer music such as heavy metal or rap.	Result (iii) I T
My favourite is rock or pop music; eg The Beatles.	Result (iii) J T
I particularly enjoy easy-listening music; eg Frank Sinatra.	Result (iii) X T
Jazz would be my number-one choice.	Result (iii) R T
My preference would be for classical music or opera.	Result (iii) Y T

790 **Which of these activities appeals most?**

I'd choose relaxing; sitting on the sofa, for example.	Result (iv) I T
My preference would be for some mild exercise, such as gardening.	Result (iv) W T
Moderate exercise, such as walking, would be my choice.	Result (iv) Q T
I would prefer more serious exercise, such as backpacking.	Result (iv) O T
Something strenuous like soccer or running would be my choice.	Result (iv) T T

791 **What sort of food do you like?**

I really just like traditional, plain food.	Result (v) T I
On the whole I prefer traditional, plain food.	Result (v) A I
I eat exotic food for a change.	Result (v) B I
I enjoy most foods, really.	Result (v) N I
I prefer a wide variety of dishes.	Result (v) M I

792 **What level of education have you reached (or do you expect to reach)?**

My education ended when I was 16.	Result (vi) I Y
No further education after leaving school at 18.	Result (vi) W Y
Some further education after leaving school at 18.	Result (vi) Q Y
Graduate degree.	Result (vi) O Y
Postgraduate degree.	Result (vi) T Y

793 **Which of these types of TV programmes do you like the most?**

Most of all I like game shows.	Result (i) I A
I couldn't do without soap operas.	Result (i) J A
I especially enjoy police dramas or comedies.	Result (i) X A
My preference is for serious dramas.	Result (i) R A
I enjoy news programmes and documentaries.	Result (i) Y A

794 **What is your view of chivalry?**

I think it's old-fashioned nonsense, to be quite honest.	Result (ii) I F
It's pretty undesirable.	Result (ii) W F
It depends; it's OK sometimes.	Result (ii) Q F
It's a desirable quality.	Result (ii) O F
I'd say it's an essential part of life.	Result (ii) T F

795 **If you had to choose just one, which of these is your favourite type of music?**

I prefer music such as heavy metal or rap.	Result (iii) I A
My favourite is rock or pop music; eg The Beatles.	Result (iii) J A
I particularly enjoy easy-listening music; eg Frank Sinatra.	Result (iii) X A
Jazz would be my number-one choice.	Result (iii) R A
My preference would be for classical music or opera.	Result (iii) Y A

796 **Which of these activities appeals most?**

I'd choose relaxing; sitting on the sofa, for example.	Result (iv) I A
My preference would be for some mild exercise, such as gardening.	Result (iv) W A
Moderate exercise, such as walking, would be my choice.	Result (iv) Q A
I would prefer more serious exercise, such as backpacking.	Result (iv) O A
Something strenuous like soccer or running would be my choice.	Result (iv) T A

797 **What sort of food do you like?**

I really just like traditional, plain food.	Result (v) T W
On the whole I prefer traditional, plain food.	Result (v) A W
I eat exotic food for a change.	Result (v) B W
I enjoy most foods, really.	Result (v) N W
I prefer a wide variety of dishes.	Result (v) M W

798 **What level of education have you reached (or do you expect to reach)?**

My education ended when I was 16.	Result (vi) J Y
No further education after leaving school at 18.	Result (vi) D Y
Some further education after leaving school at 18.	Result (vi) U Y
Graduate degree.	Result (vi) E Y
Postgraduate degree.	Result (vi) A Y

799 **Which of these types of TV programmes do you like the most?**

Most of all I like game shows.	Result (i) I B
I couldn't do without soap operas.	Result (i) J B
I especially enjoy police dramas or comedies.	Result (i) X B
My preference is for serious dramas.	Result (i) R B
I enjoy news programmes and documentaries.	Result (i) Y B

800 **What is your view of chivalry?**

I think it's old-fashioned nonsense, to be quite honest.	Result (ii) I L
It's pretty undesirable.	Result (ii) W L
It depends; it's OK sometimes.	Result (ii) Q L
It's a desirable quality.	Result (ii) O L
I'd say it's an essential part of life.	Result (ii) T L

801 **If you had to choose just one, which of these is your favourite type of music?**

I prefer music such as heavy metal or rap.	Result (iii) I B
My favourite is rock or pop music; eg The Beatles.	Result (iii) J B
I particularly enjoy easy-listening music; eg Frank Sinatra.	Result (iii) X B
Jazz would be my number-one choice.	Result (iii) R B
My preference would be for classical music or opera.	Result (iii) Y B

802 **Which of these activities appeals most?**

I'd choose relaxing; sitting on the sofa, for example.	Result (iv) I B
My preference would be for some mild exercise, such as gardening.	Result (iv) W B
Moderate exercise, such as walking, would be my choice.	Result (iv) Q B
I would prefer more serious exercise, such as backpacking.	Result (iv) O B
Something strenuous like soccer or running would be my choice.	Result (iv) T B

803 **What sort of food do you like?**

I really just like traditional, plain food.	Result (v) T Q
On the whole I prefer traditional, plain food.	Result (v) A Q
I eat exotic food for a change.	Result (v) B Q
I enjoy most foods, really.	Result (v) N Q
I prefer a wide variety of dishes.	Result (v) M Q

804 **What level of education have you reached (or do you expect to reach)?**

My education ended when I was 16.	Result (vi) X Y
No further education after leaving school at 18.	Result (vi) G Y
Some further education after leaving school at 18.	Result (vi) K Y
Graduate degree.	Result (vi) V Y
Postgraduate degree.	Result (vi) B Y

805 Which of these types of TV programmes do you like the most?

Most of all I like game shows.	Result (i) I N
I couldn't do without soap operas.	Result (i) J N
I especially enjoy police dramas or comedies.	Result (i) X N
My preference is for serious dramas.	Result (i) R N
I enjoy news programmes and documentaries.	Result (i) Y N

806 What is your view of chivalry?

I think it's old-fashioned nonsense, to be quite honest.	Result (ii) I C
It's pretty undesirable.	Result (ii) W C
It depends; it's OK sometimes.	Result (ii) Q C
It's a desirable quality.	Result (ii) O C
I'd say it's an essential part of life.	Result (ii) T C

807 If you had to choose just one, which of these is your favourite type of music?

I prefer music such as heavy metal or rap.	Result (iii) I N
My favourite is rock or pop music; eg The Beatles.	Result (iii) J N
I particularly enjoy easy-listening music; eg Frank Sinatra.	Result (iii) X N
Jazz would be my number-one choice.	Result (iii) R N
My preference would be for classical music or opera.	Result (iii) Y N

808 Which of these activities appeals most?

I'd choose relaxing; sitting on the sofa, for example.	Result (iv) I N
My preference would be for some mild exercise, such as gardening.	Result (iv) W N
Moderate exercise, such as walking, would be my choice.	Result (iv) Q N
I would prefer more serious exercise, such as backpacking.	Result (iv) O N
Something strenuous like soccer or running would be my choice.	Result (iv) T N

809 What sort of food do you like?

I really just like traditional, plain food.	Result (v) T O
On the whole I prefer traditional, plain food.	Result (v) A O
I eat exotic food for a change.	Result (v) B O
I enjoy most foods, really.	Result (v) N O
I prefer a wide variety of dishes.	Result (v) M O

810 What level of education have you reached (or do you expect to reach)?

My education ended when I was 16.	Result (vi) R Y
No further education after leaving school at 18.	Result (vi) S Y
Some further education after leaving school at 18.	Result (vi) H Y
Graduate degree.	Result (vi) P Y
Postgraduate degree.	Result (vi) N Y

811 **Which of these types of TV programmes do you like the most?**

Most of all I like game shows.	Result (i) I M
I couldn't do without soap operas.	Result (i) J M
I especially enjoy police dramas or comedies.	Result (i) X M
My preference is for serious dramas.	Result (i) R M
I enjoy news programmes and documentaries.	Result (i) Y M

812 **What is your view of chivalry?**

I think it's old-fashioned nonsense, to be quite honest.	Result (ii) I M
It's pretty undesirable.	Result (ii) W M
It depends; it's OK sometimes.	Result (ii) Q M
It's a desirable quality.	Result (ii) O M
I'd say it's an essential part of life.	Result (ii) T M

813 **If you had to choose just one, which of these is your favourite type of music?**

I prefer music such as heavy metal or rap.	Result (iii) I M
My favourite is rock or pop music; eg The Beatles.	Result (iii) J M
I particularly enjoy easy-listening music; eg Frank Sinatra.	Result (iii) X M
Jazz would be my number-one choice.	Result (iii) R M
My preference would be for classical music or opera.	Result (iii) Y M

814 **Which of these activities appeals most?**

I'd choose relaxing; sitting on the sofa, for example.	Result (iv) I M
My preference would be for some mild exercise, such as gardening.	Result (iv) W M
Moderate exercise, such as walking, would be my choice.	Result (iv) Q M
I would prefer more serious exercise, such as backpacking.	Result (iv) O M
Something strenuous like soccer or running would be my choice.	Result (iv) T M

815 **What sort of food do you like?**

I really just like traditional, plain food.	Result (v) T T
On the whole I prefer traditional, plain food.	Result (v) A T
I eat exotic food for a change.	Result (v) B T
I enjoy most foods, really.	Result (v) N T
I prefer a wide variety of dishes.	Result (v) M T

816 **What level of education have you reached (or do you expect to reach)?**

My education ended when I was 16.	Result (vi) Y Y
No further education after leaving school at 18.	Result (vi) F Y
Some further education after leaving school at 18.	Result (vi) L Y
Graduate degree.	Result (vi) C Y
Postgraduate degree.	Result (vi) M Y

817 **Which of these types of TV programmes do you like the most?**

Most of all I like game shows.	Result (i) W T
I couldn't do without soap operas.	Result (i) D T
I especially enjoy police dramas or comedies.	Result (i) G T
My preference is for serious dramas.	Result (i) S T
I enjoy news programmes and documentaries.	Result (i) F T

818 **What is your view of chivalry?**

I think it's old-fashioned nonsense, to be quite honest.	Result (ii) J Y
It's pretty undesirable.	Result (ii) D Y
It depends; it's OK sometimes.	Result (ii) U Y
It's a desirable quality.	Result (ii) E Y
I'd say it's an essential part of life.	Result (ii) A Y

819 **If you had to choose just one, which of these is your favourite type of music?**

I prefer music such as heavy metal or rap.	Result (iii) W T
My favourite is rock or pop music; eg The Beatles.	Result (iii) D T
I particularly enjoy easy-listening music; eg Frank Sinatra.	Result (iii) G T
Jazz would be my number-one choice.	Result (iii) S T
My preference would be for classical music or opera.	Result (iii) F T

820 **Which of these activities appeals most?**

I'd choose relaxing; sitting on the sofa, for example.	Result (iv) J T
My preference would be for some mild exercise, such as gardening.	Result (iv) D T
Moderate exercise, such as walking, would be my choice.	Result (iv) U T
I would prefer more serious exercise, such as backpacking.	Result (iv) E T
Something strenuous like soccer or running would be my choice.	Result (iv) A T

821 **What sort of food do you like?**

I really just like traditional, plain food.	Result (v) T J
On the whole I prefer traditional, plain food.	Result (v) A J
I eat exotic food for a change.	Result (v) B J
I enjoy most foods, really.	Result (v) N J
I prefer a wide variety of dishes.	Result (v) M J

822 **What level of education have you reached (or do you expect to reach)?**

My education ended when I was 16.	Result (vi) I F
No further education after leaving school at 18.	Result (vi) W F
Some further education after leaving school at 18.	Result (vi) Q F
Graduate degree.	Result (vi) O F
Postgraduate degree.	Result (vi) T F

823 Which of these types of TV programmes do you like the most?

Most of all I like game shows.	Result (i) W A
I couldn't do without soap operas.	Result (i) D A
I especially enjoy police dramas or comedies.	Result (i) G A
My preference is for serious dramas.	Result (i) S A
I enjoy news programmes and documentaries.	Result (i) F A

824 What is your view of chivalry?

I think it's old-fashioned nonsense, to be quite honest.	Result (ii) J F
It's pretty undesirable.	Result (ii) D F
It depends; it's OK sometimes.	Result (ii) U F
It's a desirable quality.	Result (ii) E F
I'd say it's an essential part of life.	Result (ii) A F

825 If you had to choose just one, which of these is your favourite type of music?

I prefer music such as heavy metal or rap.	Result (iii) W A
My favourite is rock or pop music; eg The Beatles.	Result (iii) D A
I particularly enjoy easy-listening music; eg Frank Sinatra.	Result (iii) G A
Jazz would be my number-one choice.	Result (iii) S A
My preference would be for classical music or opera.	Result (iii) F A

826 Which of these activities appeals most?

I'd choose relaxing; sitting on the sofa, for example.	Result (iv) J A
My preference would be for some mild exercise, such as gardening.	Result (iv) D A
Moderate exercise, such as walking, would be my choice.	Result (iv) U A
I would prefer more serious exercise, such as backpacking.	Result (iv) E A
Something strenuous like soccer or running would be my choice.	Result (iv) A A

827 What sort of food do you like?

I really just like traditional, plain food.	Result (v) T D
On the whole I prefer traditional, plain food.	Result (v) A D
I eat exotic food for a change.	Result (v) B D
I enjoy most foods, really.	Result (v) N D
I prefer a wide variety of dishes.	Result (v) M D

828 What level of education have you reached (or do you expect to reach)?

My education ended when I was 16.	Result (vi) J F
No further education after leaving school at 18.	Result (vi) D F
Some further education after leaving school at 18.	Result (vi) U F
Graduate degree.	Result (vi) E F
Postgraduate degree.	Result (vi) A F

829 **Which of these types of TV programmes do you like the most?**

Most of all I like game shows.	Result (i) W B
I couldn't do without soap operas.	Result (i) D B
I especially enjoy police dramas or comedies.	Result (i) G B
My preference is for serious dramas.	Result (i) S B
I enjoy news programmes and documentaries.	Result (i) F B

830 **What is your view of chivalry?**

I think it's old-fashioned nonsense, to be quite honest.	Result (ii) J L
It's pretty undesirable.	Result (ii) D L
It depends; it's OK sometimes.	Result (ii) U L
It's a desirable quality.	Result (ii) E L
I'd say it's an essential part of life.	Result (ii) A L

831 **If you had to choose just one, which of these is your favourite type of music?**

I prefer music such as heavy metal or rap.	Result (iii) W B
My favourite is rock or pop music; eg The Beatles.	Result (iii) D B
I particularly enjoy easy-listening music; eg Frank Sinatra.	Result (iii) G B
Jazz would be my number-one choice.	Result (iii) S B
My preference would be for classical music or opera.	Result (iii) F B

832 **Which of these activities appeals most?**

I'd choose relaxing; sitting on the sofa, for example.	Result (iv) J B
My preference would be for some mild exercise, such as gardening.	Result (iv) D B
Moderate exercise, such as walking, would be my choice.	Result (iv) U B
I would prefer more serious exercise, such as backpacking.	Result (iv) E B
Something strenuous like soccer or running would be my choice.	Result (iv) A B

833 **What sort of food do you like?**

I really just like traditional, plain food.	Result (v) T U
On the whole I prefer traditional, plain food.	Result (v) A U
I eat exotic food for a change.	Result (v) B U
I enjoy most foods, really.	Result (v) N U
I prefer a wide variety of dishes.	Result (v) M U

834 **What level of education have you reached (or do you expect to reach)?**

My education ended when I was 16.	Result (vi) X F
No further education after leaving school at 18.	Result (vi) G F
Some further education after leaving school at 18.	Result (vi) K F
Graduate degree.	Result (vi) V F
Postgraduate degree.	Result (vi) B F

835 **Which of these types of TV programmes do you like the most?**

Most of all I like game shows.	Result (i) W N
I couldn't do without soap operas.	Result (i) D N
I especially enjoy police dramas or comedies.	Result (i) G N
My preference is for serious dramas.	Result (i) S N
I enjoy news programmes and documentaries.	Result (i) F N

836 **What is your view of chivalry?**

I think it's old-fashioned nonsense, to be quite honest.	Result (ii) J C
It's pretty undesirable.	Result (ii) D C
It depends; it's OK sometimes.	Result (ii) U C
It's a desirable quality.	Result (ii) E C
I'd say it's an essential part of life.	Result (ii) A C

837 **If you had to choose just one, which of these is your favourite type of music?**

I prefer music such as heavy metal or rap.	Result (iii) W N
My favourite is rock or pop music; eg The Beatles.	Result (iii) D N
I particularly enjoy easy-listening music; eg Frank Sinatra.	Result (iii) G N
Jazz would be my number-one choice.	Result (iii) S N
My preference would be for classical music or opera.	Result (iii) F N

838 **Which of these activities appeals most?**

I'd choose relaxing; sitting on the sofa, for example.	Result (iv) J N
My preference would be for some mild exercise, such as gardening.	Result (iv) D N
Moderate exercise, such as walking, would be my choice.	Result (iv) U N
I would prefer more serious exercise, such as backpacking.	Result (iv) E N
Something strenuous like soccer or running would be my choice.	Result (iv) A N

839 **What sort of food do you like?**

I really just like traditional, plain food.	Result (v) T E
On the whole I prefer traditional, plain food.	Result (v) A E
I eat exotic food for a change.	Result (v) B E
I enjoy most foods, really.	Result (v) N E
I prefer a wide variety of dishes.	Result (v) M E

840 **What level of education have you reached (or do you expect to reach)?**

My education ended when I was 16.	Result (vi) R F
No further education after leaving school at 18.	Result (vi) S F
Some further education after leaving school at 18.	Result (vi) H F
Graduate degree.	Result (vi) P F
Postgraduate degree.	Result (vi) N F

841 **Which of these types of TV programmes do you like the most?**

Most of all I like game shows.	Result (i) W M
I couldn't do without soap operas.	Result (i) D M
I especially enjoy police dramas or comedies.	Result (i) G M
My preference is for serious dramas.	Result (i) S M
I enjoy news programmes and documentaries.	Result (i) F M

842 **What is your view of chivalry?**

I think it's old-fashioned nonsense, to be quite honest.	Result (ii) J M
It's pretty undesirable.	Result (ii) D M
It depends; it's OK sometimes.	Result (ii) U M
It's a desirable quality.	Result (ii) E M
I'd say it's an essential part of life.	Result (ii) A M

843 **If you had to choose just one, which of these is your favourite type of music?**

I prefer music such as heavy metal or rap.	Result (iii) W M
My favourite is rock or pop music; eg The Beatles.	Result (iii) D M
I particularly enjoy easy-listening music; eg Frank Sinatra.	Result (iii) G M
Jazz would be my number-one choice.	Result (iii) S M
My preference would be for classical music or opera.	Result (iii) F M

844 **Which of these activities appeals most?**

I'd choose relaxing; sitting on the sofa, for example.	Result (iv) J M
My preference would be for some mild exercise, such as gardening.	Result (iv) D M
Moderate exercise, such as walking, would be my choice.	Result (iv) U M
I would prefer more serious exercise, such as backpacking.	Result (iv) E M
Something strenuous like soccer or running would be my choice.	Result (iv) A M

845 **What sort of food do you like?**

I really just like traditional, plain food.	Result (v) T A
On the whole I prefer traditional, plain food.	Result (v) A A
I eat exotic food for a change.	Result (v) B A
I enjoy most foods, really.	Result (v) N A
I prefer a wide variety of dishes.	Result (v) M A

846 **What level of education have you reached (or do you expect to reach)?**

My education ended when I was 16.	Result (vi) Y F
No further education after leaving school at 18.	Result (vi) F F
Some further education after leaving school at 18.	Result (vi) L F
Graduate degree.	Result (vi) C F
Postgraduate degree.	Result (vi) M F

847 **Which of these types of TV programmes do you like the most?**

Most of all I like game shows.	Result (i) Q T
I couldn't do without soap operas.	Result (i) U T
I especially enjoy police dramas or comedies.	Result (i) K T
My preference is for serious dramas.	Result (i) H T
I enjoy news programmes and documentaries.	Result (i) L T

848 **What is your view of chivalry?**

I think it's old-fashioned nonsense, to be quite honest.	Result (ii) X Y
It's pretty undesirable.	Result (ii) G Y
It depends; it's OK sometimes.	Result (ii) K Y
It's a desirable quality.	Result (ii) V Y
I'd say it's an essential part of life.	Result (ii) B Y

849 **If you had to choose just one, which of these is your favourite type of music?**

I prefer music such as heavy metal or rap.	Result (iii) Q T
My favourite is rock or pop music; eg The Beatles.	Result (iii) U T
I particularly enjoy easy-listening music; eg Frank Sinatra.	Result (iii) K T
Jazz would be my number-one choice.	Result (iii) H T
My preference would be for classical music or opera.	Result (iii) L T

850 **Which of these activities appeals most?**

I'd choose relaxing; sitting on the sofa, for example.	Result (iv) X T
My preference would be for some mild exercise, such as gardening.	Result (iv) G T
Moderate exercise, such as walking, would be my choice.	Result (iv) K T
I would prefer more serious exercise, such as backpacking.	Result (iv) V T
Something strenuous like soccer or running would be my choice.	Result (iv) B T

851 **What sort of food do you like?**

I really just like traditional, plain food.	Result (v) T X
On the whole I prefer traditional, plain food.	Result (v) A X
I eat exotic food for a change.	Result (v) B X
I enjoy most foods, really.	Result (v) N X
I prefer a wide variety of dishes.	Result (v) M X

852 **What level of education have you reached (or do you expect to reach)?**

My education ended when I was 16.	Result (vi) I L
No further education after leaving school at 18.	Result (vi) W L
Some further education after leaving school at 18.	Result (vi) Q L
Graduate degree.	Result (vi) O L
Postgraduate degree.	Result (vi) T L

853 **Which of these types of TV programmes do you like the most?**

Most of all I like game shows.	Result (i) Q A
I couldn't do without soap operas.	Result (i) U A
I especially enjoy police dramas or comedies.	Result (i) K A
My preference is for serious dramas.	Result (i) H A
I enjoy news programmes and documentaries.	Result (i) L A

854 **What is your view of chivalry?**

I think it's old-fashioned nonsense, to be quite honest.	Result (ii) X F
It's pretty undesirable.	Result (ii) G F
It depends; it's OK sometimes.	Result (ii) K F
It's a desirable quality.	Result (ii) V F
I'd say it's an essential part of life.	Result (ii) B F

855 **If you had to choose just one, which of these is your favourite type of music?**

I prefer music such as heavy metal or rap.	Result (iii) Q A
My favourite is rock or pop music; eg The Beatles.	Result (iii) U A
I particularly enjoy easy-listening music; eg Frank Sinatra.	Result (iii) K A
Jazz would be my number-one choice.	Result (iii) H A
My preference would be for classical music or opera.	Result (iii) L A

856 **Which of these activities appeals most?**

I'd choose relaxing; sitting on the sofa, for example.	Result (iv) X A
My preference would be for some mild exercise, such as gardening.	Result (iv) G A
Moderate exercise, such as walking, would be my choice.	Result (iv) K A
I would prefer more serious exercise, such as backpacking.	Result (iv) V A
Something strenuous like soccer or running would be my choice.	Result (iv) B A

857 **What sort of food do you like?**

I really just like traditional, plain food.	Result (v) T G
On the whole I prefer traditional, plain food.	Result (v) A G
I eat exotic food for a change.	Result (v) B G
I enjoy most foods, really.	Result (v) N G
I prefer a wide variety of dishes.	Result (v) M G

858 **What level of education have you reached (or do you expect to reach)?**

My education ended when I was 16.	Result (vi) J L
No further education after leaving school at 18.	Result (vi) D L
Some further education after leaving school at 18.	Result (vi) U L
Graduate degree.	Result (vi) E L
Postgraduate degree.	Result (vi) A L

859   **Which of these types of TV programmes do you like the most?**

Most of all I like game shows.	Result (i) Q B
I couldn't do without soap operas.	Result (i) U B
I especially enjoy police dramas or comedies.	Result (i) K B
My preference is for serious dramas.	Result (i) H B
I enjoy news programmes and documentaries.	Result (i) L B

860   **What is your view of chivalry?**

I think it's old-fashioned nonsense, to be quite honest.	Result (ii) X L
It's pretty undesirable.	Result (ii) G L
It depends; it's OK sometimes.	Result (ii) K L
It's a desirable quality.	Result (ii) V L
I'd say it's an essential part of life.	Result (ii) B L

861   **If you had to choose just one, which of these is your favourite type of music?**

I prefer music such as heavy metal or rap.	Result (iii) Q B
My favourite is rock or pop music; eg The Beatles.	Result (iii) U B
I particularly enjoy easy-listening music; eg Frank Sinatra.	Result (iii) K B
Jazz would be my number-one choice.	Result (iii) H B
My preference would be for classical music or opera.	Result (iii) L B

862   **Which of these activities appeals most?**

I'd choose relaxing; sitting on the sofa, for example.	Result (iv) X B
My preference would be for some mild exercise, such as gardening.	Result (iv) G B
Moderate exercise, such as walking, would be my choice.	Result (iv) K B
I would prefer more serious exercise, such as backpacking.	Result (iv) V B
Something strenuous like soccer or running would be my choice.	Result (iv) B B

863   **What sort of food do you like?**

I really just like traditional, plain food.	Result (v) T K
On the whole I prefer traditional, plain food.	Result (v) A K
I eat exotic food for a change.	Result (v) B K
I enjoy most foods, really.	Result (v) N K
I prefer a wide variety of dishes.	Result (v) M K

864   **What level of education have you reached (or do you expect to reach)?**

My education ended when I was 16.	Result (vi) X L
No further education after leaving school at 18.	Result (vi) G L
Some further education after leaving school at 18.	Result (vi) K L
Graduate degree.	Result (vi) V L
Postgraduate degree.	Result (vi) B L

865 **Which of these types of TV programmes do you like the most?**

Most of all I like game shows.	Result (i) Q N
I couldn't do without soap operas.	Result (i) U N
I especially enjoy police dramas or comedies.	Result (i) K N
My preference is for serious dramas.	Result (i) H N
I enjoy news programmes and documentaries.	Result (i) L N

866 **What is your view of chivalry?**

I think it's old-fashioned nonsense, to be quite honest.	Result (ii) X C
It's pretty undesirable.	Result (ii) G C
It depends; it's OK sometimes.	Result (ii) K C
It's a desirable quality.	Result (ii) V C
I'd say it's an essential part of life.	Result (ii) B C

867 **If you had to choose just one, which of these is your favourite type of music?**

I prefer music such as heavy metal or rap.	Result (iii) Q N
My favourite is rock or pop music; eg The Beatles.	Result (iii) U N
I particularly enjoy easy-listening music; eg Frank Sinatra.	Result (iii) K N
Jazz would be my number-one choice.	Result (iii) H N
My preference would be for classical music or opera.	Result (iii) L N

868 **Which of these activities appeals most?**

I'd choose relaxing; sitting on the sofa, for example.	Result (iv) X N
My preference would be for some mild exercise, such as gardening.	Result (iv) G N
Moderate exercise, such as walking, would be my choice.	Result (iv) K N
I would prefer more serious exercise, such as backpacking.	Result (iv) V N
Something strenuous like soccer or running would be my choice.	Result (iv) B N

869 **What sort of food do you like?**

I really just like traditional, plain food.	Result (v) T V
On the whole I prefer traditional, plain food.	Result (v) A V
I eat exotic food for a change.	Result (v) B V
I enjoy most foods, really.	Result (v) N V
I prefer a wide variety of dishes.	Result (v) M V

870 **What level of education have you reached (or do you expect to reach)?**

My education ended when I was 16.	Result (vi) R L
No further education after leaving school at 18.	Result (vi) S L
Some further education after leaving school at 18.	Result (vi) H L
Graduate degree.	Result (vi) P L
Postgraduate degree.	Result (vi) N L

871 Which of these types of TV programmes do you like the most?

Most of all I like game shows.	Result (i) Q M
I couldn't do without soap operas.	Result (i) U M
I especially enjoy police dramas or comedies.	Result (i) K M
My preference is for serious dramas.	Result (i) H M
I enjoy news programmes and documentaries.	Result (i) L M

872 What is your view of chivalry?

I think it's old-fashioned nonsense, to be quite honest.	Result (ii) X M
It's pretty undesirable.	Result (ii) G M
It depends; it's OK sometimes.	Result (ii) K M
It's a desirable quality.	Result (ii) V M
I'd say it's an essential part of life.	Result (ii) B M

873 If you had to choose just one, which of these is your favourite type of music?

I prefer music such as heavy metal or rap.	Result (iii) Q M
My favourite is rock or pop music; eg The Beatles.	Result (iii) U M
I particularly enjoy easy-listening music; eg Frank Sinatra.	Result (iii) K M
Jazz would be my number-one choice.	Result (iii) H M
My preference would be for classical music or opera.	Result (iii) L M

874 Which of these activities appeals most?

I'd choose relaxing; sitting on the sofa, for example.	Result (iv) X M
My preference would be for some mild exercise, such as gardening.	Result (iv) G M
Moderate exercise, such as walking, would be my choice.	Result (iv) K M
I would prefer more serious exercise, such as backpacking.	Result (iv) V M
Something strenuous like soccer or running would be my choice.	Result (iv) B M

875 What sort of food do you like?

I really just like traditional, plain food.	Result (v) T B
On the whole I prefer traditional, plain food.	Result (v) A B
I eat exotic food for a change.	Result (v) B B
I enjoy most foods, really.	Result (v) N B
I prefer a wide variety of dishes.	Result (v) M B

876 What level of education have you reached (or do you expect to reach)?

My education ended when I was 16.	Result (vi) Y L
No further education after leaving school at 18.	Result (vi) F L
Some further education after leaving school at 18.	Result (vi) L L
Graduate degree.	Result (vi) C L
Postgraduate degree.	Result (vi) M L

877 **Which of these types of TV programmes do you like the most?**

Most of all I like game shows.	Result (i) O T
I couldn't do without soap operas.	Result (i) E T
I especially enjoy police dramas or comedies.	Result (i) V T
My preference is for serious dramas.	Result (i) P T
I enjoy news programmes and documentaries.	Result (i) C T

878 **What is your view of chivalry?**

I think it's old-fashioned nonsense, to be quite honest.	Result (ii) R Y
It's pretty undesirable.	Result (ii) S Y
It depends; it's OK sometimes.	Result (ii) H Y
It's a desirable quality.	Result (ii) P Y
I'd say it's an essential part of life.	Result (ii) N Y

879 **If you had to choose just one, which of these is your favourite type of music?**

I prefer music such as heavy metal or rap.	Result (iii) O T
My favourite is rock or pop music; eg The Beatles.	Result (iii) E T
I particularly enjoy easy-listening music; eg Frank Sinatra.	Result (iii) V T
Jazz would be my number-one choice.	Result (iii) P T
My preference would be for classical music or opera.	Result (iii) C T

880 **Which of these activities appeals most?**

I'd choose relaxing; sitting on the sofa, for example.	Result (iv) R T
My preference would be for some mild exercise, such as gardening.	Result (iv) S T
Moderate exercise, such as walking, would be my choice.	Result (iv) H T
I would prefer more serious exercise, such as backpacking.	Result (iv) P T
Something strenuous like soccer or running would be my choice.	Result (iv) N T

881 **What sort of food do you like?**

I really just like traditional, plain food.	Result (v) T R
On the whole I prefer traditional, plain food.	Result (v) A R
I eat exotic food for a change.	Result (v) B R
I enjoy most foods, really.	Result (v) N R
I prefer a wide variety of dishes.	Result (v) M R

882 **What level of education have you reached (or do you expect to reach)?**

My education ended when I was 16.	Result (vi) I C
No further education after leaving school at 18.	Result (vi) W C
Some further education after leaving school at 18.	Result (vi) Q C
Graduate degree.	Result (vi) O C
Postgraduate degree.	Result (vi) T C

883 **Which of these types of TV programmes do you like the most?**

Most of all I like game shows.	Result (i) O A
I couldn't do without soap operas.	Result (i) E A
I especially enjoy police dramas or comedies.	Result (i) V A
My preference is for serious dramas.	Result (i) P A
I enjoy news programmes and documentaries.	Result (i) C A

884 **What is your view of chivalry?**

I think it's old-fashioned nonsense, to be quite honest.	Result (ii) R F
It's pretty undesirable.	Result (ii) S F
It depends; it's OK sometimes.	Result (ii) H F
It's a desirable quality.	Result (ii) P F
I'd say it's an essential part of life.	Result (ii) N F

885 **If you had to choose just one, which of these is your favourite type of music?**

I prefer music such as heavy metal or rap.	Result (iii) O A
My favourite is rock or pop music; eg The Beatles.	Result (iii) E A
I particularly enjoy easy-listening music; eg Frank Sinatra.	Result (iii) V A
Jazz would be my number-one choice.	Result (iii) P A
My preference would be for classical music or opera.	Result (iii) C A

886 **Which of these activities appeals most?**

I'd choose relaxing; sitting on the sofa, for example.	Result (iv) R A
My preference would be for some mild exercise, such as gardening.	Result (iv) S A
Moderate exercise, such as walking, would be my choice.	Result (iv) H A
I would prefer more serious exercise, such as backpacking.	Result (iv) P A
Something strenuous like soccer or running would be my choice.	Result (iv) N A

887 **What sort of food do you like?**

I really just like traditional, plain food.	Result (v) T S
On the whole I prefer traditional, plain food.	Result (v) A S
I eat exotic food for a change.	Result (v) B S
I enjoy most foods, really.	Result (v) N S
I prefer a wide variety of dishes.	Result (v) M S

888 **What level of education have you reached (or do you expect to reach)?**

My education ended when I was 16.	Result (vi) J C
No further education after leaving school at 18.	Result (vi) D C
Some further education after leaving school at 18.	Result (vi) U C
Graduate degree.	Result (vi) E C
Postgraduate degree.	Result (vi) A C

889 **Which of these types of TV programmes do you like the most?**

Most of all I like game shows.	Result (i) O B
I couldn't do without soap operas.	Result (i) E B
I especially enjoy police dramas or comedies.	Result (i) V B
My preference is for serious dramas.	Result (i) P B
I enjoy news programmes and documentaries.	Result (i) C B

890 **What is your view of chivalry?**

I think it's old-fashioned nonsense, to be quite honest.	Result (ii) R L
It's pretty undesirable.	Result (ii) S L
It depends; it's OK sometimes.	Result (ii) H L
It's a desirable quality.	Result (ii) P L
I'd say it's an essential part of life.	Result (ii) N L

891 **If you had to choose just one, which of these is your favourite type of music?**

I prefer music such as heavy metal or rap.	Result (iii) O B
My favourite is rock or pop music; eg The Beatles.	Result (iii) E B
I particularly enjoy easy-listening music; eg Frank Sinatra.	Result (iii) V B
Jazz would be my number-one choice.	Result (iii) P B
My preference would be for classical music or opera.	Result (iii) C B

892 **Which of these activities appeals most?**

I'd choose relaxing; sitting on the sofa, for example.	Result (iv) R B
My preference would be for some mild exercise, such as gardening.	Result (iv) S B
Moderate exercise, such as walking, would be my choice.	Result (iv) H B
I would prefer more serious exercise, such as backpacking.	Result (iv) P B
Something strenuous like soccer or running would be my choice.	Result (iv) N B

893 **What sort of food do you like?**

I really just like traditional, plain food.	Result (v) T H
On the whole I prefer traditional, plain food.	Result (v) A H
I eat exotic food for a change.	Result (v) B H
I enjoy most foods, really.	Result (v) N H
I prefer a wide variety of dishes.	Result (v) M H

894 **What level of education have you reached (or do you expect to reach)?**

My education ended when I was 16.	Result (vi) X C
No further education after leaving school at 18.	Result (vi) G C
Some further education after leaving school at 18.	Result (vi) K C
Graduate degree.	Result (vi) V C
Postgraduate degree.	Result (vi) B C

CQ

895 **Which of these types of TV programmes do you like the most?**

Most of all I like game shows.	Result (i) O N
I couldn't do without soap operas.	Result (i) E N
I especially enjoy police dramas or comedies.	Result (i) V N
My preference is for serious dramas.	Result (i) P N
I enjoy news programmes and documentaries.	Result (i) C N

896 **What is your view of chivalry?**

I think it's old-fashioned nonsense, to be quite honest.	Result (ii) R C
It's pretty undesirable.	Result (ii) S C
It depends; it's OK sometimes.	Result (ii) H C
It's a desirable quality.	Result (ii) P C
I'd say it's an essential part of life.	Result (ii) N C

897 **If you had to choose just one, which of these is your favourite type of music?**

I prefer music such as heavy metal or rap.	Result (iii) O N
My favourite is rock or pop music; eg The Beatles.	Result (iii) E N
I particularly enjoy easy-listening music; eg Frank Sinatra.	Result (iii) V N
Jazz would be my number-one choice.	Result (iii) P N
My preference would be for classical music or opera.	Result (iii) C N

898 **Which of these activities appeals most?**

I'd choose relaxing; sitting on the sofa, for example.	Result (iv) R N
My preference would be for some mild exercise, such as gardening.	Result (iv) S N
Moderate exercise, such as walking, would be my choice.	Result (iv) H N
I would prefer more serious exercise, such as backpacking.	Result (iv) P N
Something strenuous like soccer or running would be my choice.	Result (iv) N N

899 **What sort of food do you like?**

I really just like traditional, plain food.	Result (v) T P
On the whole I prefer traditional, plain food.	Result (v) A P
I eat exotic food for a change.	Result (v) B P
I enjoy most foods, really.	Result (v) N P
I prefer a wide variety of dishes.	Result (v) M P

900 **What level of education have you reached (or do you expect to reach)?**

My education ended when I was 16.	Result (vi) R C
No further education after leaving school at 18.	Result (vi) S C
Some further education after leaving school at 18.	Result (vi) H C
Graduate degree.	Result (vi) P C
Postgraduate degree.	Result (vi) N C

901   **Which of these types of TV programmes do you like the most?**

Most of all I like game shows.	Result (i) O M
I couldn't do without soap operas.	Result (i) E M
I especially enjoy police dramas or comedies.	Result (i) V M
My preference is for serious dramas.	Result (i) P M
I enjoy news programmes and documentaries.	Result (i) C M

902   **What is your view of chivalry?**

I think it's old-fashioned nonsense, to be quite honest.	Result (ii) R M
It's pretty undesirable.	Result (ii) S M
It depends; it's OK sometimes.	Result (ii) H M
It's a desirable quality.	Result (ii) P M
I'd say it's an essential part of life.	Result (ii) N M

903   **If you had to choose just one, which of these is your favourite type of music?**

I prefer music such as heavy metal or rap.	Result (iii) O M
My favourite is rock or pop music; eg The Beatles.	Result (iii) E M
I particularly enjoy easy-listening music; eg Frank Sinatra.	Result (iii) V M
Jazz would be my number-one choice.	Result (iii) P M
My preference would be for classical music or opera.	Result (iii) C M

904   **Which of these activities appeals most?**

I'd choose relaxing; sitting on the sofa, for example.	Result (iv) R M
My preference would be for some mild exercise, such as gardening.	Result (iv) S M
Moderate exercise, such as walking, would be my choice.	Result (iv) H M
I would prefer more serious exercise, such as backpacking.	Result (iv) P M
Something strenuous like soccer or running would be my choice.	Result (iv) N M

905   **What sort of food do you like?**

I really just like traditional, plain food.	Result (v) T N
On the whole I prefer traditional, plain food.	Result (v) A N
I eat exotic food for a change.	Result (v) B N
I enjoy most foods, really.	Result (v) N N
I prefer a wide variety of dishes.	Result (v) M N

906   **What level of education have you reached (or do you expect to reach)?**

My education ended when I was 16.	Result (vi) Y C
No further education after leaving school at 18.	Result (vi) F C
Some further education after leaving school at 18.	Result (vi) L C
Graduate degree.	Result (vi) C C
Postgraduate degree.	Result (vi) M C

907 Which of these types of TV programmes do you like the most?

Most of all I like game shows.	Result (i) T T
I couldn't do without soap operas.	Result (i) A T
I especially enjoy police dramas or comedies.	Result (i) B T
My preference is for serious dramas.	Result (i) N T
I enjoy news programmes and documentaries.	Result (i) M T

908 What is your view of chivalry?

I think it's old-fashioned nonsense to be quite honest.	Result (ii) Y Y
It's pretty undesirable.	Result (ii) F Y
It depends; it's OK sometimes.	Result (ii) L Y
It's a desirable quality.	Result (ii) C Y
I'd say it's an essential part of life.	Result (ii) M Y

909 If you had to choose just one, which of these is your favourite type of music?

I prefer music such as heavy metal or rap.	Result (iii) T T
My favourite is rock or pop music; eg The Beatles.	Result (iii) A T
I particularly enjoy easy-listening music; eg Frank Sinatra.	Result (iii) B T
Jazz would be my number-one choice.	Result (iii) N T
My preference would be for classical music or opera.	Result (iii) M T

910 Which of these activities appeals most?

I'd choose relaxing; sitting on the sofa, for example.	Result (iv) Y T
My preference would be for some mild exercise, such as gardening.	Result (iv) F T
Moderate exercise, such as walking, would be my choice.	Result (iv) L T
I would prefer more serious exercise, such as backpacking.	Result (iv) C T
Something strenuous like soccer or running would be my choice.	Result (iv) M T

911 What sort of food do you like?

I really just like traditional, plain food.	Result (v) T Y
On the whole I prefer traditional, plain food.	Result (v) A Y
I eat exotic food for a change.	Result (v) B Y
I enjoy most foods, really.	Result (v) N Y
I prefer a wide variety of dishes.	Result (v) M Y

912 What level of education have you reached (or do you expect to reach)?

My education ended when I was 16.	Result (vi) I M
No further education after leaving school at 18.	Result (vi) W M
Some further education after leaving school at 18.	Result (vi) Q M
Graduate degree.	Result (vi) O M
Postgraduate degree.	Result (vi) T M

Take the CQ Test

913 Which of these types of TV programmes do you like the most?

Most of all I like game shows.	Result (i) T A
I couldn't do without soap operas.	Result (i) A A
I especially enjoy police dramas or comedies.	Result (i) B A
My preference is for serious dramas.	Result (i) N A
I enjoy news programmes and documentaries.	Result (i) M A

914 What is your view of chivalry?

I think it's old-fashioned nonsense to be quite honest.	Result (ii) Y F
It's pretty undesirable.	Result (ii) F F
It depends; it's OK sometimes.	Result (ii) L F
It's a desirable quality.	Result (ii) C F
I'd say it's an essential part of life.	Result (ii) M F

915 If you had to choose just one, which of these is your favourite type of music?

I prefer music such as heavy metal or rap.	Result (iii) T A
My favourite is rock or pop music; eg The Beatles.	Result (iii) A A
I particularly enjoy easy-listening music; eg Frank Sinatra.	Result (iii) B A
Jazz would be my number-one choice.	Result (iii) N A
My preference would be for classical music or opera.	Result (iii) M A

916 Which of these activities appeals most?

I'd choose relaxing; sitting on the sofa, for example.	Result (iv) Y A
My preference would be for some mild exercise, such as gardening.	Result (iv) F A
Moderate exercise, such as walking, would be my choice.	Result (iv) L A
I would prefer more serious exercise, such as backpacking.	Result (iv) C A
Something strenuous like soccer or running would be my choice.	Result (iv) M A

917 What sort of food do you like?

I really just like traditional, plain food.	Result (v) T F
On the whole I prefer traditional, plain food.	Result (v) A F
I eat exotic food for a change.	Result (v) B F
I enjoy most foods, really.	Result (v) N F
I prefer a wide variety of dishes.	Result (v) M F

918 What level of education have you reached (or do you expect to reach)?

My education ended when I was 16.	Result (vi) J M
No further education after leaving school at 18.	Result (vi) D M
Some further education after leaving school at 18.	Result (vi) U M
Graduate degree.	Result (vi) E M
Postgraduate degree.	Result (vi) A M

919 **Which of these types of TV programmes do you like the most?**

Most of all I like game shows.	Result (i) T B
I couldn't do without soap operas.	Result (i) A B
I especially enjoy police dramas or comedies.	Result (i) B B
My preference is for serious dramas.	Result (i) N B
I enjoy news programmes and documentaries.	Result (i) M B

920 **What is your view of chivalry?**

I think it's old-fashioned nonsense, to be quite honest.	Result (ii) Y L
It's pretty undesirable.	Result (ii) F L
It depends; it's OK sometimes.	Result (ii) L L
It's a desirable quality.	Result (ii) C L
I'd say it's an essential part of life.	Result (ii) M L

921 **If you had to choose just one, which of these is your favourite type of music?**

I prefer music such as heavy metal or rap.	Result (iii) T B
My favourite is rock or pop music; eg The Beatles.	Result (iii) A B
I particularly enjoy easy-listening music; eg Frank Sinatra.	Result (iii) B B
Jazz would be my number-one choice.	Result (iii) N B
My preference would be for classical music or opera.	Result (iii) M B

922 **Which of these activities appeals most?**

I'd choose relaxing; sitting on the sofa, for example.	Result (iv) Y B
My preference would be for some mild exercise, such as gardening.	Result (iv) F B
Moderate exercise, such as walking, would be my choice.	Result (iv) L B
I would prefer more serious exercise, such as backpacking.	Result (iv) C B
Something strenuous like soccer or running would be my choice.	Result (iv) M B

923 **What sort of food do you like?**

I really just like traditional, plain food.	Result (v) T L
On the whole I prefer traditional, plain food.	Result (v) A L
I eat exotic food for a change.	Result (v) B L
I enjoy most foods, really.	Result (v) N L
I prefer a wide variety of dishes.	Result (v) M L

924 **What level of education have you reached (or do you expect to reach)?**

My education ended when I was 16.	Result (vi) X M
No further education after leaving school at 18.	Result (vi) G M
Some further education after leaving school at 18.	Result (vi) K M
Graduate degree.	Result (vi) V M
Postgraduate degree.	Result (vi) B M

925 **Which of these types of TV programmes do you like the most?**

Most of all I like game shows.	Result (i) T N
I couldn't do without soap operas.	Result (i) A N
I especially enjoy police dramas or comedies.	Result (i) B N
My preference is for serious dramas.	Result (i) N N
I enjoy news programmes and documentaries.	Result (i) M N

926 **What is your view of chivalry?**

I think it's old-fashioned nonsense, to be quite honest.	Result (ii) Y C
It's pretty undesirable.	Result (ii) F C
It depends; it's OK sometimes.	Result (ii) L C
It's a desirable quality.	Result (ii) C C
I'd say it's an essential part of life.	Result (ii) M C

927 **If you had to choose just one, which of these is your favourite type of music?**

I prefer music such as heavy metal or rap.	Result (iii) T N
My favourite is rock or pop music; eg The Beatles.	Result (iii) A N
I particularly enjoy easy-listening music; eg Frank Sinatra.	Result (iii) B N
Jazz would be my number-one choice.	Result (iii) N N
My preference would be for classical music or opera.	Result (iii) M N

928 **Which of these activities appeals most?**

I'd choose relaxing; sitting on the sofa, for example.	Result (iv) Y N
My preference would be for some mild exercise, such as gardening.	Result (iv) F N
Moderate exercise, such as walking, would be my choice.	Result (iv) L N
I would prefer more serious exercise, such as backpacking.	Result (iv) C N
Something strenuous like soccer or running would be my choice.	Result (iv) M N

929 **What sort of food do you like?**

I really just like traditional, plain food.	Result (v) T C
On the whole I prefer traditional, plain food.	Result (v) A C
I eat exotic food for a change.	Result (v) B C
I enjoy most foods, really.	Result (v) N C
I prefer a wide variety of dishes.	Result (v) M C

930 **What level of education have you reached (or do you expect to reach)?**

My education ended when I was 16.	Result (vi) R M
No further education after leaving school at 18.	Result (vi) S M
Some further education after leaving school at 18.	Result (vi) H M
Graduate degree.	Result (vi) P M
Postgraduate degree.	Result (vi) N M

931 **Which of these types of TV programmes do you like the most?**

Most of all I like game shows.	Result (i) T M
I couldn't do without soap operas.	Result (i) A M
I especially enjoy police dramas or comedies.	Result (i) B M
My preference is for serious dramas.	Result (i) N M
I enjoy news programmes and documentaries.	Result (i) M M

932 **What is your view of chivalry?**

I think it's old-fashioned nonsense, to be quite honest.	Result (ii) Y M
It's pretty undesirable.	Result (ii) F M
It depends; it's OK sometimes.	Result (ii) L M
It's a desirable quality.	Result (ii) C M
I'd say it's an essential part of life.	Result (ii) M M

933 **If you had to choose just one, which of these is your favourite type of music?**

I prefer music such as heavy metal or rap.	Result (iii) T M
My favourite is rock or pop music; eg The Beatles.	Result (iii) A M
I particularly enjoy easy-listening music; eg Frank Sinatra.	Result (iii) B M
Jazz would be my number-one choice.	Result (iii) N M
My preference would be for classical music or opera.	Result (iii) M M

934 **Which of these activities appeals most?**

I'd choose relaxing; sitting on the sofa, for example.	Result (iv) Y M
My preference would be for some mild exercise, such as gardening.	Result (iv) F M
Moderate exercise, such as walking, would be my choice.	Result (iv) L M
I would prefer more serious exercise, such as backpacking.	Result (iv) C M
Something strenuous like soccer or running would be my choice.	Result (iv) M M

935 **What sort of food do you like?**

I really just like traditional, plain food.	Result (v) T M
On the whole I prefer traditional, plain food.	Result (v) A M
I eat exotic food for a change.	Result (v) B M
I enjoy most foods, really.	Result (v) N M
I prefer a wide variety of dishes.	Result (v) M M

936 **What level of education have you reached (or do you expect to reach)?**

My education ended when I was 16.	Result (vi) Y M
No further education after leaving school at 18.	Result (vi) F M
Some further education after leaving school at 18.	Result (vi) L M
Graduate degree.	Result (vi) C M
Postgraduate degree.	Result (vi) M M

Table 1: Comparing your results with your partner's

Person 2

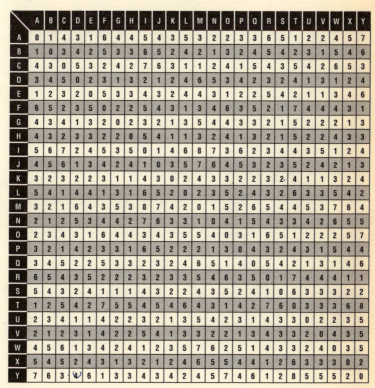

Person 1

	A	B	C	D	E	F	G	H	I	J	K	L	M	N	O	P	Q	R	S	T	U	V	W	X	Y
A	0	1	4	3	1	6	4	4	5	4	3	5	3	2	2	3	3	6	5	1	2	2	4	5	7
B	1	0	3	4	2	5	3	3	6	5	2	4	2	1	3	2	4	5	4	2	3	1	5	4	6
C	4	3	0	5	3	2	4	2	7	6	3	1	1	2	4	1	5	4	3	5	4	2	6	5	3
D	3	4	5	0	2	3	1	3	2	1	2	4	6	5	3	4	2	3	2	4	1	3	1	2	4
E	1	2	3	2	0	5	3	3	4	3	2	4	4	3	1	2	2	5	4	2	1	1	3	4	6
F	6	5	2	3	5	0	2	2	5	4	3	1	3	4	6	3	5	2	1	7	4	4	4	3	1
G	4	3	4	1	3	2	0	2	3	2	1	3	5	4	4	3	3	2	1	5	2	2	2	1	3
H	4	3	2	3	3	2	2	0	5	4	1	1	3	2	4	1	3	2	1	5	2	2	4	3	3
I	5	6	7	2	4	5	3	5	0	1	4	6	8	7	3	6	2	3	4	4	3	5	1	2	4
J	4	5	6	1	3	4	2	4	1	0	3	5	7	6	4	5	3	2	3	5	2	4	2	1	3
K	3	2	3	2	2	3	1	1	4	3	0	2	4	3	3	2	2	3	2	4	1	1	3	2	4
L	5	4	1	4	4	1	3	1	6	5	2	0	2	3	5	2	4	3	2	6	3	3	5	4	2
M	3	2	1	6	4	3	5	3	8	7	4	2	0	1	5	2	6	5	4	4	5	3	7	6	4
N	2	1	2	5	3	4	4	2	7	6	3	3	1	0	4	1	5	4	3	3	4	2	6	5	5
O	2	3	4	3	1	6	4	4	3	4	3	5	5	4	0	3	1	6	5	1	2	2	2	5	7
P	3	2	1	4	2	3	3	1	6	5	2	2	2	1	3	0	4	3	2	4	3	1	5	4	4
Q	3	4	5	2	2	5	3	3	2	3	2	4	6	5	1	4	0	5	4	2	1	3	1	4	6
R	6	5	4	3	5	2	2	2	3	2	3	3	5	4	6	3	5	0	1	7	4	4	4	1	1
S	5	4	3	2	4	1	1	1	4	3	2	2	4	3	5	2	4	1	0	6	3	3	3	2	2
T	1	2	5	4	2	7	5	5	4	5	4	6	4	3	1	4	2	7	6	0	3	3	3	6	8
U	2	3	4	1	1	4	2	2	3	2	1	3	5	4	2	3	1	4	3	3	0	2	2	3	5
V	2	1	2	3	1	4	2	2	5	4	1	3	3	2	2	1	3	4	3	3	2	0	4	3	5
W	4	5	6	1	3	4	2	4	1	2	3	5	7	6	2	5	1	4	3	3	2	4	0	3	5
X	5	4	5	2	4	3	1	3	2	1	2	4	6	5	5	4	4	1	2	6	3	3	3	0	2
Y	7	6	3	0	6	1	3	3	4	3	4	2	4	5	7	4	6	1	2	8	5	5	5	2	0

Table 2: Determining your final CQ score

Total test score	Your CQ	Total test score	Your CQ
0	172	25	94
1	169	26	91
2	166	27	88
3	163	28	86
4	159	29	83
5	156	30	80
6	153	31	77
7	150	32	74
8	147	33	71
9	144	34	68
10	141	35	65
11	138	36	63
12	134	37	60
13	131	38	57
14	128	39	54
15	125	40	51
16	122	41	48
17	119	42	45
18	116	43	42
19	113	44	40
20	109	45	37
21	106	46	34
22	103	47	31
23	100	48 or more	28
24	97		

CHAPTER 5

What your results mean

GETTING TO KNOW YOU

Harry (78) and Sylvia (77) were introduced to each other by mutual friends after their respective partners died. With a shared enjoyment of ballroom dancing, they have started to spend more time in one another's company.

Both of them acknowledge that, after a lifetime with their previous partners, they knew a great deal about them. But, as Sylvia points out, 'Although I care very much for Harry, there is a huge amount about him that I just don't know. So we thought we'd use the CQ Test as a way of finding out more about each other.'

In fact Harry and Sylvia achieved the highly compatible score of 125, their main differences being in the areas of the levels of education each had reached and the types of food they prefer. Sylvia left school at 16 while Harry stayed on until he was 18 and then went to university. They agreed that this was of little relevance, since 60 years ago educational opportunities were far more limited; in fact Sylvia is far more adept than Harry at crosswords, for example.

They learn that Harry is a fan of plain cooking while Sylvia prefers something more exotic. This does not seem to be a major issue for either of them and they agree that meeting one another was a very good thing.

Now that you have completed the test you should have arrived at a CQ score that will be somewhere between 28 and 172. In fact, as discussed earlier, there is a 50% chance that it will be in the range of 90 to 110 (see diagram in Chapter 3). As we have noted, the CQ scores have been scaled in relation to a 'normal' distribution such that the average is 100. Scores above 100 indicate higher than average CQs and scores below 100 indicate lower than average CQs.

If all this sounds like high-powered statistics, then it will be easier just to refer your scores to the following table for interpretation:

145+ Freak identity

Scores as high as this do not occur in the normal course of events. This would probably mean that the same person has completed the CQ Test twice, perhaps with an interval of a couple of weeks, as we explained earlier in the book. Identical twins are also likely to yield CQs at this extreme compatible end, regardless of whether they are raised together or apart. This is because they have identical genetic make-up, and most of the attributes measured by the CQ Test – including attitudes and religious and political beliefs – are known to have a strong genetic component.

If, by rare chance, two unrelated individuals produced a CQ score of above 145, they could be described as 'like two peas in a pod', seeing eye-to-eye on virtually every important issue. The chances of hitting it off well in the long-term would be very good indeed.

130–144 Extremely compatible

A CQ score this high is shared by only around 2% of couples. Clearly you have an exceptionally high degree of similarity with the other person and there is every likelihood that if you are not already soul-mates, then you could easily become so. In the context of this book, you probably already have some kind of relationship with that person. What your score would then imply is that you are unusually well suited to each other and the prospects for continued contentment are rosy.

If, on the other hand, you are taking the test with a prospective partner, then the omens are exceptionally good. This is certainly a relationship worth pursuing. As discussed above, the high CQ does not guarantee that the 'chemistry' between you will be right and that you are bound to 'fall in love' in the romantic sense of the term; but, if you do happen to fall in love, you should be reassured that you have done so with somebody who is 'right' for you.

115–129 Very compatible
Your CQ is shared by fewer than 20% of the population, which can be regarded as a very good platform for a long-term relationship. Our sample of (mostly happily) married counsellors averaged a score of 116, which is the sort of level to be expected in a good working relationship. Of course, relationships can and do break down for a great variety of reasons, but the prospects for a match based on this degree of similarity are very good indeed. Again, a newly established couple with this level of CQ should have renewed confidence that they are definitely on the right track.

100–114 Above average in compatibility
CQ scores in this range, particularly those towards the upper end of band, are also fairly promising, being higher than 50% of all possible relationships. As a couple, you will find sufficient points of contact to allow for the possibility

that lasting love could bloom. It is also conceivable that there could be one or two issues that need to be dealt with, but this should not prove impossible. If you are already 'an item', then you might have an idea where these differences lie and have already addressed them. In that case, you should not feel disconcerted, for your score is sufficient as the foundation for a very satisfactory future.

85–99 Below average in compatibility

Distant warning bells are sounding here, especially towards the lower end of this CQ band. You would be more compatible, theoretically speaking, with at least half of the world's population. This is not to say that a workable relationship is impossible; just that you might have to work at it a bit harder than most. If you have already worked through your problems and your relationship has stood the test of time, then don't let this discovery faze you. You might well defy the statistical predictions, in exactly the same way that an individual who has been refused life insurance on the basis of a medical exam might live a long and healthy life. However, if you have not yet become involved with this other person, a CQ score in this range might reasonably tell you to pause for thought.

70–84 Rather incompatible

The warning bells are much louder now. We are entering territory where there is a distinct likelihood of strains developing in the long-term. Only around 20% of couples would have CQs scores lower than this. Perhaps you enjoy scrapping from time to time, or perhaps you are the exception that proves the rule. Perhaps you are firmly in the grip of such powerful lust or infatuation that there is little you can (or want to) do about it. If so, then carry on despite us and let nature take its course. If, on the other hand, you are considering setting up a new relationship with this person, then you would have to do so in the full knowledge that scientific research gives you a less than even chance of success.

Below 70 Incompatible

Now the warning bells are deafening. A score such as this definitely puts you in the CQ doldrums. Perhaps you are completing the test with an 'ex' just to confirm you did the right thing in splitting up. If not, you probably don't need us to tell you about the 'chalk and cheese' nature of your relationship. Of course we might be wrong, in which case just tell us to mind our own business; all we can say is that if you get on famously together you are defying the odds. If you enter a relationship with a person despite a CQ score in this range, you are flying in the face of probability and we recommend that you don't make long-term plans such as holidays for next year or shared property deals.

The above descriptions will give you some idea of how to interpret your CQ. The banding in groups is, of course, arbitrary, so if you find yourself on the cusp, you might also want to read the interpretation for the band bordering on your own. This is because your true position may be somewhere in between.

What should you do about your result?

We are aware that many of the people taking this test will be established couples. In this case, the CQ will probably be telling you something you already know, whether or not you wish to be reminded. But what should you do if the result is a revelation? If the surprise is in the positive direction (a CQ score higher than you were expecting), then there is no great problem. You may have just gained a sense of proportion; the realisation that most other couples also have their differences but still manage to rub along alright.

The bigger question is what to do if your CQ score turns out to be catastrophic when you thought you had a very happy relationship. The answer in this instance is to ignore the CQ. If your relationship seems to be ticking over OK then don't let any outsiders (including us) tell you otherwise. There could be many reasons why the result seems wrong. The most obvious is that somebody's calculations have gone off the rails. You will discover this if you follow the procedure recommended in Chapter 6 for looking in more detail at your respective answers. From time to time, though, the CQ will fail as an accurate diagnosis in the individual case, however valid it may be in general. Its primary usefulness is in giving an advance indication as to how well a couple are likely to do in the long run. In this capacity it is indicative, not definitive.

Diagnosing your differences

CHURCH CHAP

Rob (33) and Gary (31) moved in together 18 months ago. Both have had relationships before but have never lived with another partner.

They have good jobs and enjoy a comfortable lifestyle with a cat to keep them company. Rob agrees with Gary that their attraction for each other was mainly physical in the first place but they soon realised they also had a lot in common.

They took the CQ Test for fun and were intrigued by their score of 125 – which marks them out as being highly compatible – so they decided it would be interesting to learn more about the strengths and weaknesses of their relationship.

On most issues they were in complete agreement, which they admit surprised them both. Their areas of greatest difference were those of occupation and religion. Rob is a lawyer while Gary works as a decorator; and while Gary goes to church on an occasional basis, Rob admits to being fairly anti-religious.

The differences in occupation don't bother them, but they discover that Rob is a little sceptical about Gary's religious convictions. (Gary had no idea that Rob felt that way.) When they talk it through, Gary explains that going to church was part of his upbringing and it's something he really believes in. Rob concludes that a bit of diversity is a good thing. We can't all be identical and, if we were, the world would be a dull place.

The confidential test in Chapter 4 has been constructed in such as way as to make it virtually impossible for your partner to discover how you answered each individual question. The only information they can glean is how well you are suited overall. However, some couples may be less coy, preferring to compare notes on how they answered the various items, and perhaps using the differences as a starting point for discussion of what is working and not working in the relationship.

For this reason, we present the CQ once again, as an open test for couples who wish to look in more detail at their compatibility. If you prefer, you may answer together; perhaps using different colour pens, or one partner using a tick and the other a cross to indicate their responses.

In Chapter 7, in the Tests of Importance section, we look at just how important individual items are to you both. So don't panic if you and your partner seem to have lots of areas where your opinions differ; these differences may not bear any real significance to your relationship. You may, however, find having a difference of view on a certain item is more important to one of you than the other realised, and this needs to be addressed.

Completing Chapters 6 and 7, comparing your answers, and giving yourselves time to sit and discuss them, can be a good way of airing (and perhaps resolving) your differences. It is important to give yourselves adequate time – perhaps up to 2 hours – and to be prepared for some difficult subjects coming up that are painful or awkward to discuss. Please don't attempt such an analysis without knowing that you'll be able to talk things through calmly and meaningfully together, being as supportive to each other as possible.

The Open CQ Test

Now each of you answer the following questions. choosing the answer that best fits you:

Q1 How would you describe your height?
(a) I'd say I am quite tall.
(b) I'm above average.
(c) My height is about average really.
(d) I'm below average height.
(e) I'd describe myself as quite short.

Q2 Being honest, which of these best describes you?
(a) I'm really quite overweight.
(b) I'd say I am a little overweight.
(c) Compared to other people's my weight is about average.
(d) I'd describe myself as slim.
(e) I'm pretty skinny really.

Q3 How would you say your IQ compares to other people's?
(a) I'd describe myself as bright.
(b) I'm somewhat more intelligent than average.
(c) My level of intelligence is about average.
(d) I'd say I am a bit below average.
(e) I think of myself as being a little dull really.

Q4 Which of these types of TV programmes do you like the most?
(a) Most of all I like game shows.
(b) I couldn't do without soap operas.
(c) I especially enjoy police dramas or comedies.
(d) My preference is for serious dramas.
(e) I enjoy news programmes and documentaries.

Q5 What sort of sex drive do you have?

(a) My sex drive is pretty non-existent.

(b) I'd say my sex drive is reasonably low.

(c) I'd describe my sex drive as about average really.

(d) I think my sex drive is above average.

(e) To be honest I'm absolutely insatiable.

Q6 What do you think about children?

(a) I dislike them, to be honest.

(b) I think other people's children are OK.

(c) I've no strong feelings one way or the other.

(d) I may want my own children one day.

(e) I definitely want my own (or already have them).

Q7 What job do you do (or plan to)?

(a) I'm a professional; eg doctor, teacher.

(b) My role is managerial; eg business manager, police inspector.

(c) My job is clerical, in admin or in customer service; eg secretary, chef.

(d) I'm a skilled tradesperson; eg motor mechanic, decorator.

(e) I work in a manual job; eg labourer, cleaner.

Q8 What is your view of chivalry?

(a) I think it's old-fashioned nonsense, to be quite honest.

(b) It's pretty undesirable.

(c) It depends; it's OK sometimes.

(d) It's a desirable quality.

(e) I'd say it's an essential part of life.

Q9 How would you rate your appearance?

(a) I think I'm very attractive.

(b) I'd call myself rather attractive.

(c) Compared to other people, I'd say I'm average.

(d) I'd describe myself as rather plain.

(e) I'm very plain really.

Q10 Which of the following best describes your view of drinking?

(a) It's completely unacceptable.

(b) OK for other people but not for me.

(c) I drink occasionally.

(d) I drink quite often.

(e) To be honest I think I drink a bit too much.

Q11 How would you describe your political views?

(a) I'd describe myself as being far left.

(b) You could label me left of centre.

(c) I'm pretty neutral really, or not interested in politics.

(d) I would say I am right of centre.

(e) The best description of me would be far right.

Q12 If you had to choose just one, which of these is your favourite type of music?

(a) I prefer music such as heavy metal or rap.

(b) My favourite is rock or pop music; eg The Beatles.

(c) I particularly enjoy easy-listening music; eg Frank Sinatra.

(d) Jazz would be my number-one choice.

(e) My preference would be for classical music or opera.

Q13 How essential to you is sexual fidelity in a relationship?

(a) To me it's essential.

(b) I'd say it is important.

(c) I suppose the odd lapse is OK.

(d) I think you have to expect affairs.

(e) I'd want to have an open and swinging relationship.

Q14 What do you think of pornography?

(a) I think it's disgusting.

(b) To be honest I prefer to avoid it.

(c) It's OK sometimes.

(d) It's harmless fun really.

(e) I actually think it's a great turn-on.

Q15 How do you feel about keeping pets?

(a) I hate them (or am allergic to them).

(b) I don't really like them.

(c) Some I like, others I don't.

(d) I enjoy them if it's practical and acceptable where I live.

(e) I can't imagine life without having a pet.

Q16 Which of these activities appeals most?

(a) I'd choose relaxing; sitting on the sofa, for example.

(b) My preference would be for some mild exercise, such as gardening.

(c) Moderate exercise, such as walking, would be my choice.

(d) I would prefer more serious exercise, such as backpacking.

(e) Something strenuous, like soccer or running.

Q17 Which of the following best describes your view of parties?

(a) I actually prefer being alone.

(b) Small groups are OK.

(c) I think a few parties are OK.

(d) I'm quite fond of parties.

(e) I love wild parties.

Q18 What is your view of smoking?

(a) I think it's totally intolerable.

(b) I feel it's fairly undesirable.

(c) It's OK for other people to smoke.

(d) I'm a light smoker.

(e) I'd describe myself as a heavy smoker.

Q19 How religious would you say you are?

(a) I'm active and committed to my religion.

(b) I go to church or a place of worship sometimes.

(c) I worship in private.

(d) I'm not really religious and never worship.

(e) I'd say I was actively anti-religious.

Q20 What sort of food do you like?

(a) I really just like traditional, plain food.

(b) On the whole I prefer traditional, plain food.

(c) I eat exotic food for a change.

(d) I enjoy most foods, really.

(e) I prefer a wide variety of dishes.

Q21 In your view, is money important?

(a) No, you can't buy happiness.

(b) I just need enough money to live.

(c) I want to be comfy.

(d) I'd like to be rich.

(e) Yes, I want to be very rich.

Q22 Which of the following best describes the type of relationship you'd prefer?

(a) A casual friendship is fine.

(b) I'd prefer a lasting friendship.

(c) I would favour a short-term affair.

(d) My preference would be for an intimate long-term relationship.

(e) I would choose marriage.

Q23 How experienced are you sexually?

(a) I am still a virgin.

(b) To be honest I'm rather inexperienced.

(c) I've had no complaints so far.

(d) I would class myself as an experienced lover.

(e) I'd say I'm really hot stuff.

Q24 What level of education have you reached (or do you expect to reach)?

(a) My education ended when I was 16.

(b) No further education after leaving school at 18.

(c) Some further education after leaving school at 18.

(d) Graduate degree.

(e) Postgraduate degree.

Gap scores

You will notice that each of the 24 questions in the test has five possible answers. These are arranged so that the response options that are further apart represent greater discrepancies, and the gaps can vary from 0 (same response given by both of you) to 4 (opposite ends of the list chosen). Any two responses that are next to each other score 1, those removed by two places are scored 2, those 3 notches apart score 3, and if opposite ends are chosen the item is scored 4.

Take Q18 for example, 'What is your view of smoking?' If you both choose the same answer, there is a zero discrepancy between you. If one of you chooses 'I think it's totally intolerable' and the other 'I'd describe myself as a heavy smoker', then there is a gap of 4 points. If one of you says 'I think it's totally intolerable' and the other says 'I feel it's fairly undesirable', there is a gap of 1 point. If one says 'I think it's totally intolerable' and the other 'It's OK for other people to smoke' then the gap is 2 points, and so on. 'I feel it's fairly undesirable' paired with 'I'd describe myself as a heavy smoker' scores 3.

You should now go through your answers to all 24 questions putting a number between 0 and 4 beside them. You can check that you have done this correctly by working out your CQ by hand. Total up all the 'gap' scores (to give a number between 0 and 96, but most likely in the region of 15–30). If you refer this to Table 2 (on page 196), you should obtain a CQ score that is not too far removed from the one you previously arrived at if you took the confidential test in Chapter 4. Don't worry if it is a few points different; you're unlikely to remember precisely how you answered each question the first time round. However, if it differs by as much as 10 points, something may have gone wrong with your calculations (or somebody is giving very different answers the second time around).

Gaps of either 0 or 1 for any particular item indicate that you and your partner are pretty well matched in this area.

However, gaps of 2 or more suggest poorer compatibility. In some areas, such a discrepancy may be more consequential than it is in others, or more or less relevant to you than to another couple (see Chapter 7).

After you've determined the areas in which you are either well or poorly matched, take some time to discuss each in turn. We've provided guidance below for each of the 24 questions, but remember that circumstances are likely to differ greatly from couple to couple. Some couples aren't concerned by a huge gap in the music they like; others are. The golden rule is that if you are happy, celebrate your differences rather than dwell on them.

Below we look at what could be going on within a relationship when you have a gap of 2 places or more (ie, at least one answer between your own answers) in the CQ Test. We examine each question item individually, in the order they appear in the test.

1. Height
Generally speaking, couples feel more comfortable together if the man is taller than the woman. A difference of around 5 inches in this direction is typical and works well. Most people would answer this question by comparing themselves with others of the same gender, so if a woman who considered herself quite tall (compared to other women) was in a relationship with a man who saw himself as quite short, this could be an indicator of an imperfect match. If the woman is taller than the man this is said to defy the 'cardinal rule' of mating and dating. If he is radically taller than her, people make jokes about having to stand on a box to kiss. Neither situation is necessarily cata-strophic to a relationship, but it may be a minor irritation or

impediment. People in general seem most comfortable when they encounter couples who are broadly the same height, so it could be that even though you are happily oblivious to your size difference others may be less so.

Of course, men who are unusually short and women who are exceptionally tall have a much smaller pool of partners to choose from and sometimes it will be necessary to settle for a partner who is less than ideal in this respect. There is little truth in the idea that short men are difficult because they are always trying to compensate for their height. However, high-achieving men who are short sometimes seem to sport 'trophy wives' – who are strikingly taller than themselves – in a bid to increase their own 'standing'. If that is the real reason for attaching themselves to a tall woman (rather than just the law of averages operating) then it does not bode well for the future of the relationship.

2. Weight

In much the same way that we have a tendency to form relationships with people of a similar height to ourselves, the happiest couples are often those who have comparable builds. Sometimes a couple start out with similar builds, then one puts on a great deal of weight or goes on a diet, resulting in an imbalance. Notoriously, this can threaten the relationship in ways that were not anticipated by the couples themselves. For example, a husband who fancied his wife because she was plump may fall out of love with her when she becomes slim, or a wife who 'married down' because she perceived herself as unattractively fat might aspire to other men with the new self-esteem she acquires having lost weight.

Although genetics are known to influence our bodyweight, our build ultimately depends on what (and how much) we eat, and how much we exercise. Eating can be an important social activity in our lives; sharing a meal with someone you love is an agreeable way of sustaining the relationship. However if your build is very different from your partner's, it is probable that your eating habits will be dissimilar too, and it might not be easy to plan meals together. In a similar way, having a very different build from your partner probably suggests that one of you is less active than the other, possibly leading to problems if one of you wants to go out for a walk while the other is content to sit watching TV.

3. Intelligence

IQ scores are distributed in the same way as CQs, such that 50% of the population have an IQ that is above average (100) while 50% are below average. Yet the great majority of people answering this question say that they are of average intelligence or above. Clearly, there is a certain amount of immodesty or self-delusion at play. Despite people's reluctance to own up, it is in fact pretty important for two people to be of approximately the same level of intelligence if they are to have a successful and long-lasting relationship. IQ strongly influences how we communicate – and what we talk about when we do so – and since solid relationships depend, amongst other factors, upon mutually fulfilling communication, you'll tend to do best by being with someone who's roughly the same level of intelligence as yourself. Sense of humour and entertainment preferences are also related to intelligence, and so will be more similar when a couple have comparable IQs.

An IQ difference in favour of the male partner may be less destructive than one in which the woman is the brighter of the two. This is because many women put a great deal of premium on their partner's accomplishments and capacity to provide resources (which of course relate to IQ), whereas men rate youth, beauty, and sex appeal (fertility markers) as more important criteria. Indeed, a trade-off between these two commodities is common in all cultures, not least our own. But still there is a limit to how far the gap can be stretched.

As a case in point, *The Sunday Times* recently reported that Booker prize-winning author Salman Rushdie had dumped his model girlfriend, who was more than 20 years his junior, because 'he no longer found her intellectually challenging'. Marilyn Monroe's unlikely marriage to playwright Arthur Miller lasted longer than many people expected, yet it was her second husband, the baseball-player Joe Di Maggio with whom she felt most comfortable across the years and who was chief mourner at her funeral (both of them perhaps being physical types).

4. Preferred TV programmes

A liking for similar types of TV programmes was actually a strong indicator of happy relationships when we conducted our research into the CQ Test. If you like very different programmes, of course, there's one very simple answer:get a second TV set, perhaps for the bedroom. But while that might be a short-term answer, it's one that could be the harbinger of other difficulties. Watching TV on your own is OK, but it's better when you're with someone else; it's one of the social things happy couples do. By watching TV separately you're denying yourselves the opportunity of spending time relaxing together.

Of course, there are some typical male–female differences in TV viewing preferences, which raise the likelihood of gaps appearing. We didn't include the more obvious preferences, such as men tending to like westerns and war films, and women tending to prefer programmes about royalty, celebrities, fashion and lifestyle. But of the items used in the CQ Test, women are more likely to enjoy soaps, game shows and dramas, while men tend to prefer news and documentaries, police dramas and comedies. So a discrepancy for this item is not the end of the world, unless you spend a high proportion of your time watching TV.

Perhaps the best way to deal with differences of taste is to search for programmes that you agree upon or negotiate trade-offs at the beginning of the evening, along the lines of: 'I'll let you watch *Horizon* tonight, if we can watch *Friends* on Friday.' Alternatively, you might compensate by finding some other leisure activity that you both enjoy doing together.

5. Libido

Sex means different things to different people. In some relationships it is extremely important, while in others it may be less relevant. But while it is undeniable that better sex can make better relationships, what is most important is that partners share similar levels of desire, whether rampant or disinterested.

It's a complicated area, though. If you have a significant 'gap' it may be helpful (though somewhat challenging) to try to get to the bottom of whether you have differing sex drives, or whether one of you simply doesn't want to have sex with the other. Problems in the bedroom are frequently the result of difficulties elsewhere. When things go wrong in a relationship, it can result in one of the partners 'going off' sex. It may be that one of you is beginning to transfer your desires to someone else. Or it may be that there is another problem, which this test might reveal, that is preventing one of you from becoming intimate with the other. Discussing issues in other areas, even if they seem at first sight unconnected with the physical aspect of your relationship, can help.

Incidentally, it helps some couples to know that sexual activity within a relationship typically declines over time. Burning desire often gives way to friendly familiarity at best. It has been calculated that the 'half-life' of sex within Western marriage is approximately 5 years, meaning that for every five years a couple is married, they are likely to be having sex about half as often as they were before. For example, if they start off with a rate of 8 times a week on honeymoon, it will be about 4 times a week after five years of marriage, twice a week after 10 years of marriage and once a week by their 15th anniversary. Clearly, at this rate a great many marriages are pretty much celibate by middle age. This is not just an effect of age, but also a loss of excitement as a result of over-familiarity.

Loss of libido is best accepted as a fact of life and perfectly natural but, again, it helps if the pace of decline is parallel for the two partners. Problems arise when one partner's libido declines at a faster rate than the other's. There are many possible physical reasons for this, including pregnancy, ill-health or lack of sexual satisfaction, and it may be helpful to speak to your doctor.

6. Attitudes towards children

If you and your partner's views on the subject of having children differ greatly, you probably don't need us to tell you that you've got a problem. It's a highly emotive subject, frequently made more so because partners often do not truly know where each stands on the matter until after they have committed to each other. It certainly isn't as simple as saying all women will probably want children, and men probably won't mind too much if they do have children. Statistics suggest that women are more likely than their male partner to be the one wanting children but that's not always the case.

Those who hold opposing views on the desire to have a child would probably do well to think hard before entering a relationship. If they are already together, then it is an issue that would almost certainly benefit from time with a counsellor. You yourselves are probably too close to the problem to be able to form objective views. It may be good to tackle it sooner rather than later. It's definitely not a dilemma to sweep under the carpet.

7. Occupational type

A significant gap for this item may indicate the potential for problems about perceived status. Although we may be inclined to think that we now live in a relatively classless society, we still tend to compare ourselves with others. Trying to be close to someone with an altogether different type of occupation can be challenging. At the extremes, a professional person could come home mentally drained but still full of her or his work, while a labourer might reach the front door physically exhausted, but with the job left firmly back at the workplace.

While you'll undeniably be happiest in a relationship with someone whose occupation either is or was similar to your own, it may also seem that we have little choice about what we do for a living. Perhaps one way of overcoming differences in this area is to recognise them, and find ways of accommodating each other's needs. Imagine what it would be like to lead the other person's life and see if you can give to them what you would like to be given yourself if the tables were turned.

8. View of chivalry

Some despise the very idea of it, to others it is central to their nature: whichever side of the chivalry fence you come down on, it's indisputably the case that a man who likes to hold doors open for women is likely to get short shrift from a female who considers it demeaning. Conversely, a woman who enjoys the idea of 'ladies first' is unlikely to get much out of a relationship with a man with the manners of a pig. Good relationships can accommodate small differences, but a large gap in your answers to this question may well suggest that you'll experience mismatches in other areas of your lives together, too.

In the CQ Test, the chivalry question represents general attitudes towards feminism and the division of gender roles. The woman who thinks chivalry outmoded is inclined to favour equality in matters such as income, working hours and the sharing of domestic chores and child rearing. She is unlikely to get on well with the kind of man who expects his wife to stay at home and look after the children while he 'brings home the bacon'. Hence, although chivalry might seem like a minor issue in itself, it is important as a proxy for the whole area of attitudes towards the role of women in society. One of the reasons for choosing chivalry as an item is that there is no overall difference as to whether men or women are more favourable towards the idea.

9. Appearance

While it's definitely not true that attractive couples are happier than those less well blessed on the looks front (you only have to look at tabloid pictures of all those film stars who are breaking up for proof of that), there's a good deal of evidence pointing to the fact that people who rate similarly in the attractiveness stakes tend to form more stable partnerships. Some of the research that established this used wedding pictures cut so as to disconnect the couple, who were then separately rated for attractiveness by judges unaware of the original pairings. Married couples tend be rated as similar in attractiveness.

Other studies used observers in singles bars, where it was found that a wide discrepancy in attractiveness reduced the chances that a couple would go off together. When people are asked to choose pictures of people they would like to meet, they again go for individuals whom independent judges rate as similar in degree of attractiveness. Presumably, we recognise our own limitations and are reluctant to put ourselves forward for the knockback that is likely to result from aiming too high.

Interestingly, women are inclined to rate themselves as higher in attractiveness than men are. This may be because self-esteem and grooming affect scores on this item as well as natural beauty and sex-appeal. It is customary for those with higher opinions of their attractiveness to go to greater lengths over their appearance and this self-pride also needs to be reciprocated. A woman who has spent a couple of hours getting ready to go out is unlikely to be impressed by her man if he has soup on his tie and a haircut long overdue. Thus, for a variety of reasons, those whose answers are closest together on the 'appearance' item are those most likely to thrive as a couple.

10. Drinking habits

Couples who share a similar take on drinking are likely to be most content. In general, teetotallers aren't well matched with boozers. Although drinking copious amounts of alcohol can in the extreme be a solo activity, most of us drink with others. Similarly, those who don't drink tend to seek the company of others of the same disposition. Drinkers are likely to be party-loving extraverts; those who do not drink have more chance of being quiet introverts. Therefore, drinking behaviour touches indirectly on personality and lifestyle, and a gap in this item indicates a more general incompatibility between a couple.

Intriguingly, our research among a small group of practising counsellors suggested that sometimes drinkers can have happy relationships even if their partner doesn't drink. This may be because a heavier drinker needs a sober partner to keep them on the straight and narrow, or perhaps the typically more timid abstemious partner benefits from the social glow surrounding their more sociable other half. Our study was not conclusive, however, so perhaps we are best to assume, as most research confirms, that you'll be at your happiest when your partner shares your taste (or distaste) for alcohol.

If the test reveals that one partner may have a problem with drink, or could be an alcoholic, then he or she should seek professional help.

11. Political views

It takes little savvy to realise that Margaret Thatcher would be an unsuitable bedmate for Fidel Castro. Fewer women than men are actively passionate about politics, yet when a gap in this item is revealed by the CQ Test, they tend to be more bothered.

Men, it would seem, are little concerned about the political views of their partner, but our research found that women are much happier when their male partner shares their political convictions, however strong. So if you're a woman looking for a male partner, try to find out how he votes before you get too serious. If you're with someone whose political outlook is widely different from your own, make sure you can live with his values, because your chances of talking him around to your own point of view are negligible.

12. Music preferences

With so many types of music, five answers clearly cannot incorporate every taste. Many people complain that their personal preference is omitted from the list. However, as with all the CQ Test items, we had to find a scale on which the musical genres could be arranged that would be ordinal (ie greater distances would signal greater communication problems). In this particular instance the musical genres are ranked by their rhythmic and harmonic complexity, and therefore the degree of listener investment that is necessary to appreciate them. It is partly a question of intelligence, but also partly one of temperament. Rock music has great sensory impact and is therefore preferred by extravert, sensation-seeking individuals, whereas classical music tends to be preferred by more mature, conservative, introvert types of people.

Whatever the reasons, what is clear is that people with adjacent tastes can more easily tolerate each other's preferences than those far removed on the scale. Few people like both gangsta rap and Mozart and it is hard to imagine two people with such disparate tastes sharing the same space. If you differ greatly in this area, at the very least invest in a Walkman. Better still, get two.

13. Importance of sexual fidelity

Perhaps not surprisingly, sharing a view on the importance of sexual fidelity was the number-one item in the CQ Test when it came to predicting what makes relationships happy. Our research showed that both males and females are unlikely to achieve high levels of satisfaction with their relationship if they find themselves with a partner who has a view on fidelity that differs greatly from their own. The important detail here is that having a similar view does not imply that both partners should agree that sexual exploration is out of the question. It does indicate, however, that if one partner has a roving eye, then for a happy relationship the other partner should have a similar outlook on life; there needs to be clear agreement that such an open relationship is mutually acceptable.

If you have a substantial gap in this area, it is clearly the partner with a higher expectation of an exclusive relationship who is more likely to be hurt. This factor is critical to long-term happiness; if you discover you have very different views, you may benefit from seeing a counsellor, as it could be a thorny problem to resolve on your own.

14. Pornography

Our findings on this item have brought a number of knowing looks when we have reported them to women. Our research showed that men are perfectly capable of considering their relationships to be happy and also find the idea of pornography a turn-on, even if their wife considers it distasteful. But while some women like pornography and others don't, a woman is very unlikely to be happy in a relationship with a man whose views are significantly different from hers.

So what can you do if your gap in this area is a substantial one? Many women find porn threatening because they think it means their partner doesn't love them or find them sufficiently attractive. But this is not necessarily so. Everyone is capable of being turned on by external stimuli (such as a picture), although it will come as no surprise that men are about three times as likely as women to seek out pornographic images. Accommodate one another's viewpoints if you can but, at the very least, try to reassure each other that they should have no real bearing on your own feelings towards each other.

15. Attitude towards pets

What do you do if you and your partner have very different views on the idea of keeping a pet? It's not an easy area in which to reach a compromise; adults who grew up with pets often feel something is missing in life without a dog or cat about the house. Conversely, adults whose childhoods didn't include a pet are often happy to live their lives in an animal-free environment. Pet haters who become unwilling pet owners because of their partners are likely to grin and bear it. However, if you desperately want a pet, but don't want to upset a partner by insisting, you may well feel something is missing in your life.

If you and your partner have a disagreement in this area, try to think laterally to help meet the needs of your other half. Even though you may not care for animals yourself, owning a dog is a great way of getting exercise. Cats aren't very demanding, particularly if you find someone to take care of them when you go away. If you want a pet, perhaps you can find a way of bringing an animal into your life on a part-time basis. Offer to walk someone else's dog now and then, or volunteer to feed their cat when they go away. It's usually possible to find compromises in life, and hardly ever necessary to deny yourself something you know is important to you.

16. Preferred activities

So one of you is a couch potato while the other is an aspiring athlete? Does it really matter? What's to stop one of you going to the gym every day while the other lounges around watching TV? Some couples manage to accommodate such discrepancies, but they can cause problems. If you are keen on exercise you undoubtedly enjoy the sense of well-being as a result; and it certainly contributes to general health and physical attractiveness. However, if you are making an effort to enhance your attractiveness, you may feel resentful of a partner who refuses to go to similar lengths. Alternatively, someone less motivated to exercise might resent a partner who finds it easy. Although we all know exercise is good for us, some may have withdrawn from it after 'failing' at it at school. Others may have a physical impairment which makes them embarrassed or less able to engage in physical activity.

Since exercise is patently a sensible thing, a gap in this area needs to be addressed by both partners. Go for a walk together, no matter how brief. Perhaps build in some exercise when you go on holiday. Even a kick-about in the park with the kids can do you good. Not everyone can be an Olympic athlete, but we all have the responsibility to get enough exercise to ensure our lives are as long, healthy and happy as they can be.

17. Liking for parties

While it's not a recipe for total disaster, couples with very differing preferences in this area are likely to experience problems. While we all differ in our desire to socialise, even the least intense relationship is likely to wither and fade if both partners would really rather be on their own. Our need to be with others (or not) is programmed into us from birth and you can probably think of examples of people at both extremes: some live an almost hermit-like existence, while others are the life and soul of every party. A liking for parties, then, is a marker for the personality trait of extraversion, which is partly genetic. Generally speaking, people who love socialising get on better with others who are equally gregarious; introverts may enjoy going to a concert together, or just be happy reading together at home.

If you're in a relationship with someone who has very different priorities when it comes to socialising, the best solution is to seek a compromise, without either of you having to do your own thing. Maybe you can agree to go to a party on Saturday night and stay in the rest of the week? Go to the pub, but choose a quieter one where the less extravert of the two of you won't drown in a sea of others. Do all you can to avoid leading separate social lives. It doesn't work and will almost certainly build suspicion and resentment in the mind of the partner who stays at home.

18. Smoking habits

If you're a man and you've turned to this section because you and your partner have widely differing opinions about smoking, you probably already know that it doesn't really bother you that much. Whether you're a non-smoker yourself and have a smoking partner, or vice versa, it's unlikely to give you great cause for concern. If you're a woman though, it's likely to be a very different kettle of fish. In actual fact, if your partner smokes but you don't, it could be having a significant impact on the happiness of your relationship. Our research indicated that having a similar opinion about smoking to her partner's ranked high on the list of predictors of whether a woman is likely to be happily married. Non-smoking women, it seems, particularly hate to kiss a man who smells like a chimney, though there are men who feel the same way about female smokers.

Smoking is an addictive habit, and one that is notoriously difficult to stop. As the non-smoking female partner of a male smoker, you're likely to be more bothered than you sometimes let on. Whilst it's admirable to be so selfless, if you carry on suffering in silence, resentment will almost certainly start to stew up in you. To give him his due, your partner probably doesn't realise how it makes you feel, so it may be sensible to open up a little. You probably won't stop him smoking (although if he secretly wants to give up, you could always help him) but for the sake of your relationship it could be a good idea to agree some terms. Perhaps he shouldn't expect you to empty his ashtray. Maybe he could only smoke in one part of the house – or even outside if that suits you both better. If smoking bothers you, talk about it rather than sitting there fuming.

19. Religious commitment

Couples with big gaps on this item normally either don't get together in the first place, or have resolved their diversity at an early stage of their relationship. In general, it is not easy for us to form lasting relationships with those whose religious views differ greatly from our own, and they are one way of expressing our sense of values – our view of what's right and what's wrong. Two people with widely differing perspectives in this area are only likely to get on if the non-religious partner has a similar moral outlook to his or her more religious other half. Even then, a person who believes in evolution is bound to have difficulty in relating intellectually with a Biblical fundamentalist.

Although we hear occasional stories of committed church-going women falling for imprisoned murderers, these are the exception rather than the rule, and probably come about mainly because such women believe they can change the men. In general, the happiest relationships are those between people who have shared values and beliefs, and mutual morals.

20. Food preferences

At first sight this may seem a trifling factor in a relationship when compared with the overriding importance of something like sexual fidelity, yet our research shows that happily married couples have an uncanny propensity towards sharing the same tastes in food. Strange though this may seem in a day when market research tells us that fewer and fewer people sit down to eat together (because everyone's lives are so busy), sharing a meal with someone is an important contributor to nurturing your relationship. A shared meal is an opportunity to socialise, even if it is limited to saying a few words, and you're much more likely to get together to eat if you're happy with the same kinds of foods. You'll also be more inclined to enjoy restaurant meals together if you're equally happy with the type of cuisine offered by the establishment in question.

Fortunately this is an area of life where a little compromise can go a long way. Try to find some middle ground where you can both enjoy the same restaurant, even if one of you always tends to choose steak and chips while the other experiments. It may help to remember that eating together is not something you do simply because you are hungry; it's actually a great way of cementing your relationship.

21. Importance of money

For some, money is a success symbol, for others it is merely a means to an end; but for most people, sharing views with their partner on the importance of money is a significant contributor to a contented relationship. A considerable gap in this area may indicate that one of you is more ambitious than the other, or that one of you has high regard for material things while the other is more of a 'people person'. It is likely to become an issue only if money becomes short and the person for whom wealth is important sees things slipping away, or if one keeps spending while the other worries about it.

It is helpful to understand that someone's desire for money may be driven by all sorts of reasons other than simple greed. Money may form a kind of 'security blanket' for someone worried about what the future may bring, or it may meet a need for social status, helping them 'keep up with the Joneses'. In such cases it is better to reassure them rather than rebuke them. If you're the money-focused partner and things are not going well financially, don't assume that your other half doesn't care, but count your blessings for being with someone who'll probably help keep your spirits up when the going gets rough.

22. Preferred type of relationship

There was little question about the significance of this item in the results of our research with married couples, which of course will come as no surprise. Those who are happily married are those who truly want to be married. If you're in a long-term relationship, you're fairly unlikely to have noted a wide gap between your views and your partner's for this item. If you have, now might be a good time to talk about your different expectations.

One might more reasonably expect opposing views about the preferred type of relationship coming from two people who aren't (yet?) together. If you do discover such a disparity, you may wish to think seriously about where your relationship might go. If one is keen to get married while the other wants to be no more than friends, it is inadvisable to start writing the guest-list for the wedding. It's always best to know where you both stand if you're about to enter into a relationship with someone new, before your rose-tinted view of life fools you into thinking that everything is going to be fine, when the chances are that it won't.

23. Sexual experience

Most people tend to answer this question by thinking about the amount of sexual experience they have had prior to their existing relationship, if they are currently in one. Our research on married couples revealed an intriguing difference between the views of men and women on this subject. Women who are happy in their relationship are happy, it would seem, regardless of whether their partner has had the same, less or more sexual experience than them. Men on the other hand showed a marked difference. They were noticeably more likely to be happy with a woman who had broadly the same amount of experience as themselves, than one who was either less or more experienced than themselves. It seems to put paid to the myth that experienced men are attracted to virgins. Those considering starting a relationship might compare the notches on one another's bedposts before doing so: if the woman has either led a very sheltered or wildly amorous life in the past, she may choose to be discreet about it rather than boastful.

24. Education level

It is usually the case that we reach a level of education broadly in line with our level of intelligence. However, this is not unfailingly true; and it is a dangerous assumption to make that someone is slow-witted simply because they left school at 16. Things have certainly changed over the years, with younger people more likely to go to university than those in previous generations. However, on the basis that most people have long-term relationships with someone of their own age-group, their educational opportunities are likely to have been broadly equivalent. A person with a postgraduate degree is less likely to find long-term happiness with someone who failed school exams. Like it or not, our education has a lot to do with who we are and, broadly speaking, we choose to be with others who are like ourselves; this is the basis for the whole CQ Test.

If you're already in a happy relationship, you probably won't have had a hugely different educational background from your partner or have already found some way to cope with your differences. But if you're thinking about settling down with someone who differs greatly from you in this respect, make sure you both know what you're doing. At the very least, talk it over, so that resentments do not emerge later which might spoil your relationship.

CHAPTER 7

Do your differences matter?

HEALTH MATTERS

Steve (43) and Di (42) are five years short of celebrating their silver wedding anniversary and, having married in their early twenties, wonder where the years have gone. They have two sons, Greg (16) and James (14). Steve works as a marketing manager for an electricity company, while Di is an administrative assistant at the local hospital. Their CQ score of 116, after each completed the confidential test, suggests that they are very compatible, which doesn't altogether surprise them since they're really pretty happy together.

When they then took the open test in order to see where they differ, once again there were no great surprises. Smoking, music and their perceptions of their physical builds are what set them apart. Steve is a smoker, while Di is not, but he hasn't realised until now how much his smoking really bothers her. Di is slim, but Steve sees himself as really quite overweight. And while Di likes pop music, Steve is much more into jazz. On talking things through, Steve discovers that Di is, in fact, concerned about his smoking and his weight problem from a health point of view: she worries that Steve is doing himself long-term harm. Steve thinks he may be able to cut down on the smoking with support from Di, and he also decides to limit his unhealthy lunches at the pub. On the matter of music they agree to differ.

Once you and your partner have taken the CQ Test a second time, in its open form, you'll probably have

233

discovered that you have differences – perhaps quite big ones – in some areas of your life. It's not unusual and it would be surprising if you found yourselves so alike that you disagreed on absolutely nothing. Chapter 6 looked at what those differences could mean, and how you might go about addressing them in a way that strengthens your relationship. In this chapter we provide you and your partner with a way of finding out how important it is if you don't see eye-to-eye on a particular subject.

You'll probably have discovered that you disagree on one or more of the items in the CQ Test. Perhaps they are matters on which you are perfectly happy to differ. But how do you determine whether one of you is in fact more concerned than the other about the issue?

When we researched the CQ Test with married couples we discovered that, in some areas, men were perfectly content with women whose views on a particular subject conflicted with theirs, while their partners were a lot more uneasy about it. Equally, there were issues where women are happy to be with men whose preferences differed from their own, but those men were less tolerant of the problem.

A good example is politics. Men can be happily married to women whose political views are opposite to their own but, for a woman, the happiest relationship is one where her partner votes the same way she does.

If you find from the CQ Test that your political views are unmatched, for instance, are you equally relaxed about this? Or does it maybe matter more to one of you than the other?

The Tests of Importance
For each of the CQ Test's 24 questions, you'll find a

matching five-question 'test of importance' designed to be completed by you and your partner. There's no need to be secretive about your answers, as the purpose of these tests is to encourage you to talk through your differences so as to discover whether they are of equal significance to you both.

Many of the questions are quite provocative – so you should find little difficulty in either agreeing or disagreeing with them – and there are certainly no right or wrong answers. You will probably find that you are happy to accept opposing views in some areas of the CQ Test while other differences could give one of you greater cause for concern.

When to take the Tests of Importance

There is probably little value in taking the tests until you and your partner have used the CQ Test to identify where you differ among its 24 items, so we would recommend the following process:

1   Take the CQ Test confidentially to determine your CQ score. This will show you how compatible the two of you are in general. You should only proceed to the second (open) test stage if you both agree that it would be illuminating to find out where you differ, as it could lead to the raising of sensitive issues.

2   Take the CQ Test in its open form, which you'll find on page 205. This will give you an indication of the areas in which you and your partner differ. There may be several, so make a note of them so you can move on to see how significant they are to each of you.

3   Use the Tests of Importance, which begin on page 237,

following the instructions below. You'll only need to answer the questions for those items of the main CQ Test in which you have a gap of two or more points.

4 Allow yourselves a good amount of 'quality time' in order to discuss the outcome of the tests and agree on some next steps, even if one of those is simply to find enough time to talk things through further.

How to take each Test of Importance

For each question, take it in turns to read the five statements, noting down the letter corresponding to each one and whether you agree or disagree with it. When both you and your partner have done so, calculate your totals using the method shown beneath the test.

After each question you decide to answer, compare your totals with the table below to see how significant the item is to you. (It is important to compare your answers with the following table as you go, rather than at the end of this section.)

Your total	How important you feel it is to share a common view about the item.
0–1	Hardly important at all
2–3	Fairly important
4–5	Very important

You may discover that what is relatively unimportant to one of you could be a more significant issue to the other. When you've discovered each other's feelings about your differences, it's time to talk.

Q1 Is it important to you that you and your partner are around the same height?

(a) I sometimes feel uncomfortable when I'm around someone whose height is very different from mine.

(b) Thinking about couples I know, I'd say the happiest are those who are around the same height as each other, perhaps the men being a little taller than the women.

(c) It's possible to feel physically attracted to someone regardless of how much taller or shorter than me they are.

(d) I am most likely to feel attracted to someone who is around the same height as me.

(e) To be honest, it has never occurred to me to think about the height of my partner.

Score 1 point for each statement if you agree with (a), (b) and (d) and disagree with (c) and (e).

Q2 Is it important for you and your partner to have similar builds?

(a) I can feel uncomfortable when I'm around some-one whose build is very different from my own.

(b) What counts is what's inside; someone who is skinny can be blissfully happy with a partner who is overweight.

(c) 'Laurel and Hardy' relationships rarely work; happy couples almost always have similar body types.

(d) In an ideal world I'd feel happiest being with a partner whose physical build was just like mine.

(e) I'd be happy to share my life with someone whose build was very much heavier or lighter than my own.

Score 1 point for each statement if you agree with (a), (c) and (d) and disagree with (b) and (e).

Q3 What difference does it make to your relationship if one person sees themselves as brighter than the other?

(a) Two people with significantly different levels of intelligence are unlikely to connect properly.

(b) If a friend who left school at 16 wanted to marry a rocket scientist, I'd say, 'Go ahead'.

(c) People who are not so bright often feel inferior in the company of those who are quick-witted.

(d) What has intelligence got to do with happiness? Two people can be completely different, yet still be blissfully happy with each other.

(e) Clever people just feel frustrated when they're around those who aren't so intelligent.

Score 1 point for each statement if you agree with (a), (c) and (e) and disagree with (b) and (d).

Q4 Is it relevant if your partner and you have different television viewing preferences?

(a) I'll happily watch anything on TV, even when it's not really my cup of tea.

(b) If someone needed to watch TV in a different room because of their conflicting tastes it might lead to difficulties in their relationship.

(c) It's good when someone else controls the remote, because you see things you might otherwise not have watched.

(d) Since watching TV is a common social activity, it's important that both partners in a relationship enjoy the same kinds of programmes.

(e) People resent watching things they don't enjoy on TV simply because their partners want to watch them.

Score 1 point for each statement if you agree with (b), (d)

and (e) and disagree with (a) and (c).

Q5 How much does it matter to you if you and your partner have different sex drives?

(a) I sometimes feel uncomfortable about the level of my sex drive when I compare it with my partner's.

(b) Love will find a way, even when two people have very different sex drives.

(c) I worry that my desire for sex seems different from other people's.

(d) If a relationship is to be a happy one, it is essential that both partners should have similar views about the amount of sex they have.

(e) It really wouldn't bother me if my partner and I had opposing views about the amount of sex we have.

Score 1 point for each statement if you agree with (a), (c) and (d) and disagree with (b) and (e).

Q6 Would it make life difficult if you and your partner didn't agree about wanting children?

(a) I can't think of a happy couple who disagree about whether they want to have children.

(b) If I wanted to have children and my partner didn't, I'd still be just as happy with my relationship.

(c) When one person wants children and the other doesn't, it inevitably leads to problems.

(d) My ideal relationship would be one where my partner and I were of one mind when it comes to wanting children.

(e) I believe that two people's love for each other is more important than one wanting to have a child and the other being reluctant.

Score 1 point for each statement if you agree with (a), (c)
and (d) and disagree with (b) and (e).

**Q7 How relevant is it if you and your partner have different types
of occupation?**

(a) What you do at work has nothing to do with who you
are, so people can be happy together no matter what
their jobs are.

(b) Someone whose work is demanding might feel their
partner didn't understand them if their job was less
challenging.

(c) I know couples who are happy together despite having
occupations whose demands differ widely.

(d) Couples with different levels of occupation are bound to
have less in common than those whose positions are
broadly equivalent.

(e) A person whose occupation is unskilled could feel
inferior to a partner with a high-powered job.

Score 1 point for each statement if you agree with (b), (d)
and (e) and disagree with (a) and (c).

**Q8 How would it affect your relationship if one of you feels more
strongly than the other about chivalry?**

(a) A man who has been brought up to behave chivalrously
can always change his ways if he falls in love with an
ardent feminist.

(b) If a man offers his seat to a woman who is offended by
his action, it might make them both feel cross.

(c) I can't see a couple being happy if they hold opposite views
about the idea of 'traditional' male or female behaviour.

(d) So long as people are in love, sharing views on chivalry is
not important.

(e) Women whose expectation is that males will behave as gentlemen are unlikely to be happy in relationships with men who behave otherwise.

Score 1 point for each statement if you agree with (b), (c) and (e) and disagree with (a) and (d).

Q9 Do you think it's an issue if either you or your partner regards themselves as more good-looking than the other?

(a) I tend to feel sorry for people who aren't particularly good-looking.

(b) I'm not really conscious of whether the people close to me are either attractive or unattractive.

(c) I tend to make instant judgements about how good-looking people are.

(d) It's possible to do well in life and to be happy, regardless of whether you're attractive or not.

(e) There's never an excuse for not looking your best.

Score 1 point for each statement if you agree with (a), (c) and (e) and disagree with (b) and (d).

Q10 What do you think about couples who have clashing views about drinking?

(a) I don't believe it would affect our happiness together if my partner's taste for drink differed substantially from mine.

(b) Someone who likes a good drink will only be happy when they're with a similar partner.

(c) Most of the happy couples I know have broadly similar views on alcohol; they either both drink, or they both tend to abstain.

(d) If one person is a drinker, it often helps if they have a sober partner.

(e) If a person who is virtually teetotal finds themselves with a partner who is quite a drinker, there's bound to be trouble.

Score 1 point for each statement if you agree with (b), (c) and (e) and disagree with (a) and (d).

Q11 Would it affect the happiness of your relationship if you and your partner had conflicting political views?

(a) Couples with conflicting political beliefs should have no difficulty enjoying happy long-term relationships.

(b) I can get angry or frustrated when someone I am fond of has political opinions that differ widely from mine.

(c) I can't understand why people who love one another should choose to read daily newspapers which have opposite viewpoints.

(d) It's important that partners vote for the same party at election time, since they're more likely to be happy if they do.

(e) I'm happy to spend time in the company of people whose views on politics are opposite to mine.

Score 1 point for each statement if you agree with (b), (c) and (d) and disagree with (a) and (e).

Q12 Do you think it matters if you and your partner don't like the same kind of music?

(a) Someone who's a fan of gentle, soothing music would never be able to put up with a partner who was devoted to heavy metal or rap.

(b) People's taste in music says a lot about them, so a couple could be incompatible if they liked totally different styles.

(c) I can think of happy couples who have completely opposite tastes in music.

(d) Having to listen to a great deal of music that you didn't enjoy would be intolerable.

(e) I don't mind what type of music is playing as long as it's not too intrusive.

Score 1 point for each statement if you agree with (a), (b) and (d) and disagree with (c) and (e).

Q13 What's your view on the importance of you and your partner agreeing about sexual fidelity?

(a) It's possible for two people to be happy even if one of them is having an affair.

(b) A couple can never be happy if one partner is a cheater and the other isn't.

(c) It doesn't really matter whether a couple are faithful to each other or not; all that matters is that they keep their indiscretions to themselves.

(d) I don't know happy couples where one partner is having an affair with someone else.

(e) Of the happy couples I know, just about all are either totally faithful to each other, or know about and accept, one or the other's affairs.

Score 1 point for each statement if you agree with (b), (d) and (e) and disagree with (a) and (c).

Q14 How important is it if you and your partner disagree about pornography?

(a) A person who has a distaste for pornography should be able to tolerate a partner who enjoys it.

(b) If a conservative person suddenly discovered that their partner was turned on by pornography, it could spell disaster for their relationship.

(c) People who like pornography should keep it a secret from partners who don't.

(d) Why should someone feel shocked or offended if they discover that their partner is turned on by pornography?

(e) Some people are turned on by pornography, while others are offended by it; but people will only be happy if their partner has a similar outlook.

Score 1 point for each statement if you agree with (b), (c) and (e) and disagree with (a) and (d).

Q15 How important is it if you don't share a love of pets?

(a) Someone who doesn't like pets shouldn't have to put up with them just because their partner thinks otherwise.

(b) When one person loves pets and the other can't stand them, it won't be easy to find a mutually satisfactory compromise.

(c) If I was starting a new relationship, it would make little difference to me if my new partner shared my views on pets.

(d) It wouldn't matter that two people had opposite feelings about pets, so long as their love for each other was great enough.

(e) Animal lovers would resent having to live without pets, simply because their partners disagreed with the idea of having them.

Score 1 point for each statement if you agree with (a), (b) and (e) and disagree with (c) and (d).

Q16 How important do you think it is if you and your partner don't share a similar enthusiasm for physical exercise?

(a) People who don't enjoy exercising often don't understand those who do.

(b) Some like exercise, others don't. A couple can be happy together even when they have opposite views on the subject.

(c) Those who are keen on keeping fit sometimes look down on those who aren't.

(d) Since exercise is important for good health, partners are unlikely to be happy with each other if one is more inclined to keep themselves fit than the other.

(e) It isn't important to me if my partner's views on physical exercise are different from mine.

Score 1 point for each statement if you agree with (a), (c) and (d) and disagree with (b) and (e.).

Q17 How important is it for you and your partner to see eye-to-eye on socialising?

(a) If they have differing desires to party, it's sensible for one person to stay at home while the other goes out with friends.

(b) If two people differ in their wish to socialise, they're unlikely to be able to have a happy relationship.

(c) You can reach compromises with your partner about many things in life, but the amount of socialising you do is not really one of them.

(d) If one person loves to party but the other wants to stay at home, it's a recipe for unhappiness.

(e) When one partner is a party animal, and the other painfully shy, it can be a good thing. The one who likes a good time can bring the other person out of their shell.

Score 1 point for each statement if you agree with (b), (c) and (d) and disagree with (a) and (e).

Q18 Does it matter if one of you is a smoker, and the other is not?

(a) A non-smoker could never live with a heavy smoker.

(b) I can't think of any couples I know who differ in their smoking habits, but are happy with their relationship.

(c) When one partner smokes and the other doesn't, it's always possible to find a happy compromise.

(d) Anyone who smokes will feel uncomfortable when they are around those who don't.

(e) Those who don't smoke should respect the rights of those who do.

Score 1 point for each statement if you agree with (a), (b) and (d) and disagree with (c) and (e).

Q19 Do you care if you and your partner have different levels of religious conviction?

(a) People who aren't religious can find it hard to tolerate those who are.

(b) Religion is such a personal thing that it's fine to have a relationship with someone whose belief differs widely from your own.

(c) Those who feel strongly about their religion can be inclined to behave in a superior manner to those who don't.

(d) When partners differ greatly in their views about religion, they are unlikely to have a happy relationship.

(e) If a religious friend asked for my advice about marrying someone who was non-religious, I'd tell them that things would probably work out fine.

Score 1 point for each statement if you agree with (a), (c) and (d) and disagree with (b) and (e).

Q20 Does it matter if you and your partner have different tastes in food?

(a) Eating is such an everyday activity that I think it would be hard for a couple to find a suitable compromise if they liked different things.

(b) If a couple loved one another, but their food preferences were very different, they'd find a way to meet in the middle.

(c) Someone who enjoys exotic food would find it hard to live with a partner whose tastes were for plainer fare.

(d) People grow up with different preferences, but you're never too old to try eating something new.

(e) If you don't try different food, you'll always prefer something plain.

Score 1 point for each statement if you agree with (a), (c) and (e) and disagree with (b) and (d).

Q21 Does it matter if either you or your partner is more money-conscious than the other?

(a) If a couple are to be happy it's critical that they have similar views about the importance of money.

(b) When money's unimportant to someone, they're unlikely to be happy with a partner whose goal in life is to become rich.

(c) It wouldn't affect the happiness of my relationship if my partner had a very different opinion about the importance of money.

(d) I can think of couples who are perfectly happy, even though one partner is more money-driven than the other.

(e) There will always be problems in relationships where one partner is less ambitious than the other.

Score 1 point for each statement if you agree with (a), (b) and (e) and disagree with (c) and (d).

Q22 Do you think it's important that you and your partner should agree on the type of relationship you have?

(a) It's essential that partners want the same kind of relationship if they are to be happy together.

(b) If two people love one another, it doesn't matter if one expects more from the relationship than the other.

(c) When someone is keen to get married but their partner isn't, their relationship will soon collapse.

(d) Of the couples I know, I can't think of any who are happy if one partner is less committed to the relationship than the other.

(e) Marriage is just a piece of paper, so it doesn't affect a relationship when one partner is reluctant to commit.

Score 1 point for each statement if you agree with (a), (c) and (d) and disagree with (b) and (e).

Q23 What impact would it have on your relationship if you and your partner had differing amounts of prior sexual experience?

(a) It's best for couples to have had roughly matching levels of sexual experience in their past lives.

(b) If someone hasn't had as much sexual experience as their partner, they'll relish the thought of everything they still have to learn about lovemaking.

(c) Someone who has had a lot of sexual experience will get bored or frustrated with a partner who is more of a novice.

(d) A person less sexually experienced than their partner could consider that the more experienced one was a bit 'cheap'.

(e) A person who has had more sexual experience than their partner will probably enjoy passing on their knowledge.

Score 1 point for each statement if you agree with (a), (c) and (d) and disagree with (b) and (e).

Q24 If you and your partner have different amounts of education, can you truly be happy together?

(a) It doesn't matter how much or how little schooling anyone has had; we learn from each other all the time.

(b) Someone who hasn't had a great deal of education is likely to feel inferior to someone else who has.

(c) Education doesn't make the person; people can get on with each other regardless of their educational backgrounds.

(d) Couples who have had very different amounts of education are seldom happy together.

(e) People who are highly educated may become frustrated with those who aren't.

Score 1 point for each statement if you agree with (b), (d) and (e) and disagree with (a) and (c).

What to do next

Having diagnosed your differences, then discovered how significant they are, you'll definitely need to talk through the implications. In only one instance should you feel no great need to do so, and this is if you both come out as regarding any differences as 'Hardly important at all'. With any other combination of results, you really do need to sit down and discuss things, even if they might seem trivial to one of you. Please do your best to set aside the time it will take to come to a proper understanding of your personal situation.

Here are some suggestions that could help when it's time to talk:

1   Begin by recognising the strengths of your relationship. The CQ Test will almost certainly have shown you to be well matched in many areas, perhaps even the majority of the 24. So spend some time considering the things that are going well for you and don't be afraid to pat yourselves on the back for your compatibility in these areas.

2   Move on to your areas of difference but try to do so in a way that is totally non-accusatory. If your partner thinks it's significant that only one of you likes exercise, don't say, for example, 'That's because you reckon I'm lazy, fat and ugly.' Not helpful. Keep things neutral and avoid getting personal or putting words into your partner's mouth. Try something like 'I hadn't realised that you'd prefer it if we were both similarly keen to exercise'. When your partner says something that surprises or hurts you, try repeating it back to him or her as you understand it, rather than accusing them of anything they didn't really mean. That way, you can both carefully pursue a subject however sensitive, avoiding any misunderstandings, and arrive at some level of acceptance of each other's views.

3   Recognise that every successful relationship depends upon an equal effort being made by both partners to keep things on track. People change all the time, in response not only to the passage of time, but also to the people around them and the events taking place. And

when two people are changing, the relationship between them is bound to be affected. But don't just accept that you have no control or influence over the direction in which your relationship goes. A car whose driver has taken his hands off the steering wheel will soon crash. You can, and should, recognise that you have the power to steer your relationship.

4 Accept and welcome the fact that you now both see each other more clearly than before you set out on this voyage of mutual self-discovery. All change takes time, so if you're in agreement about tackling issues and resolving differences, give yourselves long enough to make sure it can happen. Look for ways in which you might be able to reach compromises over issues on which you don't agree. Decide, perhaps, to introduce changes into your life, which could lead to things becoming better for you both. However, 'coming together' doesn't usually mean that one person stands still waiting for another. You'll get there much faster if you're both moving at the same time. Meeting in the middle should mean just that.

5 Finally, recognise that help is always available if you find issues impossible to resolve on your own. Such assistance might come from an understanding friend or relative, or it could come from a professional. Don't be afraid to ask for help if you feel you need it, and it's always better to ask for it sooner rather than later. Counsellors are much happier to help at the first signs of cracks appearing in a relationship than when an appointment at their office is the last call on the way to the divorce courts. If you need help, do ask for it.

LOOKING FOR LOVE

Jayne (36) is single but doesn't want to be. She has her own house, a good job and a busy social life but just doesn't seem to meet the right men. She lived with Brian, who was ten years older than her, for seven years but they drifted apart when she realised how much she wanted to have children, whereas Brian already had a family from his prior marriage.

Jayne used the questions in the CQ Test to help her pin down her views, opinions and goals and has now started to use the test as a way of breaking the ice with men she dates. She says that some have found it strange to begin with, but nearly all have been agreeably surprised to find that it has enabled them to talk about issues that normally wouldn't be discussed until much further on in a relationship.

Although it is early days, Mike, a management consultant whose CQ score with Jayne is 125, seems a distinct possibility for long-term happiness. And he is keen to have children, too.

Appendix

The CQ Test and Cybersuitors.com

As the Internet assumed increasing importance in the 1990s, it was soon clear that online dating would gain wide acceptance. As a way of enabling people to establish contact with each other it was unparalleled. But it wasn't an entirely new phenomenon. Computer dating appeared for the first time when computers began to become relatively commonplace. In the mid 1960s, students at Harvard University started a computer-dating service called Operation Match, while a competitive service known as Contact was established by students just across town at MIT. Both required their 'clients' to complete printed questionnaires, the responses to which were fed into a mainframe computer. For a US $10 membership fee, those who joined received the contact details of at least five people whom they could date.

The Internet, of course, made the concept of such a service even more powerful by putting the matching process into the hands of the members themselves. The benefits of subscribing to an online dating service are significant; you are matched against a huge sample of potential mates. There is the advantage of being able to enjoy online dating whatever the time of day and wherever you happen to be. Online dating also provides a convenient means of 'meeting' new people if you find socialising difficult or impractical.

When in May 2000 Jon Cousins and Caroline Chamberlain set out to establish their online dating agency Cybersuitors.com, they were very much new kids on an already busy block. But it seemed that the existing websites principally enabled people to find someone of a certain height and weight; of some specific religion; with similar leisure interests, etc. With one or two exceptions, none had really grasped the nettle of determining what it is that leads to happy relationships, or been able to turn this understanding into a methodical system that could then predict the happiness of those potential couples.

So that was precisely what Jon and Caroline set themselves to do. With Glenn Wilson's help, they first established a scientifically tested way of forecasting the compatibility of two people. It was necessary to conduct a sample trial test involving a significant number of people, giving us a picture of how people's answers would be distributed and confirming the test's reliability. The large sample of test results came from building their website – Cybersuitors.com – then despatching 15,000 postcards to businesses in the UK and US inviting groups of co-workers to find out who was most compatible with whom.

The thinking behind Cybersuitors.com was straightforward: everyone who joined would take the CQ Test, and their answers would be compared with those of every other member to find suitable matches. However, even matching just 1,000 males with 1,000 females takes nearly thirty million calculations. They eventually managed to get the technology up to speed.

Once they'd recruited their 'critical mass' of 150 members, things started to move quickly. The CQ Test generated a good amount of press coverage on BBC TV in the UK, followed by articles in the *Observer* and various tabloids. Jon Cousins and Glenn Wilson were interviewed on TV in the United States. The New Zealand magazine, *The Listener*, featured the CQ Test on its front cover, and Germany, Norway and Argentina also took up the story. The result of this unexpected coverage was a flood of people signing up to the website, at that stage being offered free of charge (an investment in building up the database).

With the benefit of a substantial amount of feedback from Cybersuitors.com members, it has been possible to form a good understanding of what happens when people meet through an online dating service. The thinking behind the CQ Test enables you to gain an instant snapshot of how much you have in common with someone at the same time as finding out whether you click or not. A high CQ score alone is not enough to ensure that you could be happily married to a particular person, but it would be equally inadvisable to rely on 'chemistry' alone.

Cybersuitors.com arms its members with the information necessary to make a decision on both aspects; CQ and chemistry. As you are looking at the photo of a potential mate and reading a description of them, you see a score showing your compatibility with them, using the scientifically validated CQ. It is then up to the member to decide how to weight these sources of information and who to email with a view to eventually meeting.

Just like this book, Cybersuitors.com cannot tell you with whom you'll fall in love, but it can increase the chances it will be a good idea if you do. We all deserve lasting love, and Cybersuitors.com can help you find it.

Further reading

Bereczkei, T. Gyuris, P. Koves, P & Bernath, L. (2002) 'Homogamy, genetic similarity, and imprinting'. *Personality and Individual Differences*, 33, 677–690.

Fisher, H.E., Aron, A., Mashek, M.A., Li, H. & Brown, L.L. (2002) 'Defining the brain systems of lust, romantic attraction, and attachment'. *Archives of Sexual Behaviour*, 31, 413–419.

Lykken, D.T. (1993) 'Is human mate selection adventitious or the result of lawful choice?: A twin study of mate selection'. *Journal of Personality and Social Psychology*, 65, 56–68.

Marazziti, D. et al (1999) 'Alteration of the platelet serotonin transporter in romantic love'. *Psychological Medicine*, 29, 741–745.

Wilson, G.D. & Barrett, P.T. (1987) 'Parental characteristics and partner choice: Some evidence for Oedipal imprinting'. *Journal of Biosocial Science*, 19, 157–161.

Wilson, G.D. & Cousins, J.M. (2003) 'Partner similarity and relationship satisfaction: Development of a compatibility quotient'. *Sexual and Relationship Therapy*, 18, (in press).

Wilson, G.D. & McLaughlin, C. (2001) *The Science of Love*. Fusion Books, London.

About the authors

Glenn D. Wilson was born in 1942 in Christchurch, New Zealand. While studying for his Ph.D at the University of London he began working with renowned psychologist Professor Hans Eysenck, pioneer of IQ, and the two later collaborated on a series of books and articles.

Glenn is currently Reader in Personality at the University of London's Institute of Psychiatry and Adjunct Professor with the University of Nevada, Reno. He has published more than 100 articles and 30 books – including *The Science of Love* (Fusion Press, 2001) – and is one of Britain's best-known psychologists.

Jon Cousins was born in 1956 in West London. After a career in advertising, in 2000 he began working with business partner Caroline Chamberlain and Glenn Wilson on ideas for an online dating agency – Cybersuitors – using psychological matching. Jon lives on a canal boat in central London and also in San Diego, California.

The Science of Love
Glenn D. Wilson and Chris McLaughlin

What is love? Why do we fall in love with the people that we do? What makes love last – and fade? What happens when love goes wrong? And what are the emotional consequences of living without love?

Psychologist Glenn D. Wilson and journalist Chris McLaughlin unite to examine the latest international scientific research on love, attraction and sexual behaviour. They reveal absorbing and controversial insights into the causes and complexities of human emotion, and the differences betweeen the mating games of men and women.

As people live longer, are they less content to settle for an imperfect ideal? Will this lead to serial relationships replacing lifelong partnerships? Can men and women ever live happily together?

The Science of Love helps unravel some of the mysteries of love: that extraordinary feeling that causes both agony and ecstacy, but which ultimately 'makes the world go round'.

ISBN: 1-901250-54-7
UK: £9.99 net
www.fusionpress.co.uk

Men, Women, Love and Romance
Under the Covers of the Bedroom Revolution
Stephen Whitehead

Romance is not dead, but it has changed. Over the last decade women have ushered in a bedroom revolution marked by a new sexual confidence. They have new expectations about themselves, their romantic opportunities and their sexuality and men have to adapt if they are to succeed in forming meaningful relationships.

In this up-to-the-minute instruction book, Stephen Whitehead warns that the 'traditional male' has no place in the new gender game and those men who don't recognise this will become the dodos of the new millennium.

With frank, entertaining interviews and acute analysis, Whitehead examines what women now want and what men have to do to keep up. He also guides us through the new ways to find romance – from text flirting to cyberdating. Democratic love is the new ideal, and this book tells you what it is, how to find it and how to keep it.

ISBN: 1-904132-22-7
UK: £10.99 net
www.fusionpress.co.uk